# The Tertiary Education Imperative

# GLOBAL PERSPECTIVES ON HIGHER EDUCATION

VOLUME 38

*Series Editors:*

Philip G. Altbach, *Center for International Higher Education,*
  *Boston College, USA*
Hans de Wit, *Center for International Higher Education,*
  *Boston College, USA*
Laura E. Rumbley, *Center for International Higher Education,*
  *Boston College, USA*

*Scope:*

Higher education worldwide is in a period of transition, affected by globalization, the advent of mass access, changing relationships between the university and the state, and the new technologies, among others. *Global Perspectives on Higher Education* provides cogent analysis and comparative perspectives on these and other central issues affecting postsecondary education worldwide.

This series is co-published with the Center for International Higher Education at Boston College.

# The Tertiary Education Imperative

*Knowledge, Skills and Values for Development*

Für Elbre,
Vielen Dank für die
Einladung -
Alls Gute
Jamil

**Jamil Salmi**

SENSE PUBLISHERS
ROTTERDAM/BOSTON/TAIPEI

A C.I.P. record for this book is available from the Library of Congress.

ISBN: 978-94-6351-126-1 (paperback)
ISBN: 978-94-6351-127-8 (hardback)
ISBN: 978-94-6351-128-5 (e-book)

Published by: Sense Publishers,
P.O. Box 21858,
3001 AW Rotterdam,
The Netherlands
https://www.sensepublishers.com/

All chapters in this book have undergone peer review.

*Printed on acid-free paper*

# TABLE OF CONTENTS

Foreword      vii
     *Philip G. Altbach*

Introduction      xi

Chapter 1: The Changing Context: New Challenges, New Opportunities      1

     Introduction: Knowledge and Innovation as Drivers of Economic and
         Social Development      1
     Changing Labor Markets in the Digital Era      2
     The Evolving Tertiary Education Ecosystem      7
     Conclusion: Challenges and Opportunities      28

Chapter 2: The Contribution of Tertiary Education: Theory vs. Reality      31

     Role and Benefits of Tertiary Education      31
     The Reality of Tertiary Education in Developing Countries: Long-Standing
         and New Challenges      45

Chapter 3: Designing and Implementing System-Wide Reforms      71

     Ignition Phase      72
     Elaboration of a Vision for the Future of the Tertiary Education System      74
     Formulation of a Set of Strategic Measures      76
     Launch of the Reform      106
     Ensuring the Sustainability of the Reform      111

Chapter 4: Ensuring Financial Sustainability: What is at Stake?      119

     Elements of a Sustainable Financing Strategy      120
     Strategic Decisions Influencing Financing Requirements      121
     Resource Mobilization Options      134
     Resource Allocation Mechanisms      156
     Conclusion      161

Chapter 5: Role of the Donors      163

     What Works: Lessons of Experience from Donor Interventions      163
     Roadmap for Donor Support in Tertiary Education      167

Conclusion: The Reform Imperative      171

TABLE OF CONTENTS

References                                                          175

Appendices                                                          183

About the Author                                                    195

# FOREWORD

Postsecondary education is vital to both economies and societies worldwide. Evidence from research over the past few decades has shown repeatedly that nations without effective postsecondary institutions have been—and will continue to be—left behind in the global knowledge economies of the 21st century. Postsecondary education is understood by societies across the planet as a requisite for social mobility. These elements—economic drivers and social pressures—have combined to create mass postsecondary education systems worldwide and, at the same time, have emphasized the importance of the small but quite important research university sector. As Jamil Salmi points out in this comprehensive volume on the vital contribution of universities and other tertiary education institutions, postsecondary education has become a central element of both national education systems worldwide and the global knowledge economy. This has serious implications for developing countries keen on achieving the Sustainable Development Goals.

## TERTIARY EDUCATION AS A GLOBAL POLICY CONCERN

This volume emerged from a research initiative of the United Nations in recognition of the central role of postsecondary education systems. It is one of a number of insightful reports commissioned by international agencies over the past several decades, including the World Bank, UNESCO, and the OECD. One of the first reports that argued that postsecondary education was key for economic and social development was *Higher Education in Developing Countries: Peril and Promise,* co-sponsored by UNESCO and the World Bank, and published by the World Bank in 2000. Salmi himself was instrumental in writing *Constructing Knowledge Societies: New Challenges for Tertiary Education,* published by the World Bank in 2002. This volume provided further evidence and useful guidance relating to the importance of postsecondary education. In the years since, postsecondary education has been recognized as a key element for development and increasingly integrated into educational planning by governments. During this same period, enrolments dramatically expanded, as young people and their families recognized the importance of postsecondary education for achieving expanded opportunities and social mobility.

Given these dynamic and sustained global demands for more and better post-secondary education, it is surprising that the World Bank's pending 2018 World Development Report, the first such report dedicated to education, does not include postsecondary education as an integral part of the education spectrum. Similarly the Organization for Economic Cooperation and Development (OECD) recently closed its highly regarded higher education journal and abolished its Institutional

Management in Higher Education program. UNESCO, as well, has diminished its higher education engagements over the past decade. In this context, it is imperative for global scholars of higher education to continue the discourse that can support improved and sustainable development and reform efforts for the sector. The sector is growing, as government and societies demand more and better tertiary education, whether international organizations choose to remain relevant to that growth or not. Salmi's volume, therefore, could hardly come at a better moment.

## MASSIFICATION AND PRIVATIZATION

Massification—expanded enrollment to over 35% of the traditional age cohort for higher education—has had dramatic implications for postsecondary education worldwide, although the specific circumstances vary significantly by country and region. The rise of private providers in the tertiary sector has been one widespread development. Indeed, private postsecondary education, both for-profit and non-profit, is the fastest growing segment of the sector worldwide. As Salmi points out in this book, Latin America and Asia are increasingly dominated by private, often for-profit provision—with Western Europe and North America less affected. Public postsecondary education has increasingly been privatized, with tuition and fees increasing in many countries as a way of financing institutions. Government funding has been replaced or supplemented by student tuition. Student debt has become an issue of public concern in many countries. There are outliers to these trends, however. Switzerland and the Nordic countries still regard postsecondary education as a public good and provide full government support, keeping tuition free or at a very low cost. Funding patterns, policy orientations to postsecondary education, governance structures, and other realities differ considerably worldwide. One of the strengths of this book is that it examines both general trends and specific patterns of development—thus providing valuable comparative perspectives that can be used by policymakers and institutional leaders in both industrial and developing nations.

## FUTURE CHALLENGES

Without question, postsecondary education will continue to face dramatic challenges in the coming decades. Expansion will go on, especially in the developing and emerging economies—putting pressure on financing and quality assurance for tertiary education in nearly all countries around the world. Most countries will need a highly trained workforce to contribute to increasingly sophisticated economies, and it will be incumbent on governments and institutions to better align their education opportunities with the outcomes expected by graduates, society, and the labor market.

Challenges such as the role of distance provision of postsecondary education, the appropriate levels of internationalization, including the use of English as a language of global communication, efficient and effective funding models, adequate governance arrangements, the role of general education in the mix of postsecondary provision, and many other issues face postsecondary education. This volume provides valuable guidance for thinking through these key challenges.

*Philip G. Altbach*
*Founding Director*
*Center for International Higher Education*
*Boston College*

# INTRODUCTION

...All regions and countries can benefit from progress toward a knowledge-based economy, which does not depend heavily on material resources, places less of a burden on ecosystems and is more sustainable than other economic models. By shifting to a knowledge-based economy, societies can move from the age of scarcity to the age of abundance. Knowledge does not deplete with use but rather increases as it is shared among people. Through technological innovation, we can help usher in a more sustainable future...

(Ban Ki-Moon, UN Secretary General, 24 April 2014)

The Brazilian aviation company, Embraer, is the world leader in the production of regional jets. The success of the country's emblematic firm can be traced back to the creation of ITA, the National Aeronautic Engineering School, in the early 1950s. Established in close partnership with MIT, and widely considered today as Brazil's top engineering school, ITA has trained the scientists, engineers and technicians who helped build Embraer into a leading global company.

Typhidot is a revolutionary method to diagnose typhoid fever. Invented by scientists at the Malaysian University of Science in Penang (USM), Typhidot is credited with saving thousands of lives. Compared with traditional methods for detecting the disease, Typhidot is faster, more reliable, cheaper, and it does not require cold storage. USM's Center for Medical Innovations and Technology Development, from which Typhidot originates, is dedicated to finding innovative ways of diagnosing infectious diseases in an effective, quick and affordable manner.

Until the beginning of this decade, most practicing teachers in Palestinian primary schools were poorly prepared and did not have a university degree. After new regulations required all teachers to have both a university degree and a relevant professional teaching qualification, three West Bank universities worked together, with support from a renowned British teacher training institution, to radically overhaul their pre-service teacher training program, introducing a competency-based approach and a school experience element. A quasi-experimental study carried out after three years of implementation found very high value added for the new pre-service teaching program.

These are but three examples to illustrate the unique and vital contribution that tertiary education makes to economic and social development. But notwithstanding this crucial developmental role, for several decades traditional human capital theory challenged the need for public support of tertiary education on the grounds that graduates captured important private benefits—notably higher salaries and lower unemployment—that should not be subsidized by taxpayers. Influenced by this argument, many multilateral and bilateral donor agencies focused their support on basic education rather than investing as well in the expansion and improvement of tertiary education systems in developing countries.[1]

In the 1990s, however, a growing body of research demonstrated the importance of going beyond rate-of-return analysis to measure the full value of tertiary education as a fundamental pillar of sustainable development. By focusing primarily on the private returns of government spending, rate-of-return analysis failed to capture the broader social benefits accruing to society, which are important to recognize and measure. These include research externalities, entrepreneurship, job creation, good economic and political governance, and the positive effects that a highly educated cadre of workers has on a nation's health and social fabric (Birdsall, 1996; World Bank, 2002).

Building on these findings, the path-breaking 2000 report entitled *Higher Education in Developing Countries: Peril and Promise* called for scaling up investment in tertiary education and research to equip developing countries with the knowledge and the qualified manpower needed to fight poverty and accelerate economic growth (World Bank and UNESCO, 2000). Written by a distinguished group of independent experts with financial support from UNESCO and the World Bank, the report had an important impact at three levels. First, it helped reorient donor policies to give greater attention to tertiary education in partner countries. Second, it unleashed several reform initiatives in the developing countries themselves. Third, it paved the way for increased South-South networking and collaborative activities (Salmi, 2016a).

Fifteen years later, the world of tertiary education has changed significantly. Developing countries have seen tremendous enrollment growth, especially in the private sector. Many of them are facing an exponentially rising demand as more young people graduate from high school as a result of successes in implementing the Education for All agenda. In Europe, the Bologna process has led to the creation of a regional "higher education space" facilitating the circulation of students and academics. In Asia, the most dynamic economies have been at the forefront of efforts to place tertiary education at the center of their development strategy.

Tertiary education finds itself at another crossroad today, as national systems are pulled in several directions by a combination of factors bringing about both opportunities and challenges. The forces exercising new pressures on tertiary education can be divided into three groups: crisis factors, rupture factors, and stimulation factors.

The crisis factors are the direct results of the economic and financial crisis that started in 2007–2008. Since then, the fiscal situation has seriously deteriorated in many countries and governments almost everywhere have significantly cut their tertiary education budget. At the same time, households have had fewer resources to allocate to finance their private education expenditures. Furthermore, in many countries, the slowing down of the economy has led to rising graduate unemployment.

Compounding these elements of financial crisis are disruption factors such as those pointed out in a 2013 report proposing the image of "an avalanche" to describe the radical changes affecting how tertiary education institutions will be conducting their teaching and research activities in the future (Barber et al., 2013). Among these rupture factors are (i) technological innovations such as flipped classrooms and other strategies for more interactive learning, (ii) mass online open courses (MOOCS) reaching hundred of thousands of students all over the world, (iii) increased competition from for-profit and corporate universities that provide professional qualifications closely linked to labor market needs, and (iv) new accountability modalities like the global rankings, that allow for different kinds of comparisons of the performance of universities across all continents.

On a positive note, tertiary education institutions are also exposed to stimulus factors in the relatively few countries that, notwithstanding the financial crisis, have continued to give priority to the development of their knowledge economy and have protected their tertiary education budget for that purpose. Under the influence of the global rankings, several governments—for example China, France, Germany, Russia and South Korea—are supporting "excellence initiatives" that translate into a large influx of additional resources for their nation's leading universities. In Sub-Saharan Africa, a new regional project funded by the World Bank, with parallel financing from several bilateral and multilateral donors, is supporting the development of centers of excellence to boost the research capacity of the leading universities in the Region.

Against this background, the launch of the Sustainable Development Goals by the United Nations in September 2015 has given renewed consideration to the importance of education for development and the urgency of putting in place viable financing strategies. This book, which focuses on the tertiary education level, is divided into five chapters.[2] The first one examines the evolving context in which tertiary education systems operate. Chapter 2 reviews the contribution of tertiary education to economic and social development, contrasting the theoretical impact that it could have and the actual state of tertiary education systems in most developing countries. Chapter 3 proposes a sequence for designing and implementing tertiary education reforms, based on international experience. Chapter 4 concentrates on the financial sustainability aspects of tertiary education reform. Finally, Chapter 5 discusses the important role that the donors can play in support of tertiary education reform in developing countries.

The book carries the following main messages:

- The innovative application of knowledge has become a fundamental driver of social progress and economic development. Advanced knowledge and modern technologies are also influencing the pace of competition and transforming the nature of labor market needs through substantial shifts in the configuration and content of jobs.
- Tertiary education is indispensable for the effective and efficient creation, dissemination, and application of knowledge and for building institutional, professional and technological capacity.

- The tertiary education ecosystem is evolving at an increasingly rapid pace, influenced by elements of uncertainty, complexity and disruption, such as changing demographics, global competition, political volatility, diminished public funding, greater private involvement, growing accountability demands, alternative delivery modes and game-changing technologies.
- In this challenging context, developing countries can either become economically marginalized, incapable of using advanced technology and unable to compete on the global scene because their tertiary education systems are insufficiently developed and under-performing, or they can strengthen their capacity to create and apply knowledge through well-trained graduates and relevant research produced by a diversified and increasingly international tertiary education system.
- To reduce the performance gaps faced by their tertiary education systems, developing countries governments need to design and implement significant reforms. International experience suggests that an appropriate reform sequence includes the following steps: (i) ignition phase to sensitize all stakeholders to the urgency of the reform; (ii) elaboration of a vision for the future of the tertiary education system; (iii) formulation of a set of strategic reforms; (iv) launch of the reforms; and (v) structural measures to ensure the sustainability of the reforms, especially its long-term financial viability.
- To achieve long-term financial viability, developing countries must not only improve resource mobilization through a combination of public and private funding but also adopt an expansion strategy that encourages institutional diversification—non-university institutions and private providers—and increased reliance on online learning opportunities.
- Through knowledge sharing, capacity building and resource mobilization, the donor community can accompany partner countries in their efforts to expand coverage and improve the effectiveness and responsiveness of their tertiary education system.

## NOTES

[1] This book adopts the OECD definition of tertiary education as representing "a level or stage of studies beyond secondary education. Such studies are undertaken in tertiary education institutions, such as public and private universities, colleges, and polytechnics, and also in a wide range of other settings, such as secondary schools, work sites, and via free-standing information technology-based offerings and a host of public and private entities" (Wagner 1999: 135). Under the new ISCED 2011 education classification, tertiary education contains four levels: short-cycle tertiary (level 5), Bachelor's (level 6), Master's (level 7) and Ph.D. (level 8).

[2] This book builds on a report prepared for the United Nations by the author. Available at http://report.educationcommission.org/resource-materials/

# CHAPTER 1

# THE CHANGING CONTEXT

*New Challenges, New Opportunities*

### INTRODUCTION: KNOWLEDGE AND INNOVATION AS DRIVERS OF ECONOMIC AND SOCIAL DEVELOPMENT

If investments in factories were the most important investments in the industrial age, the most important investments in an Information Age are surely investments in the human brain. (Larry Summers)

Among the most influential changes that the past decades have brought is the increasing role that knowledge and innovation have come to play as major drivers of growth in the context of the global economy (OECD, 2015a). Technological progress has become the main driver of growth of GDP per capita, allowing output to increase faster than labor and capital (EOP, 2016). Innovation stimulates the development of new firms and job creation; it fuels rises in productivity and leads to economic growth. Innovative economies are more productive, better able to sustain higher living standards and reduce poverty, more resilient in times of crisis and have a stronger capacity to transform themselves.

The World Bank's analytical framework for studying and explaining the dynamics of knowledge-driven development identifies the converging roles of four contributing factors: the macroeconomic incentive and institutional regime, the information and telecommunication infrastructure, the national innovation system, and the quality of human resources (World Bank, 1999).

Along similar lines, the new OECD Innovation Strategy (2015a) suggests that innovation can only flourish in an economic and regulatory environment that has the following characteristics:

- A skilled workforce that can foster new ideas and generate new technologies, bring them to the market, and implement them in the workplace, and that is able to adapt to technological and structural changes across society.
- A sound business environment that encourages investment in technology, that enables innovative firms to experiment with new ideas, technologies and business models, and that helps them to grow, increase their market share and reach scale.
- A strong and efficient system for knowledge creation and diffusion that invests in the systematic pursuit of fundamental knowledge.
- Policies that encourage innovation and entrepreneurial activity.

- A strong focus on governance and implementation. The impact of policies for innovation depends heavily on their governance and implementation, including the trust in government action and the commitment to learn from experience.

Knowledge is indispensable not only for economic growth but also for social development purposes. Countries without a minimum institutional, scientific and technological capacity to apply research results are likely to lag in realizing key social and human benefits such as increased life expectancy, lower infant mortality, and improved health, nutrition, and sanitation. Such countries will be increasingly vulnerable to emerging environmental threats (World Bank, 2002).

Knowledge and knowhow play an equally essential role as the principal engine of social innovation, defined as the efforts of firms, universities, government agencies and NGOs towards designing and applying new business models and offering services that help improve the life of vulnerable communities and groups in society. Social innovation manifests itself through innovative initiatives, products and processes aiming at finding new solutions to society's complex challenges that are durable and equitable from the viewpoint of the most vulnerable groups.

This includes the development of *frugal* innovations that seek to create greater social value in developing countries while minimizing the use of scarce financial and natural resources. From the low-cost water purifier invented by the Tata Group in India to the mobile payment service pioneered by the Kenyan telecom operator Safricom, frugal solutions can reach hundreds of millions of people at the bottom of the economy pyramid in ways that create more value while minimizing resource use and facilitating greater collaboration and engagement by local communities (Radjou, 2014).

Against this background of the dynamics of the knowledge economy, this chapter examines the changing labor market and the evolving tertiary education ecosystem, with a focus on the new accountability requirements, the effects of globalization on tertiary education, the impact of the new education technologies, and the political convulsions affecting tertiary education.

CHANGING LABOR MARKETS IN THE DIGITAL ERA

The Fourth Industrial Revolution was the main theme of the 2016 Davos meeting organized by the World Economic Forum. Observers underlined the importance of recent developments in fields that were previously separated but are now becoming increasingly intertwined, such as artificial intelligence and machine learning, robotics, nanotechnology, 3-D printing, and biotechnology and genetics (WEF, 2016). This rapid evolution in the business and production spheres is likely to cause widespread disruptions in labor markets.

In designing their future programs and courses, tertiary education institutions must therefore take notice of the considerable transformation that the labor market is undergoing in the digital era. These developments are going to translate into tremendous changes in the skill sets needed to succeed in the new work landscape. The changes will be of three types: disappearance of existing jobs, emergence of new jobs, and transformation of existing positions and, therefore, needed skills.

In the first instance, the WEF report notes that many jobs will be threatened by redundancy as robots and intelligent machines become increasingly available to replace human beings in many tasks. A recent study published by two Oxford University professors looked at 700 professions at risk of disappearing over the next ten to twenty years as a direct result of the growing integration of robotics, artificial intelligence and information technology (Frey and Osborne, 2013). Their estimates indicate that up to 47% of total employment in the US labor market is likely to be affected by job computerization brought about by advances in machine learning and mobile robotics.

> For context, every 3 months about 6 percent of jobs in the [US] economy are destroyed by shrinking or closing businesses, while a slightly larger percentage of jobs are added—resulting in rising employment and a roughly constant unemployment rate. The economy has repeatedly proven itself capable of handling this scale of change, although it would depend on how rapidly the changes happen and how concentrated the losses are in specific occupations that are hard to shift from. (EOP, 2016, p. 2)

Another key result of their analysis is that the loss of jobs through computerization is inversely related to educational attainment and that positions that require creativity, high-level socio-cognitive skills and the ability to deal with complex tasks are safe from automating. Research consistently shows that the jobs that are most under risk as a result of automation are highly concentrated among lower-paid, lower-skilled, and less-educated workers. The implication is that automation will continue to put downward pressure on wages for this vulnerable group, thereby accelerating economic inequality.

While these effects may not play out as strongly in the developing economies that still have a high proportion of employment in the informal sector, they will undoubtedly affect the modern sectors of the economy, where the majority of tertiary education graduates seek employment. They will bring about increased opportunities for the development of small and medium enterprises. Also, freelancing jobs will become more numerous in a world where production is more and more project-based.

Secondly, the growth of the digital economy implies the development of a whole range of new professions. The Spanish Observatory of Employment in the Digital Era predicts that four out of five young people between 20 and 30 will work in positions, directly linked to the digital world, that do not exist yet today (El Mundo, 2016). Among the professions likely to be most in demand are smart factory engineer, chief digital officer, digital innovation specialist, data scientist, expert in big data, smart city architect, director of digital content, expert in digital risks, director of digital

3

marketing, and growth hacker. Firms will particularly looking for big data specialists and growth hackers. Big data specialists, usually trained in computer science or mathematics, analyze the large databases collected by companies as inputs into decision-making on corrective actions and strategic orientations. Growth hackers, coming from informatics, publicity or digital marketing, are trained to identify new growth areas and modalities.

Increasingly linked to the digital economy are the cultural and creative industries, which also represent areas with high potential for the emergence of small companies and employment growth in developing nations, capitalizing on the specific culture and history of each country. In the European labor market, for example, these sectors account today for 3.3% of total employment and 4.2% of Europe's GDP. The performing arts, the visual arts and music in the lead, followed by advertising, books, film, TV, architecture and newspapers.

A few developing countries, India and Nigeria for example, have already shown the way in this direction with the development of their movie industry. In Nigeria, the relatively recent success of "Nollywood" has resulted in thousands of new jobs. In 2015, the film industry employed one million people—second only to agriculture—produced 2,500 movies and generated 600 million dollars of revenue, up from 400 movies and 5 million dollars in 2002 (Onishi, 2016). Close linkages between the ICT and creative industries can also materialize, for instance in the form of digital media in art production, or ICT-enhanced tourism.

Thirdly, existing jobs are also going to experience significant changes in the skill sets required to perform effectively. As documented in several recent studies, the changes in job contents are likely to lead to growing labor market polarization. Goos and Manning's "Lousy and Lovely Jobs" (2007) analyzed the concurrent rise in employment in low-income manual occupations that do not require high education qualifications and in high-income jobs that involve high-order cognitive skills. Similarly, a more recent study prepared by the UK University Alliance (2012) looks at the spread of middle wage routine jobs and, at the same time, the expansion of high wage abstract non-routine jobs in what the researchers describe as the "hourglass economy".

The work of Harvard professors Levy and Murnane (2005) support these findings. They studied the skills requirements for the tasks performed in US firms, showing the types of skills for which there is less demand—or which have been taken over by computers and intelligent machines—and those for which there has been increased demand. In their path-breaking research, the authors divided the tasks performed in firms into five broad categories:

- Expert thinking: solving problems for which there are no rule-based solutions, such as diagnosing the illness of a patient whose symptoms are out of the ordinary;
- Complex communication: interacting with others to acquire information, to explain it, or to persuade others of its implications for action; for example, a manager motivating the people whose work he/ she supervises;

- Routine cognitive tasks: mental tasks that are well described by logical rules, such as maintaining expense reports;
- Routine manual tasks: physical tasks that can be well described using rules, such as installing windshields on new vehicles in automobile assembly plants; and
- Non-routine manual tasks: physical tasks that cannot be well described as following a set of "if-then-do" rules and that are difficult to computerize because they require optical recognition and fine muscle control; for example, driving a truck.

Figure 1 below shows the trends of the last decades for each type of task. Tasks requiring expert thinking and complex communication grew steadily and consistently over the past four decades. The share of the labor force employed in occupations that emphasize routine cognitive or routine manual tasks remained stable in the 1970s and then declined over the next two decades. Finally, the share of the labor force working in occupations that emphasize non-routine manual tasks declined throughout the period.

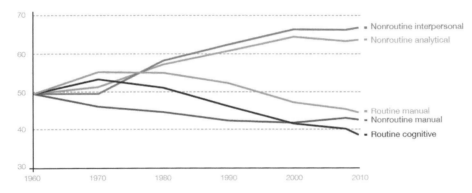

*Figure 1. Economy-wide Measures of Routine and Non Routine Task Inputs United States, 1960–2009.*
*Note: Each trend reflects changes in the numbers of people employed in occupations emphasizing that task. To facilitate comparison, the importance of each task in the US economy has been indexed to 1960, the baseline year. The value in each subsequent year represents the percentile change in the importance of each type of task in the economy. Source: Levy and Murnane (2005, 2013)*

Therefore, the evolution in the skills requirements for both new and existing jobs will not only affect the professional content of the curriculum but also have momentous implications in terms of generic competencies that graduates are expected to possess, as revealed by a meta-analysis of twenty-first century skills carried out by the World Economic Forum (WEF, 2015). Building on the *fundamental literacies* that any 21st century person needs to acquire during their primary and secondary education, such as literacy and numeracy, scientific literacy, ICT literacy, financial literacy, cultural and civic literacy, university graduates must master *complex competencies* to be able to contribute effectively to addressing today's challenges. The four key complex competencies are (i) critical thinking and problem solving skills, (ii) creativity, (iii) communication, and (iv) collaboration. Critical thinking is the ability to find and analyze relevant information to make a diagnosis of complex situations and formulate adequate responses and solutions. Creative people are capable of imagining and designing new, innovative ways of viewing and solving problems through the application, synthesis or repurposing of knowledge. This skill is of course crucial in the creative industries but it is also indispensable in any industrial or service activity where innovative processes and products can be applied to increase productivity or to find new solutions. Communication is the ability to listen, understand and explain complex phenomena and to convince others through oral, nonverbal, visual and written means. Finally, collaborative skills refer to the ability of individuals to work well in teams or within networks towards a common goal.

In addition, the ability of individuals to become successful professionals and active citizens in their rapidly changing environment is determined by their *character qualities*, also called socio-emotional skills, and commonly misnamed as "soft skills". These include (i) curiosity, (ii) initiative, (iii) persistence, (iv) adaptability, (v) leadership, and (vi) social and cultural awareness. Curiosity, an important determinant of the motivation of learners, reflects the desire to ask questions and show open-mindedness. Initiative is the ability to seek new tasks or new goals in a proactive way. Persistence (or grit) is the capacity to sustain interest and efforts in accomplishing a task or a goal. Adaptability is the capacity to modify views, methods, plans or goals in light of new information. Leadersip is the ability to inspire, guide and direct others to achieve a common goal. Finally, social and cultural awareness is the capacity to interact with other people and with the environment in a socially, culturally and ethically appropriate manner (Figure 2).

In his latest book (2009), Howard Gardner, the Harvard professor who developed the concept of multiple intelligences in the early 1980s, proposes "five minds for the future" that embody many of the complex competencies and character qualities presented above:

- The disciplined mind: the need to train and acquire the skills to become an expert in a specific professional area
- The synthesizing mind: the ability to understand, evaluate, use and communicate information from various sources in a coherent way
- The creating mind: the ability to think outside the box, break new ground, bring out new ideas, ask unfamiliar questions, and conjures up new ways of thinking
- The respectful mind: the capacity to accept and defer to the ideas of diverse groups
- The ethical mind: the capacity to do the right thing under all circumstances.

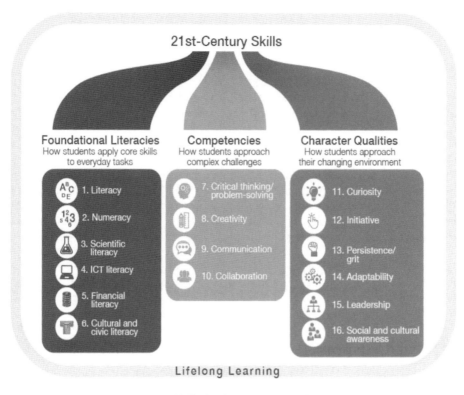

*Figure 2. Skills for the Twenty-First Century.*
*Source: WEF (2015)*

## THE EVOLVING TERTIARY EDUCATION ECOSYSTEM

### New Forms of Accountability

No good book was ever written on command, nor can good teaching occur under duress. And yet, conceding this, the fact remains that left entirely to their own devices academic communities are no less prone than other professional organizations to slip unconsciously into complacent habits, inward-looking standards of quality, self-serving canons of behavior. To counter these tendencies, there will always be a need to engage the outside world in a lively, continuing debate over the university's social responsibilities. (Derek Bok, 1990)

Until the 1980s, tertiary education institutions in the United States, the United Kingdom and Commonwealth countries were the only ones in the world with a strong tradition of external quality assurance. By contrast, most tertiary education systems elsewhere evolved without any formal quality assurance mechanism at the national level. Tertiary education institutions operated under a widely accepted notion of academic autonomy that applied not only to the relationship between universities and the State, but went all the way down to the lecture hall and the classroom.

This all started to change in the 1980s and the 1990s, as most OECD countries moved to establish some form of government-sanctioned quality assurance. Europe witnessed a considerable drive as a direct result of the Bologna process officially launched in 1999. By 2008, most countries had a functioning evaluation or accreditation agency. The successful convergence of quality assurance regulations has been one of Bologna's most noticeable outcomes.

The former socialist countries of Eastern Europe and the Soviet Union have also been keen to participate in this process. Today, most of them have a quality assurance system in place, even though the capacity is still unequal, as reflected by the fact that many of the agencies from these countries have not been accepted as full members of the European Association for Quality Assurance in Higher Education (ENQA).

In Latin America, the first quality assurance body was established in Mexico in 1991, followed two years later by a national accreditation agency in Colombia. In the following two decades, most countries in the region set up a national quality assurance body, with the exception of the Central American nations, which started with a regional accreditation agency. Today Bolivia and Uruguay are the only countries in the region without any formal accreditation body, although in the case of Uruguay the Ministry of Education is responsible for licensing new private universities.

Asia and the Middle East have experienced a similar evolution. In South-East Asia, Indonesia took the lead in establishing a national quality assurance agency in 1994, followed over the next two decades by almost all the countries in the region. Today, Myanmar is the only tertiary education system without a formal external quality assurance department or agency. In the Arab world, the first decade of the new century saw the creation of quality assurance systems in most countries, twelve out of the seventeen main countries in the region by 2010.

Africa is perhaps the region where the quality assurance movement has been slowest. By 2006, only 6 countries had a fully established quality assurance agency, Ghana, Nigeria and South Africa being the pioneers in that domain. In the past decade, however, progress has been impressive and today 23 countries count with a national quality assurance agency. The concluding declaration of a recent pan-African conference on quality assurance urges all countries that do not have with a proper QA system to put one in place as a matter of priority, especially in view of the growing importance of private tertiary education and e-learning (Jongsma, 2014).

As a result of this "quiet quality assurance revolution", countries fall today into one of the following four categories (Salmi, 2015a):

• Advanced systems whose tertiary education institutions have well-developed internal quality assurance processes with a strong focus on quality enhancement, in line with national standards defined by the external quality assurance and/or accreditation agencies, often linked to the national qualifications framework. Leading OECD economies would be in this category.

- Well-established systems relying still predominantly on external quality assurance, where a significant proportion of tertiary education institutions do not fully meet the national quality assurance standards. Many industrial and developing countries would be in this category.
- Countries that are in the process of setting up and consolidating their quality assurance system. Many developing countries and countries in transition in Eastern Europe and Central Asia would be in that category.
- Countries that have not established a formal quality assurance system. These would encompass a few countries in Asia, the Middle East, Latin America and the Caribbean and the Middle East, and about two dozen countries in Africa.

Complementing the widespread development of national and professional quality assurance agencies, new instruments of accountability have appeared or been suggested in recent years as ways of complementing the pool of information available to measure the performance and operation of tertiary education institutions (Salmi, 2015). Of particular relevance in this context are the following modalities: (i) student engagement surveys, (ii) assessment of student learning outcomes, (iii) labor market results information, and (iv) rankings.

*Student engagement surveys.* Following the example of the United States, where the first large-scale survey of student engagement (NSSE) took place in 2000, a number of countries have developed and implemented their own version of a survey aimed at ascertaining how students assess the quality of teaching and learning in their institutions. Today, student engagement surveys are carried out regularly in Australia, Canada, Germany, Ireland, the Netherlands and the United Kingdom. Pilot surveys have also been undertaken in recent years in countries as diverse as China, South Africa and South Korea.

Continuing a movement that started in the 1960s with student evaluations of their teachers, student engagement surveys include not only subjective indicators, such as the level of satisfaction of students, but also attempt to measure more objective aspects related to the degree of active engagement of students in interactive and collaborative learning activities. In countries where surveys of student engagement are conducted regularly, high school graduates tend to be better equipped to choose which college or university they would like to attend (Ramsden and Callender, 2014).

Student engagement surveys face two challenges (Klemencic and Chirikov, 2014). First, some observers have questioned their validity and reliability with respect to the ability of students to make informed judgments when asked to report learning gains, and the selection of the key factors that are supposed to determine student learning (Porter et al., 2011). Second, not all stakeholders are ready to live with the kind of transparency that these surveys imply. For instance, many US universities, including top-tier universities, have not been willing to release their NSSE results publicly. This limits the usefulness of these surveys for the universities' main stakeholders, such as employers, parents and prospective students.

*Assessment of student learning outcomes.* Unlike what happens at lower levels of education, the world of tertiary education does not have a long tradition of measuring learning outcomes. However, promising initiatives have emerged in recent years. In the United States, a growing number of institutions have been using one of three assessment instruments to try and measure added value at the undergraduate level: the ACT Collegiate Assessment of Academic Proficiency (CAAP), the ETS Proficiency Profile (EPP) and the Collegiate Learning Assessment (CLA). Similar instruments have been in use in other OECD countries, such as Australia's Graduate Skills Assessment.

A few Latin American countries—Brazil, Colombia and Mexico for example—have also been pioneers in measuring the acquisition of knowledge and competencies of undergraduate students. In Brazil, the late Paulo Renato, then Federal Minister of Education, introduced the Provão in 1996 as a voluntary test designed to compare the performance of similar programs across all universities, it was the first such national assessment system in the world. The Provão consisted of a final course examination for undergraduate students that did not count towards the graduation of the students themselves but served to evaluate the results of their program and institution. The Provão was replaced in 2004 by a new test (ENADE), applied every three year to a sample of students, which examines the test scores of both first-year and last-year undergraduate students as an attempt to measure the added value of undergraduate programs (Salmi and Saroyan, 2007). Similarly, the Colombian Assessment Institute (Instituto Colombiano para la Evaluación de la Educación), has implemented two tests (SABER-11 and SABER-PRO) since 2009 that measure students' abilities at the start and end of their undergraduate education.

In some cases, policy-makers have considered the opportunity of using students learning outcomes for quality assurance purposes. But these proposals have been met with caution by the tertiary education community, as illustrated by the controversy sparked by the 2006 report of the Spellings Commission on the Future of Higher Education in the United States. The report recommended measuring learning outcomes to complement the existing accreditation system.

> ... by law, student learning is a core part of accreditation. Unfortunately, students are often the least informed, and the last to be considered. Accreditation remains one of the least publicized, least transparent parts of higher education—even compared to the Byzantine and bewildering financial aid system. (NACIQI, 2007)

Initiatives to measure students learning outcomes in an international perspective have also been received with little enthusiasm. In 2012, the OECD conducted a pilot experience to measure the achievement of generic competencies and the acquisition of professional skills in the areas of economics and engineering in the context of the AHELO project (Assessment of Higher Education Learning Outcomes). Even though seventeen countries participated in the feasibility study and the pilot, the future of the project, presented as an alternative to the global rankings, remains uncertain (OECD, 2013).

The recent emergence of private companies specializing in testing the work readiness of young graduates has introduced a new twist with respect to the assessment of student learning outcomes. In India, for example, several large multinational firms make it compulsory for anyone interested in applying for a job to take one of these professional tests.

> More than 1.5 million people in India have taken a test called the AMCAT (Aspiring Minds' Computer Adaptive Test). The assessment measures aptitude in English, quantitative ability and logic. … It also includes a variety of situational and judgment tests, which scrutinize personality types and soft skills to see how they might apply in specific fields. (Fain, 2014)

*Labor market observatories.* Another noteworthy development has been the establishment of Labor Market Observatories (LMOs) in a growing number of developing and transition countries, following the example of the many OECD countries that have employment observatories either at the supra-national level (European Union employment observatory), the national level (e.g., Bureau of Labor Statistics in the USA, Destination of Leavers from Higher Education survey in the UK, survey university-based AlmaLaurea observatory in Italy), and the sub-national level (e.g., Learning and Skills observatory in Wales, OREF in France, Education-Employment Information system in Florida). The examples of Bulgaria, Chile and Colombia are worth mentioning in this context.

Since 2012, the Bulgarian government has published detailed data on the labor market results of university graduates. Using data from the Registry of Tertiary Students and statistics from the National Social Security administration, the Ministry of Education is able to provide a wealth of information on the types of jobs and levels of remuneration of graduates who left university in the previous five years. The database indicates, for instance, if the graduate found a job, if the position corresponds to the field and level of study, what type of employer she/he is working with, if the graduate has a permanent or temporary job, and the level of salary based on social security contributions.

Supported by the Chilean Ministry of Education and jointly run by the School of Government of the private University Adolfo Abánez and the University of Chile's Department of Industrial Engineering, *Futuro Laboral* aims to equip youths and students with academic orientation tools. *Futuro Laboral* provides information on the occupational situation of graduates of hundreds of professional and technical careers that represent 75% of technical and professional graduates. The information available to the public includes detailed data on salaries and employment opportunities. The portal displays, for each program of every tertiary education institution, detailed information on dropout rates, average time to degree, average earnings of the graduates after 4 years of graduation, current tuition fees for the program, and accreditation status of the program. Employment and earnings data are not self-reported, but gathered from the database of the national tax revenue authority. Earnings are matched to the databases of graduates provided by the tertiary education institutions. The privacy of the information is maintained, as the tax service issues only the average values for each program in each institution, provided there are at least 25 individuals in each program/institution's cohort for whom earnings data are available.

*Graduados Colombia* (*Observatorio Laboral para la Educación*) was launched in 2005 and is managed by the Ministry of Education. It collects and presents information on the demand and supply of graduates. Students, families, tertiary education institutions, researchers and the productive sector have access to statistics on the academic level of the graduates of technical institutes and universities, the salaries they receive, the average time for finding the first job, as well as the cities where they work. The website serves as a tool for students trying to choose a career, and it is also useful for tertiary education institutions intent on renewing and adapting the programs they offer according to labor market needs. *Graduados Colombia*'s site provides links to job offers in Colombia and in other countries as well as advice and tips on how to write and present a good resume. Visitors are able to look for the results of the graduate and employer surveys, as well as studies on specific disciplines and economic sectors.

These three initiatives show relevant examples of labor market observatories that aim to provide a better understanding of and match among individuals' professional aspirations, tertiary education, and occupational trends. As such, they help to address one of the main challenges of tertiary education: its relevance to individuals and societies.

*Rankings.* The power of public opinion is nowhere more visible than in the growing influence of rankings. Initially limited to the United States, university rankings and league tables have multiplied in recent years, existing today in more than 35 industrial and developing countries.[1]

> The U.S. News [& World Report] rankings have become the nation's de facto higher education accountability system—evaluating colleges and universities on a common scale and creating strong incentives for institutions to do things that raise their ratings. (Kevin Carey, 2006).

While fully acknowledging their methodological limitations, it is undeniable that the rankings have often played a useful educational role by making relevant information available to the public, especially in countries lacking a formal system of quality assurance. In Poland, for example, when the transition to the market economy started in the early 1990s, there was a thirst for information about the quality of the rapidly proliferating private education institutions. This demand for information pushed the owner of *Perspektyvy* magazine to initiate the country's first university ranking. Similarly, for many years the annual ranking published in Japan by the *Asahi Shimbun* fulfilled an essential quality assurance function in the absence of any evaluation or accreditation agency. In France, after the publication of the 2008 edition of the Shanghai ranking, while the Secretary General of the national teacher union (SNESUP) complained that it was unfair to compare the performance of universities to a race at the Olympic Games, the French Minister of Higher Education declared that "these lists of winners may not be ideal, but they do exist. … They show the urgency of reform for the [French] university" (Floc'h, 2008).

Some of the rankings include information from student engagement surveys and/or labor market observatories as key indicators. In Chile, for example, the country's main weekly magazine (*Que Pasa?*) uses the results of *Futuro Laboral* to rank universities and programs every year on the basis of the labor market outcomes of their graduates. Similarly, in Bulgaria, the Ministry of Education has developed a ranking that incorporates the labor market results of university graduates.[2]

Since the 2003 publication of the first international ranking of universities by Shanghai Jiao Tong University and the subsequent emergence of competing global league tables (THE, HEEACT, QS, etc.), students have used the results of the rankings to select study destinations while governments have increasingly relied on league tables to grant eligibility for scholarships and student loans, and even make immigration decisions.

The proliferation of rankings has provoked intense reactions, ranging from disagreements about the very principle of rankings, criticism about the methodology used to produce them, outright boycotts, and even court actions to stop their publication.

> The expansion of league tables and ranking exercises has not gone unnoticed by the various stakeholders and the reaction they elicit is rarely benign. Such rankings are often dismissed by their many critics as irrelevant exercises fraught with data and methodological flaws, they are boycotted by some universities angry at the results, and they are used by political opponents as a convenient way to criticize governments. (Salmi & Saroyan, 2007, p. 80)

Despite the controversies surrounding them, there are good reasons why rankings persist. These include the benefits of information provided to students who are looking to make an informed choice among various institutions and programs, either domestically or for studies abroad. Further, rankings contribute to promoting a culture of transparency, providing institutions with incentives to collect and publish more reliable data. Finally, rankings can be used to define stretch goals at the institutional level. In so doing, universities may find themselves analyzing key factors explaining ranking as part of their efforts to improve teaching, learning and research, proposing concrete targets to guide (but not replace) strategic planning and entering into mutually advantageous partnerships.

13

*Globalization*

Globalization, declining communication and transportation costs, and the opening of political borders have combined to facilitate increased movements of people. In the tertiary education domain, this has translated into rapidly rising numbers of international students and, more recently, a growing number of academics moving from one country to the other in pursuit of more attractive professional opportunities.

According to the OECD (2015b), more than 4 million students studied overseas in 2013, up from 1.3 in 1990 and 2.1 in 2000. The five countries with the highest proportion of international students are Australia, Austria, Luxembourg, New Zealand, Switzerland and the United Kingdom. More than half the international students enrolled worldwide come from Asia, especially China, India and South Korea. International students are predominantly present at the most advanced levels of tertiary education. Whereas the proportion of international students in OECD countries is 9% on average, 24% of students enrolled in doctoral programs are citizens of other countries.

The growing influence of the international rankings and the related movement to establish world-class universities, fueled by the various excellence initiatives launched by governments in more than 30 countries, have led to a global race for talent (Salmi, 2009a and 2016b). As documented in Wildavsky's book (2012), international mobility of advanced human capital is not only about students but also, increasingly, about academics recruited by institutions from other countries. New universities in Asia and the Middle East are competing with the likes of Cambridge and Stanford in trying to attract top faculty members. Some countries, Denmark and the Netherlands for example, have put in place accelerated visa procedures to facilitate the immigration of highly qualified professionals coming from top ranked universities.

The trend towards the rapid increase in international collaborative projects among university researchers is another important new dimension of the global tertiary education scene. Research production has increased exponentially in the past decades, and collaborative research activities have followed the same pattern. Figure 3 illustrates this trend and presents the evolution of co-authored articles, revealing a faster growth of multiple author articles than single author ones. While the number of articles published over the past decade went from 1.3 million in 2003 to 2.4 million in 2013, the number of authorships has increased at a far greater rate from 4.6 million in 2003 to 10 million in 2013 (Plume and van Weijin, 2014).

Drawing from a pioneering analysis of publications over the past three decades, Jonathan Adams announced the "fourth age of research", the age of collaborative research and international research networks, following the age of individual researchers, the age of the research institution, and the age of the national research enterprise (Adams, 2013). He went on to demonstrate that international collaborative research is of higher quality and has a greater influence than traditional research, as shown in Figure 4, which compares the citation impact of international collaborative publications and domestic publications in the United States and the United Kingdom.

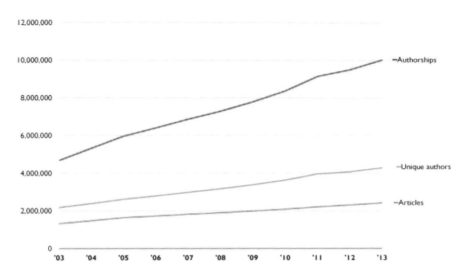

*Figure 3. Evolution of Number of Authors and Number of Joint Authors.*
*Source: Scopus database*

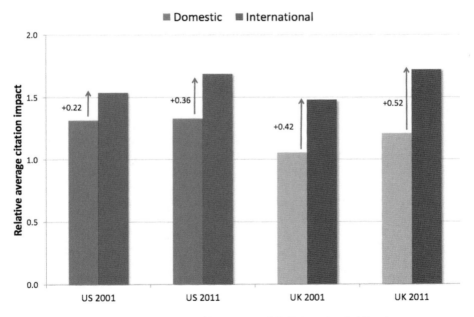

*Figure 4. Citation Impact of International Collaborative Publications.*
*Source: Thompson Reuters database*

15

Collaborative research yields faster results and facilitates a quicker transfer of these results, thereby serving the needs of both producers and users of knowledge in a more effective and efficient manner.

Finally, as part of their internationalization and resource diversification strategy, a growing number of universities in industrial countries have opened branch campuses in developing and emerging economies. These branch campuses are usually brick-and-mortar facilities delivering the same degree(s) as the mother institution to students coming predominantly from the host country. The most recent estimate puts the number of branch campuses at 229, with 20 being currently developed (C-BERT, 2015). Half of the branch campuses are affiliated to US universities; the others belong mainly to Australian, British and French universities, in declining order. In recent years, universities from emerging economies, such as India and Malaysia, have also opened branch campuses in other countries. The large majority of branch campuses have been established in the Middle East and in South-East Asia.

The main advantage, for the host country, is that its students can get access to a good quality education from a foreign university without actually needing to live overseas and pay the full cost associated with a foreign degree, as a recent global survey of transnational education found out (Knight and McNamara, 2015). Anecdotal evidence from Chinese universities confirm the growing quality of programs offered in branch campuses (Box 1).

> ### Box 1. Offering a Relevant Overseas Experience at Home: Examples from China
>
> Overseas universities with joint ventures in China are now attracting a better class of student. For example, New York University Shanghai has worked to build its reputation by promising good knowledge resources as well as international exposure and better job opportunities for graduates.
>
> More high-quality young people are now flocking to such colleges, not least because of their mature recruitment policies. According to Yang Guohua, a senior executive with the Sino-Foreign Cooperative Universities Union, "apart from accepting students based on their performance in the Gaokao, China's national college entrance examination, these universities have developed diverse ways to find students who can better meet their expectations." NYU Shanghai, for example, a joint venture launched in 2013 by NYU and Shanghai's East China Normal University, has a pre-selection process in which promising students are interviewed before the all-important exam, with the goal of enrolling the most excellent Chinese students.
>
> China has seven universities that are jointly operated by domestic and foreign institutions. The oldest, the University of Nottingham Ningbo China, was established in 2004 by Zhejiang Wanli University and Britain's University of Nottingham. The Ministry of Education has approved plans for two more in the

southern province of Guangdong. Statistics from the Sino-Foreign Cooperative Universities Union, which the joint ventures established in 2014 to advise the Chinese government on such collaboration, show that the seven universities accepted more than 7,300 Chinese students in 2015.

Jeffrey S. Lehman, vice-chancellor of NYU Shanghai, said the university fosters its students' capacity to deal with multicultural situations. To do that, "the first lesson a freshman receives is to learn how to live and communicate with someone from another country, as it's essential to share a room with a person from a different country in the first year," he said. "A fraternity with organizers from at least two nationalities is also needed to have a better fusion of cultures." Yang added that while internationalization is a distinct characteristic of such universities, "they also prepare students with a lot of knowledge on Chinese culture and general education, to ensure the young people gain a global vision while understanding the Chinese context".

With quality resources and lower tuition fees (compared with studying overseas), these universities are a good option for students who want to get an overseas education experience in China. A survey of graduates from these colleges, released during a forum in April for presidents of the Sino-foreign cooperative universities, found the employment rate was 95 percent in 2014. Seven out of 10 graduates went on to work for multinational corporations or international organizations, while more than 90 percent said they were satisfied with their joint-venture alma maters.

(Source: Zhao and Yu, 2016)

With these reasons in mind, a number of governments have offered financial and fiscal incentives to encourage foreign universities to set up branches locally. Dubai, for instance, constructed the Knowledge Village in 2003 as a free trade zone for foreign institutions interested in operating there without needing to build facilities or pay taxes.

*New Providers and New Education Technologies*

Big breakthroughs happen when what is suddenly possible meets what is desperately necessary. (Thomas Friedman)

In 2002, the World Bank's *Constructing Knowledge Societies* identified several new trends likely to translate into significant changes in the tertiary education landscape, notably the emergence of new providers and new modes of delivery. These trends have but accelerated in the past fifteen years. Three developments are particularly worth reviewing in that respect: (i) the rapid growth of for-profit providers, (ii) the multiplication of alternative modes of delivery in the form of MOOCs, and (iii) the impact of open science, big data and open education resources.

*For-Profit Providers.* The growth of for-profit providers has continued and even accelerated in a number of industrial and developing countries. In the United States, for example, enrolment in for-profit institutions increased by 235% in the past decade, reaching a market share of almost 10% of all students, according to estimates from the Carnegie Foundation for the Advancement of Teaching (Zhao, 2011). The sector represented close to 30% of all tertiary level institutions in 2011. The economic downturn as a result of the 2007-2008 financial crisis triggered a 30% jump in enrollment in the largest 11 for-profit universities in just three years, as many laid-off employees sought to retrain whereas in most states funding for public institutions was significantly cut down. Almost 80%% of the newly accredited tertiary education institutions during the 2005-2010 period were for-profits.

In many cases, the success of for-profit institutions relies on their ability to take advantage of the Internet and new technologies for designing and offering new, flexible and less expensive teaching and learning delivery models that are appealing to the mature student population that they serve in general. The University of Phoenix, whose enrolment reached a high of 600,000 in 2010 but had declined to 162,000 by 2016, is perhaps one of the most emblematic cases of a for-profit university effectively championing a blended learning model. Box 2 documents University of Phoenix' experience in Southern Arizona.

---

*Box 2. Example of For-Profit University:*
*The University of Phoenix in Southern Arizona*

Complementing the work of the University of Arizona and the local community colleges, the private, for-profit University of Phoenix (UoP) fulfills an important role in support of training and retraining for the adult population in Southern Arizona. In the words of its President, Bill Pepicello, the University owes its success to the recognition that "...education needs to be something that fits people's lives and becomes part of it... It needs to be that kind of accessibility, and many people are willing to pay a premium price for that."[3]

Over the past 30 years, UoP has developed a unique pedagogical model to fit the characteristics and needs of its adult student body (average age of students is 34), who are looking to earn a degree corresponding to their actual work activity or for starting a new career. The students go through a sequence of 6-week modules that usually combine actual class time and online learning, although UoP offers four different modalities to match the variety of learning preferences of the students (classroom, blended, online, and directed study mode with a one-on-one instructor). Faculty members do not lecture generally, but facilitate self-learning among the students. UoP has a comprehensive quality assurance and standards system to train the practitioner faculty and ensure that students achieve the prescribed learning objectives. Learning is

---

enhanced through a wide array of online resources, including a digital library, e-texts and pedagogical software (tutorials, grammar support, plagiarism checker, etc.).

(Source: OECD, 2011)

While for-profit tertiary level institutions are not allowed in many parts in the world, in those countries where they can operate legally they have also witnessed rapid growth. In Brazil, Peru, the Philippines and South Korea, for instance, enrollment in for-profit colleges and universities account today for 40 to 50% of the total student population. For-profit providers are also quite prominent in Chile, Jordan, Malaysia, Mexico, Peru, South Africa and Ukraine. Box 3 documents the role played by for-profits in Brazil.

*Box 3. Evolution of For-Profits in Brazil*

Brazil's for-profits enrolled over two million students in 2010, representing 43% of the private sector and 32% of the overall tertiary education system. By 2000, just a year after full legal approval to allow for-profit higher education, the sub-sector already enrolled 18% of the private sector's student population and 12% of the total tertiary education population. For-profit boosted its size by 537% in the 2000 to 2010 period, displacing the public sector from its second position in enrolments, while the private non-profit and the public sectors increased by only 88% and 85%, respectively.

Consistent with major trends in private tertiary education globally, the for-profit sub-sector accumulates its largest share of enrolments in the fields of social science, business and law (51%), education (17%) and health and social welfare (15%). By contrast, the public sector shows a greater concentration on education (41%), followed by social sciences et al. (15%), and engineering, production and construction (12%). For-profits tend to offer programs with low costs and high rates of return to institutional investment.

Through planned and unplanned factors, Brazil has given the private sector overall—now very much including the for-profit sub-sector—a major role in access, keeping most selective institutions in the public sector. This reality, coupled with the fact that an overwhelming 95% of for-profits are non-university institutions, has generated concern about quality in the for-profit sub-sector. However, Brazil's large-scale test of undergraduate students (Provão) found a wide range of quality in both the private and public sectors, with for-profits outperforming what conventional wisdom expected.

Trends seem to point toward continuing growth of the Brazilian for-profit sub-sector through two developments: first, more non-profit institutions have switched their legal status; and second large domestic and international publicly traded companies have incorporated non-profit institutions in their business portfolios.

(Source: Salto, 2014)

From a national policy viewpoint, the main advantage of for-profit institutions is their ability to absorb part of the enrolment expansion at no cost to the State and provide relevant professional training that is directly related to labor market needs. While available data from the US confirm that for-profit tertiary education institutions actually help increase access beyond public sector provision and often offer training opportunities in fields not always served by public institutions, concerns about quality and fraudulent practices—from questionable marketing methods to inappropriate student loans—remain (Kinser, 2009). In recent years, for-profits have been accused of exploiting minorities, poor people and veterans.

The institutions that have failed to meet regulatory standards or been accused of violating legal statutes include tiny beauty schools with staggering loan default rates and online law schools with dismal graduation rates and no bar association accreditation. Without government money, few of these institutions could attract students or stay in business. (Harris, 2016)

The 2016 trial and 25 million dollar settlement around the Trump University brought to light questionable practices, including accusations of unscrupulous exploitation of vulnerable students, high-pressure sales tactics, use of unqualified instructors and deceptive claims about the academic offerings (Barbaro et al., 2016).

*Alternative modes of delivery: the MOOCs explosion.* Awed by their potentially disruptive character, the New York Times declared 2012 "the year of the MOOCs", referring to the explosion of the so-called Massive Open Online Courses and the growing perception that they could challenge traditional universities or even threaten their very existence. Unlike traditional online courses, which charge tuition, have limited enrolment and give credits to their students, the MOOCs are supposed to be free, expected to reach thousands if not millions of students, and usually do not carry credits. Made famous by the likes of EdX (non-profit partnership between MIT and Harvard), Udacity (for-profit startup launched by Stanford Professor Ng), Coursera (for-profit organization working closely with several Ivy League universities), and FutureLearn (the UK's Open University venture into MOOCs, which overtook Coursera in 2015 as the third largest provider), the MOOCs have grown at exponential speed in the past few years. In the United States, where 400 universities have produced a total of 2,400 such online courses, the MOOCS have become an integral part of the tertiary education landscape. Worldwide, estimates indicate a total of 35 million students participating in MOOCs in 2015, compared to 18 million the previous year. Figure 5 illustrates the tremendous increase in MOOCs in the past 5 years.

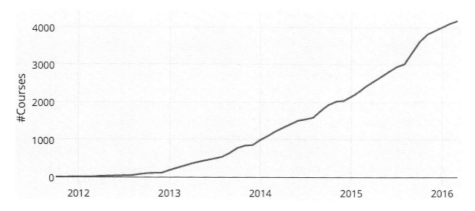

*Figure 5. Evolution of the Number of MOOCs (2012–2016).*
*Source: Class Central website https://www.class-central.com/report/moocs-2015-stats/*

Supporters of the MOOCs hail them as the most important innovation in tertiary education, with the potential of offering unlimited learning opportunities to millions of people all over the world by giving them free access to courses from the best professors in the best universities. The MOOCs come complete with exams and electronic feedback from teaching assistants. Some are also providing certificates to the students who complete the course. A few universities—Georgia Technology Institute for example—have even packaged an entire degree around MOOCs.

Not everyone is taken by the MOOCs, however. The critics point to a number of serious limitations evidenced by the low completion rates.[4] How much learning does actually take place in a course with 100,000 students? How can the MOOCs successfully help the students who most need new learning opportunities, but who at the same time are less prepared for university-level autonomous learning? How can students be effectively assessed, electronically? How can widespread cheating—apparently an endemic phenomenon with online education—be avoided? How can students combine a set of courses into a consistent program that can be recognized by other academic institutions and employers?

The results of a recent survey of students in three developing countries, Colombia, the Philippines and South Africa, shed a more positive light on the potential of MOOCs (UWN, 2016a). In contrast to findings among users of MOOCs in industrial countries, in the three developing countries included in the study, low-income and middle-income students made up 80% of MOOC users. The proportion of users who actually completed the courses was quite high (30%) and 49% of users received a certificate, with women being more likely than men to complete a MOOC or get certification. Lack of computer access or prior skills was not highlighted as a significant barrier.

At the end of the day, the success of the MOOCs will by conditioned by two factors. The first constraint is the ability of MOOCs providers to find a sustainable business model. The fact that many of them have abandoned the tuition-free approach illustrates the difficulty of maintaining a very low cost for the students while raising the resources necessary for the development of high quality online courses. The second, even more important challenge consists in developing a credible system of certification and recognition of qualifications. To operate truly as a viable alternative to on-campus studies at regular tertiary education institutions, the MOOCs must offer professional qualifications that give proper access to the labor market. In addition, students enrolled in regular on-campus programs, who want to take some of their courses online, need the assurance that their institution recognizes their MOOCs credits.

*Open science, big data and open education resources.* Open Science, defined broadly as "a systemic change in the modus operandi of doing research and organizing science," offers new opportunities for tertiary education in developing countries. The paradigm shift embodied by Open Science refers to the rapid development of interactive and collaborative modes of knowledge acquisition, generation and dissemination, facilitated by networks that rely on modern information and communication tools.[5] This recent evolution encompasses several interrelated trends and phenomena, ranging from citizen science to web 2.0., which can greatly benefit tertiary education systems and institutions. Figure 6 proposes a representation of how the various dimensions are connected and interact.

Two developments are worth mentioning here: predictive analytics and open education resources. In the first instance, big data and predictive analytics have arisen in just a few years as powerful tools to assist policy-makers and practitioners in making data-driven decisions through mathematical modeling, digital simulation and scientific computation. In particular, big data may be a promising avenue to address the issue of low internal efficiency and high dropout rates that plagues many institutions in both industrial and developing nations.

A recent survey estimated that about 40% of US universities have experimented with novel data analysis methods to follow the digital footprint of their students and detect, very early on, behavioral changes associated with potential academic difficulties (Ekowo and Palmer, 2016). Administrators and professors can use digital dashboards and "heat maps" that highlight who might be in academic trouble. Ball State University in Indiana monitors not only the academic engagement of students but also their social activities in order to identify unexpected shifts in patterns that may reflect study difficulties. Retention specialists immediately contact the students to offer academic or psychological support as needed. Special attention is given to Pell Grant beneficiaries (low income students) through a mobile app. Arizona State University's eAdvisor system, which flags students at risk of lagging behind, is credited with a significant increase in completion rates for students from vulnerable groups, from 26 to 41%, since its establishment in 2007.

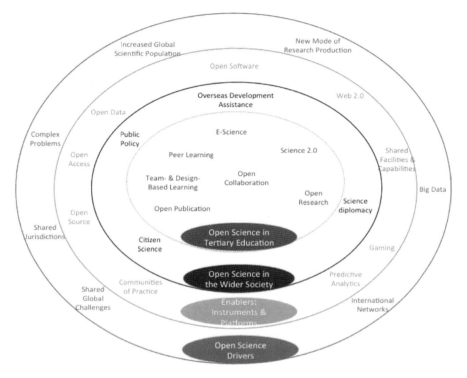

*Figure 6. Open Science and Related Developments.*
*Source: Elaborated by Jamil Salmi*

The Minnesota State Colleges and Universities system, which used to allow students to apply for enrolment until a few days before the beginning of classes, recently terminated this practice after administrators realized that students who enrolled closer to the start of the semester where more likely to fail than those who enrolled earlier (Kelderman, 2012). A new University Innovation Alliance of 11 large public universities, backed by several major foundations, was constituted in September 2014. It will use data analytics in its first set of projects, which are aimed at improving graduation rates for low-income students (Blumenstyk, 2014).

The University of Maryland System has adopted the PAR Framework's Student Success Matrix to improve student success programs through the use of predictive analyses and benchmarking collaborative to identify students at risk.[6]

Our culture of evaluation and our use of learning analytics have created a new way of thinking about learning. Our focus is not solely relegated to individual courses or processes, but rather to all of the activities that

23

contribute to educational improvement... The process of leveraging analytics and improving student outcomes requires institutions to add capacity in understanding the data, applying evidenced based research practices for the student populations served, and a willingness to measure the effectiveness of the initiatives applied. (Karen Vignare, Vice Provost for UMUC's Center for Innovation in Learning and Student Success (CILSS))

The experience of Georgia State University in Atlanta is perhaps the most telling example of the use of predictive analytics in the United States. Georgia State University (GSU), whose students are sixty percent nonwhite and many are from first generation families, uses predictive analytics to advise students on which majors they are most likely to succeed in, based on their grades in prior courses (Blumenstyk, 2014; Kamenetz, 2016). GSU relies on an early-warning system built on the analysis of 2.5 million course grades received by students over 10 years to identify the critical factors that reduce changes to graduate. For example, an academic adviser will get a red flag if a student does not receive a satisfactory grade in a course needed in her or his major, or does not take a required course within the recommended time, or signs up for a class not relevant to his or her major. As part of establishing the Graduation and Progression Success program, GSU recruited more academic advisers and managed to bring down the caseload from 700 to 1 to 300 to 1. The University has obtained impressive results: graduation rates are up 6 percentage points since 2013; to get their degree, graduates are spending on average a semester less than before, saving an estimated $12 million in tuition; and low-income, first-generation and minority students have closed the graduation rate gap, even in tough STEM majors.

Canadian universities have also started to use predictive analytics to identify and help students at risk (Chiose, 2016). At the University of Toronto, for example, the use of big data has influenced the decision to do away with the practice of allowing students with poor scores in their first term to continue taking classes with their cohort under the condition that they would take again the courses that they failed. Data on graduation rates showed that the majority of these students did not finish their degree. So moving them along did not work. Instead, the University asks them now to repeat their first year and participate in a special program called Refresh, which includes academic, professional and personal development courses. Along similar lines, the University of British Columbia has a pilot project to link the academic trajectory and preparation of incoming students with their participation in extracurricular programs, their university grades, and their labor market results.

Observers have also suggested that big data could be used effectively to map out future labor market needs and influence the shaping of curriculum and pedagogy. The city of Manchester, for instance, has tried to chart the competencies, skills and attributes in demand in the Greater Manchester area by analyzing 600,000 LinkedIn profiles of people working in the region. Tertiary education institutions could gain insights into workplace and workforce trends nationally and globally (Hristov, 2016).

Big data can also be used to organize the active participation of citizens in data collection, scientific experiments and problem resolution. In recent years, scientists have found it useful to involve volunteers and amateurs in their activities, often benefiting in unexpected ways from these non-professional contributions. One of the most relevant cases in that respect is the "fold-it" biochemistry experiment (Box 4).

---

*Box 4. Amateurs Solving Complex Science Problems:*
*the Foldit Experiment*

Foldit is a science game designed to tackle the problem of protein folding with the help of ordinary people who enjoy videogames acting as scientists. Is was developed by the Center for Game Science at the University of Washington (http://centerforgamescience.org), which creates game-based environments in order to solve important problems that humanity faces today.

Over 100,000 amateur players from all over the world, each with different backgrounds, are engaged in the Foldit game. As the official site of the game states, the best Foldit players have little to no prior exposure to biochemistry.

Playing the game implies folding proteins starting from a set of provided tools and models of proteins. Users receive scores for how good they do the fold and these scores can be seen on a leaderboard, therefore stimulating competition among players.

The game was developed with the premise that humans' pattern-recognition and puzzle-solving abilities are more efficient than the existing computer programs dealing with this kind of tasks. The data gathered can be used to train and improve computers in order to generate more accurate and faster results than they are capable of achieving at present.

So far, Foldit has produced predictions that outperform the best known computational methods. These results have been published in a Nature paper with more than 57,000 authors, most of them being non-experts in biochemistry related fields. This is a great example of how this type of gaming environment can create skilled researchers out of novices.

Other good examples of citizens' involvment in research can be also found at www.zooniverse.org, the largest global platform hosting projects in different scientific fields ranging from astronomy to zoology. The platform provides opportunities for people around the world to contribute to real discoveries, converting volunteers' efforts into measurable results. So far, the amateur scientists have contributed to a large number of published research papers and significant examples of open source data analysis can be found as useful contributions to the wider research community. Unexpected,

---

scientifically significant discoveries have been made by the voalunteers as well.

Another strong point of citizen science research is that the citizens' involvement can help research save money. A recent study made on seven Zooniverse projects followed the activities of 100,386 participants who contributed a total of 129,500 hours of unpaid labor. That would have been worth more than $1.5 million, taking into account the rate normally paid to undergraduate students.

(Source: http://fold.it/portal/; Sauermann and Franzoni, 2015)

Similarly, researchers at University College London designed a videogame to analyze the first symptoms of Alzheimer's disease. Harnessing data from the 2.4 million people who downloaded and played the game, they conducted the world's largest dementia research experiment (Gallagher, 2016).

Second, the open education movement represents a unique opportunity for tertiary education institutions and learners in developing countries to access free courses, scientific articles, software and other education resources. Since the launch of MIT's OpenCourseWare website in October 2003, the Open Education Resources movement has spread exponentially and universally. Open Educational Resources (OER) encompass all sorts of educational materials that are free to access and open for use, and that can be adapted and combined in many ways. Here are the most common two definitions of OER (OECD, 2015c, p. 17):

Open educational resources are digital learning resources offered on line (although sometimes in print) freely and openly to teachers, educators, students, and independent learners in order to be used, shared, combined, adapted, and expanded in teaching, learning and research. They include learning content, software tools to develop, use and distribute, and implementation resources such as open licenses. The learning content is educational material of a wide variety, from full courses to smaller units such as diagrams or test questions. It may include text, images, audio, video, simulations, games, portals and the like. (OECD-CERI definition)

OER are teaching, learning, and research resources that reside in the public domain or have been released under an intellectual property license that permits their free use and repurposing by others. Open educational resources include full courses, course materials, modules, textbooks, streaming videos, tests, software, and any other tools, materials or techniques used to support access to knowledge. (William and Flora Hewlett Foundation definitions)

OECD (2015c) describes OER as a genuine catalyst for innovation because they can, at the same time, drive the transformation of educational practices and facilitate new forms of interaction among teachers, researchers, learners and knowledge along many dimensions. OER represent a platform for reducing the constraints of geographical location, time and pace of learning. For tertiary education institutions and students in developing countries, relying on OER means being able to access high-quality materials at no cost or very low cost, thereby reducing the barriers to learning opportunities. Free digital resources can help improve the process of teaching and learning by bringing about new forms of learning and a richer learning experience. Teachers can work together to develop their own learning materials and create networks for supporting capacity building among other teachers as well as the educational needs of other learners.

Because of their flexibility and adaptability, OER are well suited to address some of the new challenges faced by tertiary education institutions in the 21st century discussed earlier in this Chapter. In particular, they can support the transformation of the curriculum, the application of new learning theories, and better respond to the various knowledge and competence acquisition needs of heterogeneous groups of learners. OER also help to build bridges across countries and learning communities of all kinds. They blur the frontier between formal and informal learning, and between degree-focused education and lifelong learning.

*Political Commotions*

The final trend worth mentioning is the serious deterioration of the political environment in a growing number of countries, resulting in adverse to dangerous situations for tertiary education. In particular, violence against students has erupted in unprecedented ways in recent years. Hundreds of students were abducted or killed in countries as diverse as Kenya, Mexico, Nigeria and Pakistan. The racist killing of an Indian student in Australia in 2010 led to thousands of Indian students switching to Canada as their preferred international study destination. The Scholars at Risk network registered 158 attacks in 35 countries between 1 May 2015 and 1 September 2016 (O'Malley, 2016). The attacks included 40 incidents of killings, violence and disappearances, as well as several cases of university closures or military occupation of campuses.

US colleges witnessed several massacres in the past few years. Paradoxically, this has led to more guns on campuses rather than the opposite. At the University of Texas, the dean of the Faculty of Architecture stepped down in February 2016 in protest against the imposition, by the state legislature, of the right of wearing concealed weapons in the classroom. At the University of Houston, the administration warned professors against discussing sensitive topics during class to avoid angering students who may be armed.

Reduced academic freedom is also becoming a matter of concern. As early as 2001, Professor Altbach documented how academic freedom was coming under attack even in countries with reasonable levels of democracy. From Serbia to Indonesia, from Egypt to Malaysia, or from Hong Kong to Singapore, professors expressing views or researching topics perceived as politically incorrect or inacceptable can be censored, sacked or even jailed (Altbach, 2001). This downward trend has not stopped, quite the contrary. The *Scholars at Risk* network documented gross breaches of academic freedom in many parts of the world in the past twelve months, notably in Bahrain, China, Egypt, India, Israel, Malaysia, Nigeria, Pakistan, Thailand and Turkey.[7] In the US, the September 11 terrorist attack has resulted in increased scrutiny of views not deemed to be patriotic enough and condemnation of faculty speech interpreted as critical of official US government positions (Benedict, 2009). In Russia, the justice department sued a professor of history because the research for his doctoral thesis focused on a controversial Soviet general who had turned against Stalin and allied himself with the German army, thereby challenging the orthodox view of the war between the Soviet Union and Nazi Germany (Holdsworth, 2016).

Tightened visa rules as part of the fight against terrorism have often translated into restrictions for foreign scholars and students. The Scottish universities have complained of a decrease in the number of foreign students as a result of the stricter visa regulations put in place for students seeking to study in the United Kingdom.

Finally, the massive influx of Afghan, Iraqi and Syrian refugees into Europe represents a major challenge for the local universities ill-prepared to take on significant numbers of new foreign students without matching additional budgetary resources and an appropriate framework for the recognition of the academic qualifications of the incoming refugee students.

## CONCLUSION: CHALLENGES AND OPPORTUNITIES

There has never been a time of greater promise, or greater peril. (Klaus Schwab, 2016 World Economic Forum)

The French philosopher Paul Valery observed with nostalgia that "the trouble with our times is that the future is not what it used to be". This is particularly true in the realm of tertiary education, which is in great flux. Labor markets requirements are changing drastically. Students and academics are increasingly internationally mobile, and research has gone global. New competitors threaten to displace traditional providers and new learning modalities challenge established ways of teaching and conducting research. The political environment in which tertiary education institutions operate is unstable in many places.

These global trends have brought uncertainty and disruption to tertiary education (Box 5). But they also offer remarkable new opportunities that tertiary education institutions and learners can seize. For this to happen, it is indispensable to ensure the availability of broadband connectivity and end-user devices to support the delivery of educational, research, and administrative services of tertiary education institutions in an efficient, reliable, and affordable way.

*Box 5. Welcome to the University of the Future!*

Teaching and learning will look very differently by the year 2030. We can imagine universities without majors, without academic departments, without lecture halls, and without tenure. We can imagine a professor giving a course to more than 300,000 students at the same time, online. We can imagine a robot teaching small groups of students... We can imagine students learning from each other without direct teacher involvement... Or we can imagine a student learning on her/his own, guided by an educational software based on artificial intelligence...

Are these images outlandish dreams? Actually, they are real-life examples of the radical transformation that tertiary education is undergoing today in a few institutions at the vanguard of innovative practices. While teaching approaches and learning modalities have seen very little improvement in the past decades—unlike the rapid transformation that medicine has gone through—, we are likely to witness drastic changes in the near future under the combined influence of two key factors: technological advances and labor market changes.

First, widespread progress in education technology, machine learning and data analytics is opening new avenues for interactive and design-based learning. Online platforms, simulation robots, gaming-like software, virtual reality, open digital resources, customized digital learning playlists, embedded assessment, micro-credentialing, learner profiles, and virtual mentoring, among others, will radically transform the learning experience.

Second, tertiary education institutions are faced with the challenge of preparing young people for jobs that do not exist yet. The traditional approach where teachers impart their knowledge to students in the classroom is being replaced by a dynamic learning model where students acquire generic competencies and socio-emotional skills that prepare them to identify their own learning needs and advance their professional capacity by acquiring new knowledge and skills throughout their career in a lifelong learning mode.

(Source: adapted from Salmi, 2013a)

In order to ascertain to what extent tertiary education systems in developing countries are ready in that respect, the next chapter looks at the expected role of tertiary education and at the actual state of tertiary education institutions in developing countries.

NOTES

[1]  IREG Observatory on Academic Ranking and Excellence. http://ireg-observatory.org/en/index.php/ranking-profile

[2]  http://rsvu.mon.bg/rsvu3/?locale=en

3    Quoted in Mackey, A., and B. Pallack (2009). " Private colleges growing quickly", *Arizona Daily Star*, 25 August 2009.

4    When Stanford Professor Ng offered his course on machine learning, more than 100,000 students signed up. Only 46,000 attempted the first assignment, and less than 13,000 actually completed the course.

5    This section draws on a recent study on Open Science prepared by the author for the European Commission (Salmi, 2015b).

6    http://www.parframework.org/ssmx/

7    See http://scholarsatrisk.nyu.edu/

# THE CONTRIBUTION OF TERTIARY EDUCATION

## *Theory vs. Reality*

Participation in education is not an end in itself. What matters for people and for our economies are the skills acquired through education. It is the competence and character qualities that are developed through schooling, rather than the qualifications and credentials gained, that make people successful and resilient in their professional and private lives. They are also key in determining individual well-being and the prosperity of societies.

(OECD, 2016)

### ROLE AND BENEFITS OF TERTIARY EDUCATION

In July 1945, Vannevar Bush wrote the following statement in his pioneering book *Science, the Endless Frontier*: "a nation which depends upon others for its new basic scientific knowledge will be slow in its industrial progress and weak in its competitive position in world trade." While the book was written with the United States in mind—it was one of the triggers behind the creation of the National Science Foundation a few years later in 1950—, other nations heeded the call for developing scientific capacity, especially in South-East Asia. One of the first ones was South Korea, whose tertiary education enrolment rate was barely 2% when it regained its independence in 1945. It embarked on a long journey of investment aiming at building up its education system in support of the transforming economy, starting with primary education, then secondary and finally expanding the post-secondary sector so much that today it can boast the highest level of tertiary education completion among OECD nations (60%).

It is widely recognized that the ability of a society to generate, adapt and apply knowledge is critical for sustained economic growth and improved living standards. Rapid technological progress, the spread of global value chains, and the increasing importance of knowledge-based capital mean that knowledge has become the most important factor in economic development, not only technical knowledge but also knowledge about attributes, that is the informational characteristics that support analysis and decision-making (World Bank, 1999). Comparative advantages among nations come less and less from abundant natural resources or cheap labor and increasingly from technical innovations and the competitive use of knowledge—or from a combination of both (Porter, 1990; Ranis et al., 2011). As the Norwegian

31

Prime Minister Erna Solberg observed upon taking office in early 2015, "knowledge is the key to a future after the age of oil."

The innovation strategy recently articulated by the OECD (2015) outlines five priorities, namely (i) the need to strengthen investment in innovation and foster business dynamism, (ii) the importance of investing in an efficient system of knowledge creation and diffusion, (iii) the opportunity of capturing the benefits of the digital economy, (iv) the need to foster talent and skills, and (v) the urgency to improve the governance and implementation of innovation policies. A strong tertiary education system is vital to support the second and fourth priorities.

More specifically, tertiary education supports knowledge-driven economic growth and poverty reduction strategies by (a) training a qualified and adaptable labor force, including high-level scientists, professionals, technicians, teachers in basic and secondary education, and future government, civil service, and business leaders, (b) generating new knowledge through basic and applied research, and (c) providing the platform for accessing existing stores of global knowledge and adapting this knowledge to local use. Tertiary education institutions are unique in their ability to integrate and create synergy among these three dimensions. Sustainable transformation and growth throughout the economy are not possible without the capacity-building contributions of an innovative tertiary education system, especially in low-income countries with weak institutional capacity and limited human capital (Salmi, 2012a).

This important role of tertiary education is borne out by widespread evidence showing that tertiary education graduates have better employment prospects and receive higher salaries than individuals with less education. In North America and Europe, for example, until the 2007-08 economic crisis, the unemployment problem was almost exclusively concentrated among the low skilled. According to OECD's 2012 Education at a Glance, "… tertiary-educated individuals are employed at a higher rate than people with an upper secondary or post-secondary non-tertiary education. On average, 83% of 25-64 year-olds with a tertiary education were employed in 2010, compared to 74% of those with an upper secondary education" (OECD, 2012, p.122). Similarly, earnings data continue to show a significant premium for tertiary education over upper secondary education.

The success of East Asian economies illustrates the symbiotic relationship among tertiary education, innovation, and growth through the production of research and skills. A recent World Bank report analyzed the positive links between economic growth and tertiary education as measured by the tertiary gross enrollment ratio, science test scores, levels of R&D investment, and the number of scientists and engineers relative to a country's population. Firm innovation surveys undertaken in Indonesia, the Philippines and Thailand showed that the most active innovators are those with higher levels of R&D expenditures, more highly qualified staff, and located in more R&D-intensive industries (World Bank, 2012).

As far as research is concerned, the same World Bank report on East Asia found that universities and other tertiary education institutions not only added to the knowledge stock, but also helped raise the technological capacity of low income countries and supported countries with medium technology capacity in the transition from technology assimilation to innovation through consulting services, hosting incubation facilities, and customizing foreign technologies for local requirements (World Bank, 2012).

The country studies undertaken in the context of that report revealed that, in terms of skills formation, employers expect tertiary education institutions to equip graduates with the cognitive, technical, social, and behavioral skills making them capable of bringing advanced knowledge to bear on complex problems, use that knowledge to work toward their solution, perform relevant applied research, and develop ideas for more innovative ways of designing processes and products. These competencies include client orientation, communication, problem solving, and creativity skills (World Bank, 2012).

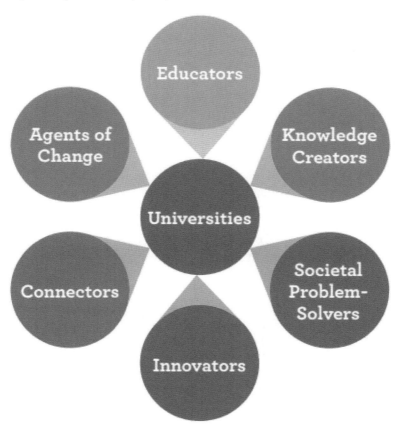

*Figure 7. Contribution of Universities in the Asian and Pacific Region.*
*Source: APRU (2016)*

A recent study of the Association of Pacific Rim Universities attempts to measure the contribution of its 45 member institutions, which are distributed across 17 countries (APRU, 2016). APRU identifies six principal roles played by member universities (7).

As *educators*, the universities "train work-ready, flexible graduates including professionals to serve their communities, educate tomorrow's leaders, offer pathways for social mobility and role models for a fairer, more cohesive society, and reach out to raise cultural, scientific and health literacy." As *knowledge creators*, they "generate cutting-edge knowledge through research, gather, interpret and maintain data over long periods of time, necessary to understand complex issues, and provide work of local cultural and social importance. As *societal problem-solvers*, they "apply research to complex societal challenges such as disaster risk reduction, health, environmental sustainability, the digital economy, and ageing." As *innovators*, APRU universities "commercialize intellectual property, collaborate with industry, and support the next generation of entrepreneurs." As *connectors*, they put "stakeholders in relationships to the latest knowledge and to each other, and build intercultural understanding across the region. Finally, as *agents of change*, they "experiment with new ideas on campus, offer support for wider reform in society, and provide a critical conscience for society."

Looking at the impact of human capital development policies at the national level is not the only way of exploring the interface between innovation and tertiary education. Recent research in Europe indicates that the regional dimension of economic development maybe as important as what happens at the national level, or sometimes even of greater magnitude. The most successful regions are those that manage to attract and retain people in employment, improve the adaptability of workers and enterprises, and increase investment in human capital through skills matching and upgrading (Ederer et al., 2011). Figure 8 illustrates how tertiary education institutions interact with the local economy.

A recent study of about 15,000 universities in 1,500 regions across 78 countries, which estimated fixed effect models at the sub-national level between 1950 and 2010, found evidence of the positive role of universities on economic growth at the local level.

> ... Increases in the number of universities are positively associated with future growth of GDP per capita... [The] estimates imply that doubling the number of universities per capita is associated with 4% higher future GDP per capita... We show that the relationship between growth and universities is not simply driven by the direct expenditures of the university, its staff and students. Part of the effect of universities on growth is mediated through an increased supply of human capital and greater innovation... The benefit of universities is not confined to the region where they are built but "spills over" to neighboring regions, having the strongest effects on those that are geographically closest. Using these results, we estimate that the economic benefits of university expansion are likely to

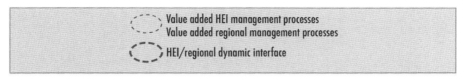

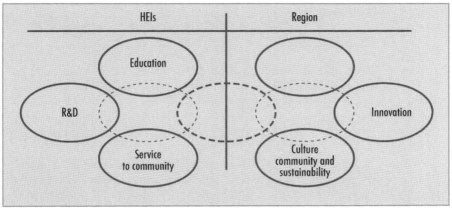

*Figure 8. Interface between Tertiary Education and the Region.*
*Source: Goddard and Chatterton (2003)*

exceed their costs… We provide suggestive evidence that universities play a role in promoting democracy, and that this operates over and above their effect as human capital producers. (Valero and Reenen, 2016, pp. 1 and 32)

In that perspective, researchers have explored the growing importance of cities, especially megacities, as drivers of economic growth (Ohmae, 1995; Florida, 2008). Beyond population size, what characterizes dynamic megacities are the presence of a significant productive capacity, a large market, relevant innovative activities, and talented people with high educational qualifications. In planning for the development of tertiary education, governments should not focus only on the national level but rather work closely with regional authorities and city municipalities in configuring the articulation between tertiary education institutions and other components of urban development.

Two caveats should be mentioned with respect to the complexity of measuring the economic contribution of tertiary education. First, the impact of universities, as assessed through the quantity and quality of graduates, is likely to be reflected in faster economic growth with a relatively substantial time lag of 20 to 30 years, as the arrival of new graduates into the labor force represents no more than 5 to 10% of the total stock. In research, by contrast, the return to investment is visible at a fairly early stage, given that research results can be more rapidly translated into new firms with new products or services and/or into new products and services in existing firms.

Second, as demonstrated by Aghion and Howitt (2006), the impact of tertiary education on growth is influenced by the state of technological advancement of the economy. Economies with a larger high technology sectors that are closer to the technology frontier will benefit more from tertiary education and research than countries in the converging state. Box 6 illustrates the importance of science in an advanced economy such as Australia.

### Box 6. The Importance of Science for the Australian Economy

Advances in the physical, mathematical and biological sciences in the past 20 to 30 years underpin A$330 billion (US$233 billion) a year of Australia's economic output. These advances also support nearly 1.2 million Australian jobs, or 10% of total employment. These findings are presented in a new report commissioned by the Office of the Chief Scientist and the Australian Academy of Science.

Without the last 30 years of advances in the biological sciences alone, the Australian economy would be 5% smaller than it is today. The burden of disease carried by its people would be 18% to 34% higher, and Australians would miss out on health improvements worth up to A$156 billion every year.

Australia's outgoing Chief Scientist, Professor Ian Chubb AC, said the reports underscore the importance of science to all Australians. "Of course the benefits of science are difficult to measure. Of course those benefits can only be partially counted in dollar terms. But of course we have to investigate them, in economic as well as human terms, because we cannot afford to ever take them for granted." We have, for the first time, a credible estimate of a phenomenon that defines our lives and underpins our prospects for growth.

Professor Andrew Holmes AM, President of the Australian Academy of Science, noted that the finding that science contributes so substantially to Australia's economy is consistent with similar analysis conducted in Australia and overseas. "Our national situation is unique, but the message for all advanced economies is clear. Scientists, and the industries which harness their discoveries, are critical to prosperity. "We need Australian science to address our own challenges, just as we need it to have access to the new knowledge uncovered overseas."

Universities Australia said that at a time when the country faces a growing burden of chronic, often preventable disease, the reports highlight the contribution of science to prevent illness—and not just treat it. The reports reveal that without the advanced biological sciences, the burden of cardiovascular disease in Australia would be between 35% and 40% higher, while the burden of cancer would be between 27% and 54% higher.

Spray-on skin, the Cochlear hearing device, and cervical cancer vaccines are some of Australia's best-known inventions. Yet the reports highlight that remarkable advances in biological sciences are being used in all sectors, not just health. For instance, developments in microbiology have helped create 'self-healing' concrete while other advances are being used to build a more resilient Great Barrier Reef.

(Source: UWN, 2016b)

A recent review of 99 studies looking at various dimensions of the impact of tertiary education on development, commissioned by DfID, came to the following main conclusion regarding the effects on earnings and economic growth (Oketch et al., 2014, p. 23):

The studies show that tertiary education has a strong impact on the earnings of graduates. There is evidence that tertiary has a stronger impact on growth than previously assumed. However, there are some inconsistencies in the results, largely due to methodological differences between studies. The impact of TE on income equality is difficult to isolate and appears to vary significantly depending on context.

Tertiary education's contribution is strong beyond the economic sphere. Nations with high level of educational attainment also enjoy important social benefits. Studies indicate that people with tertiary education are much less dependent on welfare programs. In the US, for instance, the government spends up to US$2,700 less per year on social programs for tertiary education graduates than for high school graduates (Baum, 2005).

A recent OECD publication provides useful data to support this assessment of the social benefits of tertiary education (OECD, 2012). Individuals with tertiary education also tend to be in better health, are less likely to smoke, are more actively engaged in civic life, and are less prone to engage in criminal activities. For example, for the 15 OECD countries for which sufficient data are available, ..."a 30-year-old male tertiary graduate can expect to live another 51 years, while a 30-year old man who has not completed upper secondary education can expect to live an additional 43 years" (OECD, 2012, p. 204). Adults with tertiary education are more likely to vote in democratic elections than those with lower levels of education, with a 14.8 percent gap for the 25-64 age-olds group and even higher (26.8) for young adults (25-34 year-olds). The benefits of tertiary education also extend across generations: children of parents with tertiary education are more exposed to reading, have higher cognitive skills, and are better able to concentrate during their studies. Box 7 illustrates the transformative power of tertiary education in developing countries, especially for minorities and women.

*Box 7. Transformative Power of Tertiary Education in Developing Countries: A Testimony from Guatemala*

Sindy Patricia Ramos Pocón, 23, knows what it means to be poor and go without food. As a child growing up in Villa Nueva, Guatemala City, she used to help her grandmother sell meat or cheese and bananas from her car to survive. At one point she had to leave school and work a six-day week in a tree nursery, earning US$250 a month, to keep herself fed and pay for her younger sister's education. Sindy's mother died when she was 13 and when her sick father was unable to support her she had to enter a grant-aided boarding school.

"There is too much poverty in Guatemala – 50% of the population are poor, a lot of them are indigenous, and 20–30% are in extreme poverty. "They can't buy food or other basics, it's very difficult. It's very hard for poor people to find work, especially for women. Many survive on US$2 a day and they have to try and support six or seven children on that," she explains.

Now, as the first of four siblings to enter university, she is nearing the end of a four-year undergraduate program in agricultural sciences and natural resource management in Costa Rica, and is simultaneously heading up a groundbreaking project to enable poor women to establish their own independent businesses in that country. "I wanted to help people. I have always had that dream ever since I was a little girl; I wanted to make a difference," she says.

Sindy has been supported in that journey by a scholarship from The MasterCard Foundation, which covers all her costs to study at EARTH University, Guácimo, Limón, in Costa Rica. Established in 1986, EARTH University is a private, international, non-profit institution with two bases in Costa Rica. It aims to enable young disadvantaged people from Latin America, the Caribbean, Africa and Asia to contribute to the sustainable development of their countries. The university boasts world-class technological and scientific facilities and has approximately 423 students from 42 countries, 60% of whom receive full scholarships, with the remaining receiving significant financial aid. Attitudes, values and an ethical entrepreneurial spirit are as important as technical and scientific knowledge in the curriculum.

Studying at EARTH University has given Sindy an understanding of the value of being able to work with other people. She put into practice her university research and team-working skills when she developed a project to enable unemployed women to establish their own businesses using banana stalk fibre – a waste material in plantations – to create arts and crafts for sale, to benefit local women from rural communities. The medium-term plan is to provide disadvantaged Costa Rican women, who are housewives, with an independent income so that they can help their families, but if Sindy wins the competition in December, she will use the US$10,000 to develop a brand and spread the idea to Guatemala.

The goal is for the women in the project to turn their knowledge into their own small businesses and provide financial stability to their families through ecological and sustainable products and practices – to lift them out of the kind of poverty trap that Sindy experienced when she had to drop out of school to earn a meager income, foregoing achieving educational progress. "My project challenges inequality because women are able to take charge of the whole process themselves. It is giving independence to women who otherwise would not have the possibility to work," she concludes. "And I know that's what I want to do in the future. "I used to dream but now I can see changes," she says.

(Source: Rigg, 2016)

The DfID-commissioned literature review mentioned earlier came to a similar conclusion: "a number of studies showed a positive impact of tertiary-level study on graduates' capabilities. Impact was shown in areas of health, nutrition, political participation and women's empowerment" (Oketch et al., p. 31).

In the 2001 World Development Report on Poverty Reduction, the World Bank (2001) emphasized the key role played by tertiary education institutions in imparting the norms, values, attitudes and ethics necessary to build the social capital that graduates must acquire to be able to contribute to the construction of healthy civil societies and socially cohesive cultures that underlie good governance and democratic political systems. The institutions, relationships, and norms that emerge from tertiary education are instrumental in influencing the quality of a society's interactions, which in turn fortify economic, political, and social development. Universities and other tertiary institutions are the crossroads for social cooperation, fostering strong networks, stimulating voluntary activity, and promoting extracurricular learning and innovation. In post-conflict nations, especially, reconstituting social capital is essential for assisting societies in reinventing themselves with resilient institutions and a sound moral compass (World Bank, 2002).

A related, critical issue is the ability of society to deal with the new ethical challenges brought about by scientific advances, such as genetically modified crops, stem cell and embryo research, genome editing technologies, or additive manufacturing methods. In that respect, all countries need a strong tertiary education system that grounds its graduates in philosophy and ethics to equip for the proper consideration of issues linked to emerging technologies.

Finally, it is doubtful that any low-income country can achieve the United Nations Sustainable Development Goals (SDGs) without a strong tertiary education system. In addition to the essential contribution that tertiary education can make to the goals of sustainable economic growth (SDG 8) and poverty reduction (SDG 1), advances on all the other dimensions, from developing a vibrant agricultural sector and building up a resilient infrastructure to mitigating the devastating effects of climate change and preserving the environment, cannot happen without the participation of scientists and well-trained professionals and the application of leading edge research for finding appropriate solutions to the big challenges faced by mankind. With respect to the goal of diminished inequality (SDG 10), tertiary education plays a critical role in promoting social mobility through equal educational opportunities for all groups, especially the most vulnerable groups in society (low-income groups, minorities, people with special needs, etc.). Achieving the SDGs also requires strong institutions for policy design and implementation, and well-prepared citizens who care about inclusion and sustainability.

The contribution of tertiary education is crucial, in particular, for achieving real progress in basic and secondary education. A recent study found that more than a quarter of all primary school teachers in 31 countries had not achieved the minimum education standards themselves (The Economist, 2016). Tertiary education supports the rest of the education system through the training of effective teachers and school principals, the involvement of highly qualified specialists in curriculum development and educational research, and the design of appropriate tests to assess students learning outcomes. The symbiotic linkage between tertiary education and the lower levels of schooling has the potential of stimulating a virtuous circle of capacity building in as far as the quality of tertiary education affects the quality of primary and secondary school education and is, in turn, directly influenced by the quality of secondary school graduates. As summarized by the former President of the World Bank:

> It is impossible to have a complete education system without an appropriate and strong higher education system. You have to have centers of excellence and learning and training if you are going to advance the issue of poverty and development in developing countries... the key ... is higher education, not just on the technological side, but to create people with enough wisdom to be able to use it. (James D. Wolfensohn, former President of the World Bank. (March 1, 2000))

A similar argument applies to the fundamental role of medical education and research for meeting the health sustainable development goal (SDG 3). Universities train the medical doctors, nurses, technicians, epidemiologists, public health specialists, and hospital managers who form the most important pillar of any health system. Universities and associated health institutes conduct the fundamental research and a significant share of the applied research that condition any significant progress in the fight against diseases and health hazards. Box 8 provides a powerful illustration of how universities can help resolve important health crises.

*Box 8. University Research Helping Address Public Health Issues:*
*Virginia Tech and the 2015 Flint Water Crisis*

The young scientists, mostly in their 20s, had drawn an audience so large that it spilled from the auditorium on the Virginia Tech campus into two overflow rooms. They were explaining to students, members of the faculty and guests how they were at first laughed off by government regulators about 550 miles northwest of here in Flint, Michigan, when they detected alarming amounts of lead coming from residents' taps. Siddhartha Roy, a doctoral student from India, held up a bottle of yellow-tinted Flint water. The team's role was "essentially validating what citizens had been saying for months."

Flint's public health problem stemmed from a failure to properly treat water from the Flint River, which resulted in pipe corrosion and elevated levels of lead. Lead exposure can result in health and developmental problems, particularly in children, and its toxic effects can be irreversible. The crisis is at best a tale of neglect and incompetence. At worst, critics say, it is criminal conduct that imperiled the public's wellbeing. ... But as government officials were ignoring and ridiculing residents' concerns about the safety of their tap water, a small circle of people was setting off alarms. Among them was the team from Virginia Tech.

The team began looking into Flint's water after its professor, Marc Edwards, spoke with LeeAnne Walters, a resident whose tap water contained alarming amounts of lead. Dr. Edwards had his students send testing kits to homes in Flint to find out if the problem was widespread.

Their persistence helped force officials to acknowledge the crisis and prompted warnings to residents not to drink or cook with tap water. Officials are now scrambling to find a more permanent solution to the problem than trucking in thousands of plastic jugs, and are turning to Virginia Tech for advice. The scientists "became the only people that citizens here trust, and it's still that way," said Melissa Mays, a Flint resident who has protested the water quality.

At Virginia Tech, the researchers are a source of pride. The team is a mixed group. Mostly environmental engineers, members range in experience from undergraduates to professors. Several of them were drawn to environmental engineering, Mr. Roy said, because "we have this childhood aspiration of hopefully helping people and serving society at some point."

The students began their work last summer as Michigan officials insisted that Flint's malodorous, discolored water was safe. The team mailed testing kits to Flint, and in August a group packed into Dr. Edwards's family van and set off for a site visit. Once in Flint, the group visited several homes to collect water, shipping the samples back to Virginia so they could be tested quickly on campus. "It's like a once-in-a-lifetime experience," said Colin Richards, 25, a graduate student in environmental engineering, who went on that trip. The tests revealed alarming levels of lead. Besides calling residents to advise them of the troubling results, the team posted its documents and data online at flintwaterstudy.org, an act that has helped others investigate Flint's problems. When the federal, state and local governments failed to acknowledge the scope of the problem, Dr. Edwards held a community meeting in September advising residents to stop drinking the water.

In October, government officials finally warned of the lead risk, but the Virginia Tech researchers became concerned about the possibility that the water was causing Legionnaires' disease. As it turned out, state officials had long been aware of a spike in Legionnaires' cases after the switch in water sources, but the public was not told until last month.

Joyce Zhu, a doctoral student, went to collect samples at a Flint hospital, looking for signs of the bacteria that cause Legionnaires'. "When I turned on the tap, you see this corrosive, reddish, brownish tap water," she said. "It's that moment that made it so real." Ms. Zhu said she had planned on a "typical" academic career, doing lab research with limited application off campus. But after analyzing lead-tainted water samples in the labs in Blacksburg and traveling to Flint, she said, she is considering how her career can benefit the public. "I grew up in Singapore, where clean water, you take it for granted so much," Ms. Zhu said.

State officials in Michigan initially dismissed the Virginia Tech team's findings. As they did with other whistle-blowers, they disparaged its work. In one email obtained by the researchers, a spokesman for the Michigan Department of Environmental Quality, Brad Wurfel, played down the lead risk, telling a reporter that the Virginia Tech team was known to "pull that rabbit out of that hat everywhere they go."

Now the tables have turned, and the Virginia Tech team has been enlisted to help address the crisis. Governor Rick Snyder, whose administration has been widely blamed for a failure to protect Flint's residents, has thanked Dr. Edwards and included him in a group now advising officials on permanent fixes for the Flint problem.

The Virginia Tech team is among a handful of outside researchers who have been credited with helping expose the lead problem and stop it from getting worse. Some in Flint have said they will not trust that the water is safe until the Virginia Tech researchers say so. Without Dr. Edwards and his team, residents suspect little would have been done to protect Flint from its toxic water.

(Source: Smith, 2016)

Developing countries need to build up their capacity to deal with serious health issues not only from a domestic policy viewpoint, but also in order to be able to contribute effectively to the resolution of global health crises through collaborative research. Indeed, research production has moved from being discipline-driven to problem-focused, with diverse teams of scientists from several disciplinary areas collaborating on the resolution of complex problems, which often correspond to shared challenges that affect mankind as a whole regardless of political boundaries. This evolution is best illustrated by the global health issues that have come up in recent years, from SARS to MERS to the latest Ebola epidemics in West Africa. In the case of SARS, for example, identifying the corona virus required data sharing and collaborative efforts on an unprecedented scale. This experience has radically changed how the international scientific community responds to emerging global health threats (Box 9).

*Box 9. Global Epidemics and Open Science Collaboration:*
*the SARS Epidemics*

The SARS-Coronavirus (SARS-CoV) caused an infectious disease that was first identified in people in early 2003. Scientists believe that the virus emerged from Guangdong province in China, infecting people who handled or inhaled virus droplets from cat-like mammals called civets.

By 2004, SARS-CoV disease had disappeared in humans, and scientists are not sure whether it will return. Though its stay was short, SARS-CoV changed how scientists respond to emerging infectious diseases by focusing on the need for global openness and immediate cooperation.

Prior to SARS-CoV, emerging infectious diseases were thought to take weeks or months to spread globally. SARS-CoV showed how efficiently a virus could spread through international travel. By mid-2003, SARS-CoV had spread to 29 different countries, including the United States.

Since then, scientists and public health officials around the world have worked to rapidly coordinate studies and emphasize the need to share information with colleagues at the start of infectious disease outbreaks.

(Source: US National Institutes of Health, 2015;
http://www.ncbi.nlm.nih.gov/pubmedhealth/PMHT0024856/)

To conclude this review of the contribution of tertiary education to economic and social development, Table 1 recapitulates the fundamental role that tertiary education institutions can play in supporting the achievement of the Sustainable Development Goals by fulfilling their main functions: skills development, knowledge generation and transfer, capacity building, and values formation.

In summary, although the mechanisms through which tertiary education contributes to social and economic development are not fully understood and precise measures of these contributions are not yet available, tertiary education contributes a wide range of private and social benefits, as indicated in the DfID literature review cited earlier, and summarized in Table 2 below.

When taken as a whole, the body of evidence … suggests that tertiary education plays an important role in both economic and non-economic development in lower-income contexts. For years, much of the international literature on tertiary education in lower income contexts emphasized the private benefits to individuals. However, recent studies have indicated that investment in tertiary education also yields significant social returns, both in terms of economic growth and in terms of non-economic benefits. The included studies show a consistent positive impact of tertiary education on societal institutions and on a range of capabilities that have public, as well as private, benefits. (Oketch et al., p. 48)

*Table 1. Contribution of Tertiary Education to the Sustainable Development Goals*

| SDGs | Preparation of Skilled Professionals | Knowledge Generation, Adaptation & Diffusion | Institutional Development & Capacity Building | Values & Citizenship Skills |
|---|---|---|---|---|
| 1. Poverty Ended | X | X | X | X |
| 2. Sustainable Agriculture to End Hunger | X | X | X | |
| 3. Healthy Lives | X | X | X | X |
| 4. Inclusive & Equitable Quality Education | X | X | X | X |
| 5. Achieve Gender Equality | X | | X | X |
| 6. Water & Sanitation for All | X | X | X | X |
| 7. Sustainable Energy | X | X | X | |
| 8. Inclusive & Sustainable Economic Growth | X | X | X | |
| 9. Resilient Infrastructure | X | X | X | |
| 10. Reduced Inequality | X | | | X |
| 11. Sustainable Cities | X | X | X | X |
| 12. Sustainable Consumption & Production | | X | | X |
| 13. Managed Climate Change | | X | X | X |
| 14. Sustainable Marine Resources | X | X | X | X |
| 15. Sustainable Use of Terrestrial Systems | X | X | X | X |
| 16. Peaceful & Inclusive Societies | | X | X | X |
| 17. Global Partnership for Sustainable Development | | | X | X |

*Table 2. Potential Benefits from Tertiary Education*

| Benefits | Private | Public |
|---|---|---|
| Economic | Higher salaries | Greater productivity |
| | Better employment prospects | National and regional development<br>Increased potential for transformation from low-skill industrial to knowledge-based economy – Attraction of dynamic firms |
| | Higher savings | Increased tax revenues |
| | Improved working conditions | Increased spending and consumption<br>Reduced reliance on government subsidies |
| | Professional mobility | |
| Social | Improved quality of life for self and children | Nation building and development of leadership |
| | Better decision-making | Democratic participation; increased consensus; perception that society is based on fairness and opportunity for all citizens |
| | Improved personal status | Social mobility |
| | Increased educational opportunities | Greater social cohesion and reduced crime rates |
| | Healthier lifestyle and higher life expectancy | Improved health |
| | | Improved basic and secondary education |

*Source: Adapted from World Bank (2002, p. 86)*

## THE REALITY OF TERTIARY EDUCATION IN DEVELOPING COUNTRIES: LONG-STANDING AND NEW CHALLENGES

Sixteen years after the publication of the groundbreaking report sponsored by the World Bank and UNESCO—Peril and Promise—tertiary education systems have changed significantly. In particular, developing countries have seen tremendous enrollment growth, especially in the private sector. As a result, many if not most of the issues outlined in Peril and Promise continue to challenge tertiary education systems that are financially constrained.

Problems of quality and lack of resources are compounded by the new realities faced by higher education, as higher education institutions battle to cope with ever-increasing student numbers. Responding to this demand without further diluting quality is an especially daunting challenge. … Expansion, public and private, has been unbridled, unplanned, and often chaotic. The results— deterioration in average quality, continued interregional, inter-country, and intra-country inequities, and increased for-profit provision of higher education—could all have serious consequences. (Report of the Task Force on Higher Education and Society. (World Bank and UNESCO, 2000))

To assess the performance of tertiary education in developing countries against this background, this chapter adopts a benchmarking approach that makes a fundamental distinction between (i) the results of tertiary education systems ("system performance") and (ii) the drivers of performance that account for these results ("system health"). This can be translated into the following two questions:

- How well does the tertiary education system actually produce expected outcomes at the current time (system performance)?
- How well do the tertiary education systems' key inputs, processes and enabling factors reflect conditions that are known to bring about favorable outcomes?[1]

Table 3 summarizes the principal dimensions of system performance and health in tertiary education.

*Table 3. Conceptual Framework for Benchmarking Tertiary Education in Developing Countries*

| Focus of Benchmarking | Main Dimensions of Analysis |
|---|---|
| *System Performance* | Educational Attainment<br>Equity (access, completion, outcomes)<br>Learning Achievement<br>Labor Market Outcomes<br>Research Output<br>Technology Transfer Results |
| *System Health* | Expansion Strategy<br>Curricular and Pedagogical Practices<br>Quality Assurance<br>Relevance, skills mismatch and links to the economy<br>Stewardship and Governance<br>Financing |

*Elaborated by Jamil Salmi*

*Unequal Performance*

*Educational attainment.* In the past two decades, the achievement of universal primary education and the ensuing secondary education expansion in many developing countries has contributed to accelerating demand for tertiary education.

Figure 9, which shows the evolution of tertiary education enrollment rates in various parts of the globe, illustrates these trends in a clear way.

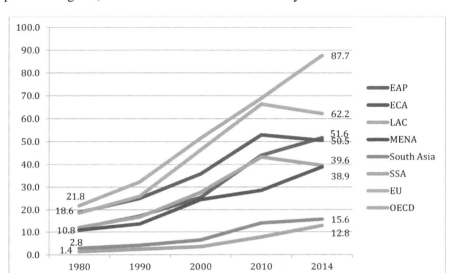

*Figure 9. Evolution of Enrolment Rates by Region (1980–2014).*
*Source: UIS*

The data reveal important differences among regions, with South Asia and Sub-Saharan Africa lagging significantly behind the other regions. As a recent report on inequality in African tertiary education underlines, … "despite the fast growth in enrollment, Africa is decades behind other regions in providing access to tertiary education (Darvas et al., 2016).

These differences are clearly reflected in the level of educational attainment of developing countries, calculated as the proportion of adults in the working age population who have completed a tertiary level degree (Figure 10).

Not only are there strong differences in tertiary education attainment and enrollment rates across regions and across countries within each region, but developing countries also face disparities in educational opportunities among income groups. Indeed, the expansion of tertiary education experienced over the last decades all over the world does not necessarily mean that tertiary education systems have become equally accessible to all social groups. Increased tertiary education rates can result from the participation of a greater proportion of students from families with a relatively high socio-economic status. To illustrate this situation, Table 4 summarizes equity data for various regions of the world, showing two key equity measures: the mean disparity ratio (enrollment rate of the top income quintile

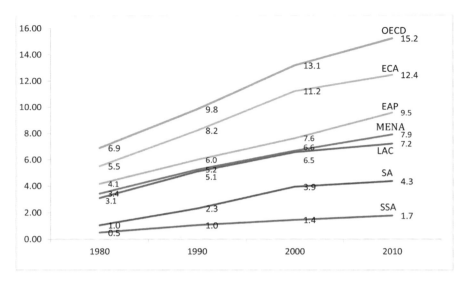

*Figure 10. Proportion of Adults (25+) Having Completed a Tertiary Education Degree.*
*Source: Barro-Lee database, World Bank Edstats*

divided by the enrollment rate of the lowest quintile) and the range of disparity ratios
from best to worst country in each region.

*Table 4. Summary Results by Region*

| Country Groupings | Mean Disparity Ratio | Range | Average Enrollment Rate in 2014 |
|---|---|---|---|
| East Asia | 16.0 | 1–61 | 51.6 |
| Eastern Europe and Central Asia | 3.5 | 1–9 | 50.5 |
| Latin America and the Caribbean | 27.0 | 3–100 | 39.6 |
| Middle East and North Africa | 28.2 | 7–89 | 23.9 |
| South Asia | 21.1 | 7–45 | 15.6 |
| Sub-Saharan Africa | 99.3 | 4–200 | 12.8 |

*Source: Salmi and Bassett (forthcoming)*

Eastern European and Central Asian countries stand out with the lowest degree
of inequality overall. Their lower levels and smaller range of inequality reflect the
positive legacy of decades of socialist policies that emphasized quality primary
and secondary education for all. In the developing world, South Asia is the most
homogenous region, owing to the fact that the region regroups a much smaller

number of countries, which are at relatively similar levels of tertiary education development. Sub-Saharan Africa shows the worst pattern of inequality in tertiary education, reflecting the strongly elitist nature of its universities. Figure 11 presents the disparity ratios for all SSA countries for which data are available.

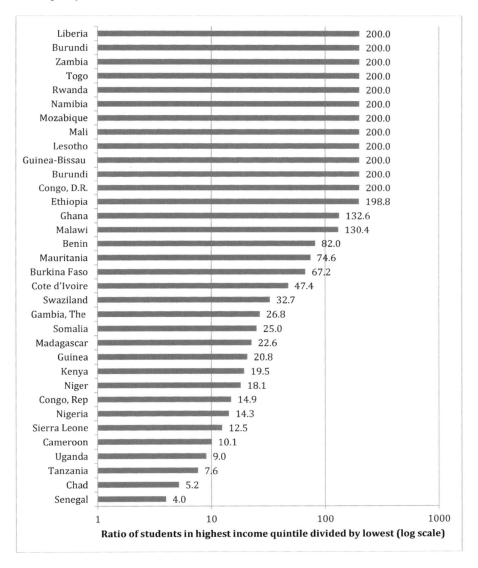

*Figure 11. Disparity Ratios in Sub-Saharan Africa.*
*Source: Household Surveys*

While the above regional and country comparisons on the basis of household survey data provide a valuable illustration of the scope of socio-economic disparities at the tertiary level, they suffer from methodological problems due to the lack of consistency across household surveys. A complementary, statistically more rigorous way of measuring socio-economic disparities is to use regression analysis to assess the importance of family socioeconomic status in shaping access to tertiary education. Using large datasets providing information on the family background of individuals across two or three generations in 68 countries, it is possible to measure the extent of intergenerational mobility in tertiary education by examining the variation in the correlation between the probability of participating in tertiary education and parents' educational attainment as a proxy of family socio-economic background (d'Hombres, 2010).

The 68 countries for which sufficient data are available consist of eight Latin American countries, 28 countries from Eastern Europe and Central Asia, nine countries from South-East Asia, and 23 OECD countries. African and Middle Eastern countries were not included because of the unavailability of recent micro data representative of the whole country. Appendix 1 presents the data sources and country sample sizes for each of the countries included in this exercise, as well as the methodology applied in this statistical analysis of the surveys.

Table 5 below reports the average relationship between participation in tertiary education and father's education for the four large regional groups analyzed in the study.

*Table 5. Intergenerational Correlations in Accessing Tertiary Education*

| Region | Relative probability to reach TE for lowest income group $\hat{\delta}^j$ | Relative probability to reach TE when father has TE $\hat{\beta}^j$ | Composite Inequality of Opportunities Index $\widehat{INE}^j = \left|\hat{\beta}^j\right| + \left|\hat{\delta}^j\right|$ |
|---|---|---|---|
| **OECD** | −0,167w | 0,285 | 0,452 |
| **LAC** | −0,276 | 0,228 | 0,504 |
| **ECA** | −0,118 | 0,246 | 0,378 |
| **SEA** | −0,104 | 0,214 | 0,318 |

*Source: d'Hombres (2010)*

The results confirm that an individual's probability of accessing tertiary education depends significantly on the educational status of his/her father. In addition, the association between family origin and access to tertiary studies varies significantly across regions. LAC countries display the highest level of inequality while SAA countries, followed by ECA countries, show the lowest figures. In the LAC region, individuals whose father has reached tertiary studies are 22.8% more likely to participate in tertiary education than their peers whose father has only secondary education. Similarly, individuals with the poorest family background are 27.6% less likely to reach tertiary studies than the reference group. In SEA, children coming from a family with a low social status have 10.4% less chances to enrol in tertiary studies as compared to the reference group, and the comparative advantage for coming from a high social status family takes the form of an additional 21.4% chance of enrolling in tertiary studies.

For the set of OECD countries, having a father with a high level of education results more than in any other region in an increase in the probability of participating in tertiary education (point estimate: 0.285). However, the disadvantage of having a father with a low educational status is much lower than in the LAC region (point estimates in absolute values: 0.167 for OECD countries versus 0.276 for LAC countries).

Socio-economic characteristics are not the only dimension of equity worth looking at. Gender balance in tertiary education is also an important aspect. Available statistics indicate that all countries have significantly increased female participation in tertiary education. In some countries, progress has been such that today there are significantly more women than men enrolled in tertiary education. This has been the trend in Eastern Europe and Central Asia, the Middle East and North Africa, as well as Latin America and the Caribbean. The two outlier regions are South Asia and Sub-Saharan Africa, where considerably fewer females are enrolled in tertiary education in comparison to other regions. Across Sub-Saharan Africa, there are only about 62 female students for every 100 male students. In South Asia, the proportion is 74%.

Box 10 illustrates the main barriers encountered by women in tertiary education in Afghanistan.

---

### Box 10. Challenges to Female Participation in Afghanistan

Progress in education in Afghanistan since the fall of the Taliban, whilst significant, has been described as 'fragile, limited in reach, depth and uncertainty of sustainability'. This is particularly true for Afghan women participating in tertiary education, within a culture that remains resistant to women's education, and where women face many significant barriers to their participation. The UN's Human Development Report for Afghanistan indicates that, in 2012, 5.8% of adult females have reached secondary or tertiary education, compared to 34% of males; female participation in the labor market is 15.7% compared to 80.3% for men.

The vital role of tertiary education in promoting a unified national identity, cross-cultural understanding, social cohesion and democracy in Afghanistan has been highlighted. However, the tertiary education participation rate in Afghanistan is one of the lowest in the world, with a gross enrolment ratio of around 5%. According to a recent World Bank study of tertiary education in

Afghanistan, women made up only 19% of students enrolled in public universities and tertiary education institutions in 2012. The report identified a number of factors contributing to women's underrepresentation in tertiary education in Afghanistan, including the lower participation of girls in secondary education reducing the eligible pool of applicants; the lack of appropriate transport, sanitation and residential facilities for women students; and inadequate child care provision.

The testimonies of Afghan women enrolled in tertiary education from recent interviews provide useful insights into the challenges that they face in seeking to pursue their education.

- My aim is to get an education to be a different person from my mother. I don't want to be locked at home like my mother. I want to be an active member of society and to help my people (Sabrina, Maidan Wardak Province).
- My main concern is the security situation in Afghanistan. If the security worsens, and the situation gets difficult for girls to get to school or university, they will be forced to abandon their education (Madina, Kunduz Province).
- We have faced cases where girls couldn't continue their higher education due to financial problems. In case girls can't pass the exam for government universities, they need to have enough budgets to attend private universities. This is very difficult for most Afghan families to afford expenses of private education (Heela, Parwan Province).
- Shortage of job opportunities is the biggest concern. When I see people have queued in lines to get a very basic job, I get concerned (Laila, Herat Province).
- Unfortunately, due to the corruption in the government … incompetent people with money and power rise to higher levels. For instance, scholarships intended for talented and distinguished students are often distributed among those who already have money, influence and power (Lailuma, Serat Province).
- Education is as important for me as water is for sustaining life. Education brings changes that brighten your world … Education causes positive changes to emerge in everyone's life (Janan, Daikundi Province).

(Source: Burridge et al., 2016)

*Quality and relevance.* The third key dimension of performance is learning achievement, which refers to the quality and relevance of the education and training experience of tertiary level graduates. This is one of the most difficult areas to measure. Unlike what happens at lower levels of education, where evaluators use widely accepted metrics, such as TIMMS or PISA, to assess student learning outcomes in an international perspective, no such instrument exists for tertiary

*Box 11. Understanding and Using Rankings to Their Best Advantage*

Just as scarcity, prestige, and having access to "the best" increasingly mark the purchase of consumer goods, the users of tertiary education are also looking for indicators that enhance their capacity to identify and access the best universities. In this race for "high quality" education, countries are striving to develop "world-class universities" that will spearhead the development of a knowledge-based economy. Because of the power of rankings, institutions are playing a game of innovating and investing in light of ranking methodologies, perhaps at the expense of their real mission and strengths, fianancial resources, and institutional capacity.

Regardless of their controversial nature and methodological shortcomings, university rankings have become widespread and are unlikely to disappear. Because they define what "world-class" is to the broadest audience, they cannot be ignored by anyone interested in measuring the performance of tertiary education institutions. The following general recommendations may help understand what rankings actually mean:

- Be clear about what the ranking actually measures.
- Use a range of indicators and multiple measures, rather than a single, weighted ranking.
- Consumers should be aware of comparing similar programs or institutions.
- Institutions can use rankings for strategic planning and quality improvement purposes.
- Governments can use rankings to stimulate a culture of quality.
- Users of the rankings data can use the rankings as one of the instruments available to inform students, families, and employers and to fuel public debates.

(Source: Salmi and Saroyan, 2007; Salmi, 2013a)

education yet, despite promising developments in recent years, as discussed in Chapter 1.

In the absence of direct measures of learning outcomes, the global rankings can be used as a useful proxy to assess the quality of tertiary education in developing countries from an international viewpoint. In spite of their methodological limitations (Box 11), international rankings identify the top universities, which significantly contribute to knowledge generation through their cutting-edge research, offer high-quality teaching with innovative curricula and teaching methods, and produce graduates who excel in the global labor market. Table 6, which shows how many developing countries universities appear in the Times Higher Education 2015-2016 ranking, reveals in an unequivocal manner that universities in the developing world operate at lower levels of performance.

*Table 6. THE Ranking Results for Developing Countries (2015–2016)*

| Country Groupings | 101–200 | 201–300 | 301–400 | 401–500 |
|---|---|---|---|---|
| East Asia and the Pacific | 0 | 4 | 1 | 4 |
| Eastern Europe and Central Asia | 0 | 0 | 0 | 0 |
| Latin America and the Caribbean | 0 | 1 | 1 | 3 |
| Middle East and North Africa | 0 | 0 | 0 | 2 |
| South Asia | 0 | 1 | 1 | 3 |
| Sub-Saharan Africa | 1 | 0 | 0 | 2 |
| Total | 1 | 6 | 3 | 14 |

*Source: Times Higher Education. https://www.timeshighereducation.com/world-university-rankings/2016/world-ranking#!/page/0/length/-1/sort_by/rank_label/sort_order/asc/cols/scores*

Out of 500 top ranked universities, only 23 come from the developing world. In addition, they are concentrated in 9 countries: China and Malaysia for South-East Asia, India, Brazil, Chile and Mexico in Latin America, Iran in the Middle East, and South Africa and Uganda in Africa. None are included in the top 100. The top ranked developing country university, University of Cape Town, is ranked 120th in the world.

While the rankings presented above provide a comparative assessment of individual universities, they do not give direct information on tertiary education systems considered as a whole. The publication since 2012 of a ranking specifically designed to focus on entire tertiary education systems—the U21 ranking—gives a useful comparative perspective for benchmarking the results of developing countries systems in relation to OECD nations.[2] This ranking, prepared by a group of experts from the University of Melbourne in Australia is based on four groups of indicators that evaluate the level of funding for tertiary education, the production of the system in terms of research and training for the labor market, international connections of tertiary education institutions, and the regulatory framework. Table 7 presents the latest (2016) and the first (2012) systems rankings, showing the top 10 countries and all the developing world countries included in the 50 ranked nations (in 2012, only 48 countries were ranked).

Among the 50 countries assessed in this tertiary education system ranking, Malaysia has the best results among all developing countries, which is consistent with its status as a high-middle income economy. China is the one that has most progressed in the past five years. None of the world's 77 low-income countries have tertiary education systems that make it into this ranking.

*Table 7. U 21 Ranking of National Tertiary Education Systems (2016)*

| Countries | 2016 Rank | Countries | 2012 Rank |
|---|---|---|---|
| USA | 1 | USA | 1 |
| Switzerland | 2 | Sweden | 2 |
| Denmark | 3 | Canada | 3 |
| United Kingdom | 4 | Finland | 4 |
| Sweden | 5 | Denmark | 5 |
| Finland | 6 | Switzerland | 6 |
| Netherlands | 7 | Norway | 7 |
| Singapore | 8 | Australia | 8 |
| Canada | 9 | Netherlands | 9 |
| Australia | 10 | United Kingdom | 10 |
| Malaysia | 27 | Malaysia | 36 |
| China | 30 | Chile | 37 |
| Chile | 33 | Argentina | 38 |
| South Africa | 37 | China | 39 |
| Brazil | 38 | Brazil | 40 |
| Argentina | 40 | Thailand | 41 |
| Mexico | 43 | Iran | 42 |
| Thailand | 44 | Mexico | 43 |
| Turkey | 44 | Turkey | 45 |
| Iran | 47 | South Africa | 46 |
| India | 49 | Indonesia | 47 |
| Indonesia | 50 | India | 48 |

*Source: University of Melbourne. (2016 and 2012). U21 Ranking of National Higher Education Systems. Melbourne Institute and Universitas. http://www.universitas21.com/ article/projects/details/152/u21-ranking-of-national-higher-education-systems*

*Box 12. The Quality Crisis in Developing Countries*

*Sub-Saharan Africa*
The reasons for poor quality are known: large enrolment of students beyond the carrying capacity of the institutions; acute lack of funding in public institutions; severe shortage of qualified faculty; poor governance; internal, institutional inefficiency; inadequate linkages with the productive sector; and a proliferation

of private, for-profit providers. The consequences are equally known: inadequate and crumbling infrastructure; programs, departments and even institutions that fail to be nationally accredited; large unemployment of graduates; abysmally poor research output; and, ultimately, higher education institutions being unable to contribute to the development of Africa.

*Malawi*
The supply of qualified graduates is inadequate in terms of both quality and absolute numbers. Higher education institutions have struggled to insulate the quality of education delivered from pressures associated with increased enrolment. Available evidence suggests that the limited increase in enrolment is not aligned with the needs of the labor market, and that universities have weak linkages with the private sector with regard to program development and curriculum review. Quality assurance systems remain under-developed.

*Egypt*
The Egyptian higher system is not serving the country's current needs well, and without far-reaching reform it will hold back Egypt's economic and social progress. The dysfunctions include poor quality of educational inputs and processes, and deficiencies and imbalances in graduate output relative to labor market requirements.

... The reality of a narrow, content-heavy curriculum delivered to very large classes in poorly equipped facilities gives rise, as a necessary condition of teacher survival in the majority of institutions, to reliance on "the recitation method" of one-way communication, "telling" rather than "asking". For students, the experience is a passive one of "listening" rather than participating in interactive and experiential modes of learning.

*Latin America and the Caribbean*
The results of LAC universities are not commensurate with the economic weight of the Region. Although the Caribbean, Central and South America account for 8.5% of the world's population and produce 8.7% of global GDP, the region's universities make up only 2.2% of the top 500 universities in the Shanghai Jiao Tong University ranking, less than 1.5% of the 400 universities in the THE rankings, and 2,6% of the 500 universities in the Leiden bibliometric ranking. The contrast between large countries like Brazil and Mexico, which have no university ranked among the top 100, and small countries such as Israel and the Netherlands, placing respectively three and two universities among the top 100 in the Shanghai ranking, is striking.

Quality in the universities of the Region is adversely affected by the insufficient academic preparation of incoming students, the low proportion of qualified full-time academics and the long duration of first degrees, resulting in high level of dropouts. Mexico, for example, is the only OECD country where university graduates have more trouble finding a job than uneducated youths, partially because of the unsatisfactory quality and lack of relevance of many academic programs. A recent survey administered by the Manpower Group reveals that 54% of Mexican firms report difficulties in finding the right talent for open jobs, reflecting the inability of the universities to develop the right competencies.

*East Asia*
The quality (and relevance) of education and training appears to be much more of a binding constraint than the quantity of students in all employers' surveys... The co-existence of significant demand for professionals, relatively high tertiary unemployment rates, and fairly long times to fill professional positions suggests skill mismatches between the labor market and the tertiary education system in some countries... Higher education graduates simply do not have the right skills.

*India*
It is a never-ending source of dismay to Indians themselves that they have only a single institute in the Shanghai Academic Ranking of World Universities (Indian Institute of Science), while China has 44. The reason for this is not hard to work out. Indian universities traditionally focused very heavily on arts and humanities; the institutions that did focus on science and engineering tended to be small and narrowly focused. Neither of those profiles wins you points in international rankings. But more broadly, infrastructure at most Indian universities is substandard, and professorial pay is more or less designed to keep bright scientific talent in the private sector.
(Sources: Barceló, 2015; Mohamedbhai, 2016; Mumbo, 2016; OECD/World Bank, 2010; Salmi, 2013d; World Bank, 2011; Usher, 2014a)

To illustrate how the quality and relevance issues that affect developing countries play out, Box 12 provides a sample of vignettes from various corners of the world.

One of the most serious problems affecting tertiary education systems in developing countries is the low academic level of incoming students. Not all nations participate in the PISA assessment program of the OECD, but the results of the few countries that have taken part clearly indicate that students in developing countries score way below the OECD average (Table 8). In Latin America, for instance, the best performing country, Chile, is 10% below the OECD average. The score of the worst performing system, the Dominican Republic, is about 60% of Singapore, the top performer in the 2015 round. In North Africa and the Middle East, Algeria, Jordan, Lebanon and Tunisia lag significantly behind. Indonesia, the only low-income East Asian country that participated, has an average score about 20% below the OECD average.

*Table 8. PISA Scores in Developing Countries and Selected High-Income Economies (2015)*

| Countries | Science | Reading | Mathematics |
|---|---|---|---|
| 1. Singapore | 556 | 535 | 564 |
| 2. Japan | 538 | 516 | 532 |
| 3. Estonia | 534 | 519 | 520 |
| 4. Chinese Taipei | 532 | 497 | 542 |
| 5. Finland | 531 | 526 | 511 |
| 6. Macao-China | 529 | 509 | 544 |
| 7. Canada | 528 | 527 | 516 |
| 8. Vietnam | 525 | 487 | 495 |
| 9. Hong Kong China | 523 | 527 | 548 |
| 10. BSJG China | 518 | 494 | 531 |
| 11. S. Korea | 516 | 517 | 524 |
| **OECD average** | **493** | **493** | **490** |
| 31. Latvia | 490 | 488 | 482 |
| 35. Hungary | 477 | 470 | 477 |
| 37. Croatia | 475 | 487 | 464 |
| 44. Chile | 447 | 459 | 423 |
| 45. Bulgaria | 446 | 432 | 441 |
| 47. Uruguay | 435 | 437 | 418 |
| 48. Rumania | 435 | 434 | 434 |
| 51. Albania | 427 | 405 | 413 |
| 54. Thailand | 421 | 409 | 415 |
| 55. Costa Rica | 420 | 427 | 400 |
| 56. Qatar | 402 | 424 | 402 |
| 57. Colombia | 416 | 425 | 390 |
| 58. Mexico | 416 | 423 | 408 |
| 59. Montenegro | 411 | 427 | 418 |
| 60. Georgia | 411 | 401 | 404 |
| 61. Jordan | 409 | 408 | 380 |
| 62. Indonesia | 403 | 397 | 386 |
| 63. Brazil | 401 | 407 | 377 |
| 64. Peru | 397 | 398 | 397 |
| 65. Lebanon | 386 | 347 | 396 |
| 66. Tunisia | 386 | 361 | 367 |

*Table 8. (Continued)*

| Countries | Science | Reading | Mathematics |
|---|---|---|---|
| 67. Macedonia | 384 | 352 | 371 |
| 68. Kosovo | 378 | 347 | 362 |
| 69. Algeria | 376 | 350 | 360 |
| 70. Dominican Rep. | 332 | 358 | 328 |

*Source: OECD PISA 2015 database https://www.oecd.org/pisa/pisa-2015-results-in-focus.pdf*

The high level of graduate unemployment experienced by many developing countries is another major source of concern. Figure 12, based on ILO statistics, shows that quite a few countries have 40% levels of graduate unemployment, or even close to 50% in the case of Panama.

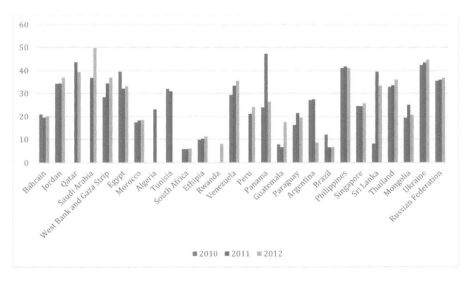

*Figure 12. Proportion of Unemployed Graduates with Tertiary Education (2010–2012). Source: ILO (2015)*

Paradoxically, unemployment for the graduates of many tertiary education programs is often associated with skills shortages in key sectors of the economy. This is notably the case in countries that export health personal.

The already inadequate health systems of Africa, especially sub-Saharan Africa, have been badly damaged by the migration of their health professionals. There are 57 countries with a critical shortage of healthcare workers, a deficit of 2.4 million doctors and nurses. Africa has 2.3 healthcare workers per 1000 population, compared with the Americas, which have 24.8 healthcare workers per 1000 population. Only 1.3% of the world's health workers care for people who experience 25% of the global disease burden. (Naicker et al., 2009)

Skill shortages also reflect the lack of relevance of existing programs in many parts of the world. In India, for example, large-scale studies of employability of engineers have found, four years in a row, worrisome gaps in the quality of training. In 2015, less than 20% of engineers trained in Indian institutions were assessed as employable for the software services sector, and less than 40% for non-functional roles such as business process outsourcing (Aspiring Minds, 2015). In East Asia, similarly, employers point to serious skills gaps, which is confirmed by prevailing patterns of wage skill premiums across low- and middle-income in the Region.

But higher education today does not sufficiently provide its graduates with the skills that firms need to increase their productivity. The quantity of higher education graduates is still too low for the labor market in countries like Cambodia, China, and Vietnam. More important than quantity, however, is quality. Across low- and middle-income East Asia, employers expect workers— particularly those with higher education—to possess the technical, behavioral, and thinking skills to increase their productivity and growth. They need science, technology, engineering, and math skills. They also need the problem-solving and creative skills to support a higher value- added manufacturing sector and the business, thinking, and behavioral skills for a higher-productivity service sector. (World Bank, 2011)

Finally, from the point of view of preparing graduates to be active citizens in democratic societies, few tertiary education institutions put sufficient emphasis on inculcating positive values as an integral part of their study programs. Even though very few studies on this aspect exist, anecdotal evidence on the academic background of professionals and politicians involved in reprehensible behaviors (corruption, fraud, harm to the environment, human rights violations, etc.) suggests that the ethical dimensions of the curriculum are generally neglected, even in top universities.

*Research and technology transfer.* Research output refers to the publications produced and the advanced training provided by universities in developing countries, measured by the number of scientific journal citations relative to a country's population and the capacity of tertiary education systems to prepare PhD graduates. Figure 13 presents the number of scientific citations of the top five countries in each region of the world and among OECD countries, relative to their population size.

The research output of developing countries is lagging dramatically behind that of OECD economies, reflecting the low performance of their research

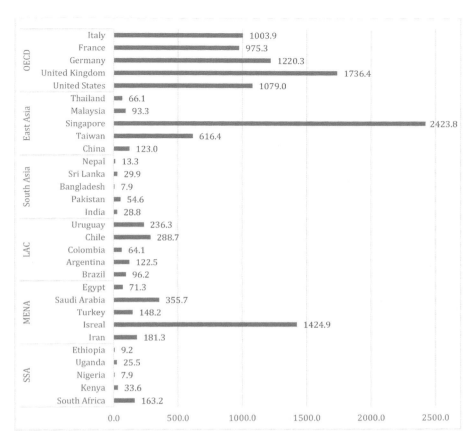

*Figure 13. Scientific Citations per One Million Inhabitants in Developing Countries (2015).*
*Source: Scimago and World Bank population data*

universities. China is the only research powerhouse among developing countries, with a production five times as high as that of India. Brazil, Iran and South Africa are the only other developing countries with a significant research output. As shown in the final section of this chapter, this situation reflects the absence of ambitious science and technology development strategies in most developing countries, limited funding for research, and the lack of critical mass in the research community.

The lagging research output of most developing countries universities is caused, to a great extent, by the lack of critical mass, as reflected in the low numbers of new PhD graduates in most developing countries (Figure 14).

The scanty presence of developing countries universities in the Shanghai ranking (Table 9), which essentially measures the research output and strength of universities,

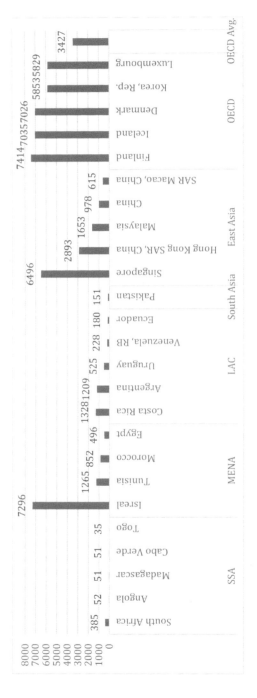

*Figure 14. PhD Graduates per Million Inhabitants (2011).*
*Source: World Bank data*

*Table 9. Shanghai (ARWU) Ranking Resultsfor Developing Countries Universities (2015)*

| Country Groupings | 1–100 | 101–200 | 201–300 | 301–400 | 401–500 |
|---|---|---|---|---|---|
| East Asia and the Pacific | 0 | 10 | 9 | 19 | 8 |
| Eastern Europe and Central Asia | 0 | 0 | 0 | 0 | 0 |
| Latin America and the Caribbean | 0 | 2 | 1 | 1 | 1 |
| Middle East and North Africa | 0 | 0 | 1 | 0 | 2 |
| South Asia | 0 | 0 | 0 | 0 | 1 |
| Sub-Saharan Africa | 0 | 0 | 2 | 0 | 2 |
| Total | 0 | 12 | 13 | 20 | 14 |

*Source: Academic Ranking of World Universities (ARWU) http://www.shanghairanking.com/ aboutarwu.html*

confirms their limited contribution in this area. The developing world does not have any university in the top 100, and does not represent more than 10% of the total number of universities among the 500 that are ranked.

The Leiden ranking, which measures not only the number of publications but also their impact (most highly cited publications), provides another assessment of the research performance of developing countries universities (Table 10). The 2016 CWTS Leiden Ranking is based on the Web of Science bibliographic database produced by Thomson Reuters. Universities worldwide are ranked according to their publication output in the Web of Science database in the following five broad scientific fields: (i) biomedical and health sciences; (ii) life and earth sciences; (iii) mathematics and computer science; (iv) natural sciences and engineering; and (v) social sciences and humanities.[3]

*Table 10. 2016 Leiden Ranking Results for Developing Countries Universities*

| Country Groupings | 1–100 | 101–200 | 201–300 | 301–400 | 401–500 |
|---|---|---|---|---|---|
| East Asia and the Pacific | 15 | 11 | 17 | 17 | 13 |
| Eastern Europe and Central Asia | 0 | 0 | 1 | 1 | 0 |
| Latin America and the Caribbean | 1 | 3 | 2 | 2 | 2 |
| Middle East and North Africa | 0 | 0 | 1 | 3 | 3 |
| South Asia | 0 | 0 | 1 | 2 | 3 |
| Sub-Saharan Africa | 0 | 0 | 0 | 0 | 3 |
| Total | 16 | 14 | 22 | 25 | 24 |

*Note: While the proportion of developing countries universities is higher than in the Shanghai ranking, this reflects essentially the progress of Chinese universities (67 ranked universities). Only a handful of universities from 12 other developing countries have a scientific output sufficient to be included: India (7), Brazil (6), Iran (6), Malaysia (4), South Africa (3), Thailand (2), Argentina (1), Chile (1), Mexico (1), Serbia (1), Slovenia (1), and Egypt (1).*

Some of the critics of the Shanghai ranking rightly argue that it is biased in favor of the hard sciences and engineering and neglects the social sciences where developing countries universities are stronger. But the few existing social sciences rankings do not show better results for the developing world. For example, in the Tilburg University ranking of the top 100 economics schools in the world, the only developing countries institutions represented are three Chinese universities.[4] Similarly, the ranking of the top 100 research business schools prepared by the University of Texas in Dallas does not includes any university from the developing world.[5] The same situation can be observed with the rankings of finance programs published by the University of Arizona: not one university from the developing world makes the cut.[6]

The situation is especially critical in Sub-Saharan Africa, where the priority given to basic education by governments and donors has adversely affected the development of tertiary education systems.

> Higher education in Africa faces severe constraints in terms of attaining critical mass of quality faculty. The average percentage of staff with PhD in public higher education institutions in Africa is estimated to be less than 20 percent (based on 10 countries in the region). Many departments do not have more than 1 or 2 senior professors, many close to the retirement age. This prevents departments and universities from being able to provide relevant higher education training (in part to develop faculty themselves), and establishing vibrant research environments. Moreover, low salaries of faculty, lack of research funding and equipment as well as limited autonomy provide disincentives for professors to stay in African universities. (World Bank, 2013)

While universities in East Asia are significantly more advanced and well resourced than their Sub-Saharan African counterparts, their contribution to innovation is still far from being adequate.

> Higher education also fails to provide the type of research needed to boost technological upgrading in firms. Governments are urging universities to go beyond simply providing skills to support innovation through research and technology... Research enables universities to produce ideas for the business community, thereby contributing to knowledge and technological innovation through basic and applied research and technology transfer. But international rankings and research output indicate that low- and middle-income East Asian higher education systems are not providing research of adequate quality. Even mere university involvement in technology adaptation and upgrading is limited in lower- and middle-income East Asia, with the possible exception of China. In Malaysia, Mongolia, and Thailand, for instance, universities are mentioned as leading in acquiring

technological innovations (in a broad sense) by only 1–2 percent of firms. (World Bank, 2011)

Finally, measures of technology transfer capture the contribution of tertiary education institutions to the development of the regions and the economy that they serve. Figure 15 shows the annual number of registered patents per one million inhabitants in the top 5 countries of each region of the world, as well as among the OECD economies. China and, to a lesser extent, Iran are the only two developing countries with a substantial output.

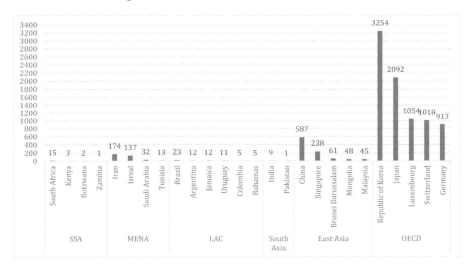

*Figure 15. Registered Patents by Origin for Developing*
*Countries (per Million Inhabitants, 2014).*
*Source: World Intellectual Property Indicators. Available from*
*http://www.wipo.int/ipstats/en/wipi/figures.html*

*The Determinants of Performance*

Conducting a comprehensive analysis of the various factors explaining the relatively poor performance of many tertiary education systems in developing countries could turn into an encyclopedic endeavor beyond the focus and scope of this report. Instead, this section proposes a series of summary tables indicating the main areas of progress in recent years and outlining the key challenges faced by tertiary education systems in developing countries (Tables 11 to 15). A more detailed discussion of generic issues and progress in addressing these issues in recent years can be found in other parts of the report (quality assurance in Chapter 1, governance in Chapter 3, and financing in Chapter 4).

*Table 11. Coverage, Access and Equity*

| Principal aspects | Strengths | Areas for improvement |
|---|---|---|
| Expansion of coverage | Rapid enrollment growth in all regions | South Asia and SSA still lagging. In most countries, lower enrollment rates for vulnerable groups |
| Institutional configuration | Degree of institutional diversification (non-university institutions, private sector) varies a lot. East Asia, Middle East and Latin America more diversified | Non-university public institutions poorly resourced and considered. Absence of pathways and bridges |
| Financial aid for low-income students | Scholarships and student loans available in many countries | Insufficient public resources |
| Non financial equity promotion measures | Very few countries with a national equity plan | Insufficient policy attention to these aspects and lack of public and institutional resources |
| Retention | A few successful schemes in individual institutions | High level of dropouts in many countries |

*Table 12. Quality and Relevance*

| Principal aspects | Strengths | Areas for improvement |
|---|---|---|
| Academic preparation and qualification of incoming students | A few developing countries have significantly improved their secondary education, as measured by PISA and TIMMS scores | In most developing countries, insufficient preparation of high school graduates |
| Licensing | Growing number of countries with requirement for all new programs | Insufficiently rigorous standards to avoid entry of fraudulent providers |
| Quality assurance/ accreditation | Significant progress in East Asia and Latin America, followed by Eastern Europe and the Middle East | Challenges to independence and professional level of accreditation agencies. SSA lagging behind. |
| Assessment of learning outcomes | Brazil, Colombia, Jordan, Mexico and Panama pioneers | Need to ensure better measure of actual competencies Insufficient use of existing instruments by tertiary education institutions |
| Evaluation of labor market outcomes of graduates | Labor Market Observatories in Chile, Colombia and Mexico as pioneers | Insufficient use of results by governments and institutions |

*Table 12. (Continued)*

| Principal aspects | Strengths | Areas for improvement |
|---|---|---|
| Curriculum and structure of degrees | A few universities, especially private ones, have aligned their programs with the Bologna process | Insufficient linkages with the productive sectors |
| Pedagogical practices | A few innovative initiatives in some universities in many countries | Still traditional teaching methods in the majority of tertiary education institutions |
| Postgraduate education | Progress in East Asia, Brazil and South Africa | Insufficiently developed in most developing countries |
| STEM programs | Pockets of excellence in a few countries, especially in leading public universities | Limited in many developing countries |

*Table 13. Research and Innovation*

| Principal aspects | Strengths | Areas for improvement |
|---|---|---|
| National science and technology vision and strategy | A few countries, especially in East Asia, have defined a long-term strategy | Lack of clear vision and comprehensive strategy in many if not most developing countries |
| Research production | Rising proportion of academics with a PhD in many public universities Centers of excellence in a few universities in most countries | Low levels in South Asia, SSA and low-income countries in East Asia and Latin America Academic in-breeding in many public universities |
| Financing of research | Recent increases in several East Asian countries and a few Latin American countries | Low level in South and Central Asia, North Africa and SSA |
| Doctoral education | Overall progress in the past decade | Slow development in most countries, especially low income |
| Focus of research activities | Efforts of national research policy agencies to link research to the needs of the economy | Overtly theoretical and academic in many universities |

67

*Table 14. Governance*

| Principal aspects | Strengths | Areas for improvement |
|---|---|---|
| Institutional autonomy | Fairly high level of autonomy regarding academic organization and management | Financial and human resources management in public institutions usually constrained by civil service regulations and salary levels |
| Accountability | Financial audits | Few accountability mechanisms to reflect actual university performance |
| Role and composition of university boards | Increasing participation of external members in several countries | Limited power of university boards in many countries |
| Selection of university presidents and leadership team members | Governance reforms of public universities in few countries Good practices in top private universities | In many public institutions, absence of objective process for selection of presidents and leadership teams on the basis of professional criteria Lack of transparency in many private institutions |
| Stability in the operation of tertiary education institutions | Stability in private institutions | Frequent conflicts and strikes in public universities, especially in Latin America, South Asia and SSA |

*Table 15. Financing*

| Principal aspects | Strengths | Areas for improvement |
|---|---|---|
| National budget contribution | - | Low level of public funding (with a few exceptions) |
| Allocation mechanisms | A few countries have introduced formula funding and/or performance based allocation mechanisms | Lack of performance criteria: no incentives to improve or be efficient |
| Efficiency in resource utilization | Financial crisis has forced public institutions to rationalize their spending | Waste of resources linked to high level of dropouts, long duration of studies, low completion rates, and inefficient deployment of academics |

*Table 15. (Continued)*

| Principal aspects | Strengths | Areas for improvement |
| --- | --- | --- |
| Distribution of public subsidies | More equitable distribution in the few countries with an effective, well-targeted scholarships and student loans program | Regressive distribution of public funding in most cases: wealthiest groups benefit in a disproportionate way in tuition-free public universities |
| Effectiveness of student loan programs | Very few countries with a well-functioning program | Most student loan schemes affected by problems of high administrative costs, low interest rates, and inefficient loan recovery |

## NOTES

[1]  This conceptual framework was developed by the author while working at the World Bank in the context of a wider policy research project on the measurement of the results of education systems. A summary presentation of the framework for tertiary education can be found in Salmi (2013e).

[2]  http://www.universitas21.com/article/projects/details/152/u21-ranking-of-national-higher-education-systems

[3]  The CWTS Leiden Ranking measures the scientific performance of 843 major universities in 53 countries. Using a sophisticated set of bibliometric indicators, the ranking aims to provide highly accurate measurements of the scientific impact of universities and of universities' involvement in scientific collaboration. The 2016 CWTS Leiden Ranking is based on Web of Science indexed publications from the 2011–2014 period. Detailed information is available at: http://www.leidenranking.com/#sthash.zFFiawq4.dpuf

[4]  https://econtop.uvt.nl/rankinglist.php

[5]  http://jindal.utdallas.edu/the-utd-top-100-business-school-research-rankings/worldRankings#20082012

[6]  http://apps.wpcarey.asu.edu/fin-rankings/rankings/results.cfm

# DESIGNING AND IMPLEMENTING
# SYSTEM-WIDE REFORMS

We must free ourselves of the hope that the sea will ever rest. We must learn to sail in high winds.

(Aristotle Onassis)

The academic literature on change in tertiary education focuses almost exclusively on issues of knowledge development, skills formation, curriculum reform and related transformational interventions to improve quality and relevance within universities (Whitehead, 1998). But little attention has been paid to the evolution and transformation of entire tertiary education systems, unlike what has happened with regard to the development of education systems at the primary and secondary levels. In 2007, for instance, McKinsey and Company carried out a study of the common characteristics of high performing basic education systems (McKinsey, 2007). In 2010, it published the results of policy research on twenty education systems showing sustained and widespread progress as a consequence of important structural reforms (Mourshed et al., 2010).

Building on the pioneering work of McKinsey and Company and the author's international experience, this report proposes an analytical framework to understand the main success factors behind successful reform strategies in tertiary education.[1] As illustrated by Figure 16, the appropriate sequence of a reform process at the tertiary level would include the following steps:

1. Ignition phase to sensitize all stakeholders to the urgency of the reform;
2. Elaboration of a vision for the future of the tertiary education system;
3. Formulation of a set of strategic reforms to translate the vision into reality;
4. Launch of the reform, taking the political dimensions into consideration; and
5. Structural measures to ensure the sustainability of the reforms, especially their long-term financial viability.

*Figure 16. Proposed Sequence for Designing, Initiating and Implementing Tertiary Education Reforms.*
*Source: Adapted from Mourshed et al. (2010)*

IGNITION PHASE

*I am all for progress. It is change I can't stand.* (Mark Twain)

McKinsey's research on the dynamics of successful education reforms points to three possible "ignition" factors which, separately or together, are most likely to generate the kind of political support required to facilitate the implementation of difficult reforms: a severe political and/or economic crisis, the publication of a high profile report on the state of the education system, and/or the appointment of a new leader. While these three factors appear to be also relevant in the context of the introduction of tertiary education reforms, an important additional driver—the global rankings—seem to play an equally powerful role among the elements likely to impulse significant change in tertiary education.

The Chilean experience is perhaps the most recent example of reforms imposed by a crisis situation partially linked to the fact that the government did not move fast enough after the publication of a high profile expert report. Since 2007, the Chilean government had operated two separate student loan systems, one for students enrolled in the 25 publicly subsidized universities (30% of total enrollment) with a low interest rate and favorable repayment conditions, and one for students attending private, non-subsidized universities (70% of enrollment) with a high interest rate and less favorable repayment conditions. In 2008, the Ministry of Education invited the OECD and the World Bank to conduct a joint assessment of the country's tertiary education system. One of the strong recommendations of the report was to eliminate the discriminatory distinction between the two groups of students from the point of view of student aid opportunities and subsidies, merge the two existing student loan schemes and offer easier repayment conditions, preferably on an income-contingent basis (OECD/WB, 2009). Unfortunately, the government was slow in considering implementation of this reform. In 2011, a vast majority of Chilean students staged street protests to demand the abolition of tuition fees and the elimination of the high interest student loan scheme. Ironically, the students used the findings of the OECD/WB report to back their requests up (Salmi, 2014).

The student protests evolved into a nation-wide wide political movement that threatened the survival of the government. In 2012, the Ministry of Education yielded and introduced a new financing law suppressing the second student loan scheme and extending the benefits of the first one to all Chilean students. In 2013, Michele Bachelet promised to introduce free tertiary education for all during her reelection campaign. Since the beginning of her second presidential mandate in February 2014, the Chilean government has sought to find a way of making true on the promise of making tertiary education free, which is no easy feat in a country where more than 70% of the students are enrolled in private universities and tertiary education institutions.

Post-conflict transitions are usually moments of acute political and economic crisis but at the same time they can present good windows of opportunity to undertake courageous reforms that may not be possible in most countries where the key stakeholders in the tertiary education community have entrenched positions that make change difficult if not impossible. In the mid-1990s, the new Minister of Higher Education of Mozambique took advantage of the positive momentum created by the end of the crippling civil war to transform the tertiary education system in a comprehensive way as part of the country's reconstruction effort (Bollag, 2003).

Pakistan offers a good illustration of how a high-profile report can trigger important reforms. In 1998-99, the founding president of the Aga Khan University of Karachi—a former Minister of Education—was part a distinguished group of independent experts who wrote an influential report on the role of tertiary education in the developing world—Peril and Promise—, with financial support from several donor agencies, including the World Bank and UNESCO (2000). Afterwards, he was instrumental in the launch of a national Task Force that elaborated a detailed vision and strategy for the transformation of the Pakistani tertiary education system. The government endorsed it, established a powerful Higher Education Commission and provided substantial funding to implement wide-ranging reforms. This led to significant progress up to the beginning of the current decade, when the growing political instability in Pakistan slowed down reform activities in tertiary education.

In the tertiary education arena, national and global rankings have increasingly played an igniting role similar to that of a high profile report. In Malaysia, for example, the 2005 edition of the ranking of world universities published by the Times Higher Education Supplement created a major controversy when it showed the country's top two universities slipping by almost 100 places compared with their results of the previous year. Notwithstanding the fact that the big drop was essentially due to a change in the ranking methodology—a little known fact at the time—the news was so traumatic to Malaysian society that a parliamentary commission of inquiry was set up to investigate the matter and the Vice-Chancellor of the University of Malaya had to step down. On the positive side, this crisis prompted the Malaysian authorities to ask hard questions about the performance of the country's universities and to undertake significant reforms, from changing the mode of selection of university presidents—from political appointment to professional competitive selection—to mobilizing additional funding for the country's top universities. Similarly, the recent Excellence Initiatives in France, Germany and Russia were prompted, principally, by the poor showing of their flagship universities in the global rankings (Salmi, 2016b).

Whether the main trigger is a crisis, a high profile report or the whiplash effect of poor results in the global rankings, the arrival of new leaders appears to be the most powerful "ignition" factors, provided the new leadership is committed to offering new solutions to long-standing problems and ensuring the sustainability of the reforms.

73

ELABORATION OF A VISION FOR THE FUTURE OF THE TERTIARY
EDUCATION SYSTEM

There is no prescription for how a country creates such a culture [of knowledge]
… But government does have a role—a role in education, in encouraging the
kind of creativity and risk taking that the scientific entrepreneurship requires,
in creating the institutions that facilitate ideas being brought into fruition,
and a regulatory and tax environment that rewards this kind of activity.
(Joseph E. Stiglitz, Nobel Prize lecture, 2001)

It is striking to observe the presence of no less than eleven Californian universities
among the top 100 universities in the Shanghai ARWU ranking. This impressive
outcome is not due to pure chance, nor does it reflect only the outstanding endeavors
of each of these eleven universities. To a large extent, it is the direct result of a clear
and wide-ranging vision elaborated in the 1960s and reflected in the much-celebrated
"Higher Education Master Plan", which sets out to define the respective roles and
contributions of the various types of institutions constituting the Californian tertiary
education system, from the junior colleges to the top research universities, together
with the pathways allowing for the fluid movement of students throughout the
system (Box 13).

---

*Box 13. Setting the Vision for Tertiary Education in California*

California pioneered the establishment of a policy framework for a state
system of higher education in the United States when it developed and
implemented its first Master Plan in 1959-60. The primary issues considered
at that time were the future roles of the public and private sectors and, in
particular, how the public sector should be governed and coordinated to avoid
duplication and waste.

The fundamental principles that emerged from the initial master plan still
shape the state's system today:

- Recognition of different missions for the four components of the higher
  education system (University of California, California State University,
  community colleges, and private universities and junior colleges),
- Establishment of a statutory coordinating body for the entire system,
- Differential admission pools for the University and State Colleges,
- Eligibility of students attending private institutions for the state scholarship
  program.
- Availability since 1965 of grants from the federal government (Pell Grants)
  for low-income students throughout the state system.

The California Master Plan for Higher Education, which is revised about
every ten years, is not a rigid blueprint to control centrally the development of

---

California's system of higher education. Rather, it sets some general parameters, focuses primarily on the boundaries among the four sectors of higher education, and strives for a system that balances equity, quality and efficiency.

Since only a handful of developing nations have formulated a comprehensive plan for the development of their tertiary education system, the first step for thinking about possible reforms in any country would consist in elaborating a vision for the future of tertiary education. The vision would define the mission and role of tertiary education and the guiding principles that would orient the growth of the system, outline policies to improve equity, quality and relevance, and channel efforts to strengthen the research capacity of the country. The vision must be informed by a thorough diagnosis of the current performance of the system in terms of quantitative development, distribution of the supply of tertiary education institutions and programs, quality and relevance of existing programs, equity in access and completion rates for various population groups, and strength of the research system.

Developing the vision is however not sufficient in itself. It must be translated into a comprehensive strategic plan that articulates quantitative targets in terms of expansion of coverage and reduction in disparities, sets out overall goals in terms of quality improvement and enhancement of the relevance of programs, and revisits the institutional configuration of the tertiary education system, as needed. The plan should also outline those reforms that are necessary to establish appropriate conditions for the effective operation of tertiary education institutions in terms of supportive quality assurance mechanisms, favorable governance and sustainable financing. In each case, the vision and the plan should aim at answering the following questions:

- What concrete quantitative targets will the government pursue with respect to overall enrollment growth, equal opportunities for students from vulnerable groups, distribution of educational attainment of the adult population, and research output?
- What is the core mission of each type of tertiary education institution? Is there sufficient differentiation among research universities, teaching universities, and non-university institutions offering shorter duration, professionally oriented programs in terms of the desirable balance among these institutions' research, teaching and service functions? Do existing articulation mechanisms provide pathways and bridges that permit flexible mobility across various types of institutions?
- Does the country want to establish a world-class university or, at least, support the development of a few centers of excellence that can conduct research at the most advanced level?
- What quality assurance instruments are needed to promote better quality and relevance across the board?

- What governance arrangements should be put in place to offer an appropriate regulatory framework to promote innovative behaviors and practices?
- What level of resource mobilization (public and private funding) would be needed to reach the objectives set by the government in a sustainable manner?

FORMULATION OF A SET OF STRATEGIC MEASURES

International experience indicates that successful reforms, when measured not only by the yardstick of implementation but, more importantly, by their impact on the performance of a tertiary education system, do not consist of a single measure or intervention (Salmi, 2012b). The more effective reforms are those designed as a set of coherent, mutually reinforcing interventions aiming at improving the operation of the entire tertiary education system. Denmark, for example, started a series of reforms in 2002-2003 that included changes in the governance arrangements at the national and institutional levels (bringing the university sector under the authority of the Ministry of Industry and Innovation, strengthening the role of the Board, moving from an elected university president to an international, competitive selection process), increased funding for tertiary education in general and university research in particular, and a number of university mergers as a way of achieving critical mass in research and boosting their scientific production in order to increase the global competitiveness of Danish universities.

Thus, developing countries keen on reforming and transforming their tertiary education system should identify and design the set of interventions most appropriate to reach their long-term goals for bringing about better results in the following key areas of performance:

- Tertiary education coverage and equity in access and success;
- Quality and relevance of tertiary education institutions, programs and courses; and
- Quantity, relevance and impact of the research output of universities.

The package of reforms would need to reflect the specific challenges and development objectives of each country in terms of enrollment growth and institutional diversification, improvement in the quality and relevance of programs, and upgrading of the research capacity of universities.

*Increasing Access and Equity*

While the financial aspects of strategies to expand tertiary education coverage in an equitable way—including scholarships and student loans—are analyzed in the next chapter, this section looks at the non-monetary policies known to help improve access and equity in tertiary education (Salmi and Malee Bassett, 2014). Governments and institutions must consider, in particular, the following interventions:

- Academic and career counseling
- Outreach and bridge programs
- Affirmative action programs
- Measures to increase retention

*Academic and career counseling.* A solid and comprehensive system of academic and career counseling represents an essential instrument to improve the transition from high school to tertiary education, especially for students from under-privileged backgrounds who often lack the information and motivation to pursue their studies. Very few developing countries have a career information and guidance system in place. It would therefore be advisable to assess the effectiveness of existing services in reaching those students who are traditionally under-represented among tertiary education graduates, either because they never enter a post-secondary education institution or because they drop out before completing their studies.

A career information and guidance system can be defined as a set of tools and services intended to assist individuals of any age to make educational, training, and occupational choices and to manage their careers (Watts and Fretwell, 2004). To operate in an effective manner, the career information and guidance system must be designed and put in place as a coherent system bringing all necessary stakeholders together, including the Ministry of Education, Ministry of Labor, Ministry of Economy, all tertiary education institutions, Chambers of Commerce, etc. It must rely on sound measurement tools for assessing quality throughout the system, including the quality of the information offered to students and graduates. The system should facilitate information access, allow for self-help and self-development, lead to increased use of information and communication technologies, and promote interaction among tertiary education institutions, the private sector and NGOs.

*Outreach and bridge programs.* Programs that link tertiary education institutions to the lower levels of education through outreach and bridge activities can also be effective in improving transition rates and raising the probability of success in tertiary education, especially for at-risk students. Outreach and bridge interventions seek to reduce the academic, aspirational, informational, and personal barriers that restrict access among students currently underrepresented in tertiary education.

The following suggestions for policy and practices that could be successful in developing countries are based on a recent review of outreach and bridge programs currently operating around the world (Savitz-Romer et al., 2009). They seek to expand upon current efforts to foster the most important kind of access–access that leads to degree completion.

- *Establish early intervention programs and policies.* Ensuring that students possess adequate skills and aspirations to successfully seek out and enroll in tertiary education must start early. Children's career and educational aspirations are formed in early years of schooling, and negative experiences and messages about their chances for entry into tertiary education likely diminish their motivation and interest.

- *Build collaborative partnerships.* The most successful outreach and bridge programs involve university-school partnerships that allow for multi-level interventions and support. The presence of a university partner in a primary or secondary school community helps to influence the aspirations of students, expectations of teachers, and enhances possibilities for creating a broader community of learners, holding great promise for improving secondary school completion rates and access to tertiary education.
- *Increase policy attention to engaging families in interventions.* It is widely recognized that parents and extended family members play a key role in influencing tertiary education aspirations. Family support, both financial and emotional, plays an important role in shaping students' aspirations, as well as their academic preparation for tertiary education. The impact of family and community on education aspiration setting is an area that warrants additional attention, especially among communities with few or no first generation college-attenders.
- *Create linked programs.* The importance of linking interventions to funding is evident in multi-tiered programs where scholarships act as incentives and rewards for successful participation. In this way, students are more likely to overcome the multiple barriers they face when pursuing tertiary education, rather than creating dichotomies among their academic, social and financial needs. A recent program in the Colombian department of Antioquia offers useful lessons in this respect (Box 14).

*Box 14. Conditional Subsidies to Increase the Transition between Secondary and Tertiary Education in Colombia*

The conditional transfer incentives program was designed and implemented in the context of a secondary education project in the Colombian department of Antioquia, with technical and financial support from the World Bank between 2009 and 2014. The main purpose of the scheme was to reduce dropout rates and increase the transition from upper-secondary to tertiary education.

Five thousand students had been randomly selected under the following criteria: (i) formal enrolment in a public high school, (ii) coming from a bottom income quintile family, (iii) being below 18 years, and (iii) not coming from a family that was already in a conditional cash program (*Familias en acción*). These students received the equivalent of 21 dollars every month, ten months a year. Continuous participation in the scheme was conditional upon the student staying in school and participating in the education for peace activities.

A preliminary evaluation of the impact of the scheme on retention and learning outcomes, conducted after three years of operation, found that dropout rates had fallen by 40% and that participants in the scheme obtained significantly higher scores in language. The authors of the preliminary impact evaluation observed an increase in the transition rate from secondary to tertiary from 23% in 2006 to 30% in 2013.

(Source: Econometria, 2013; Evaluación del Programa de Incentivos en la Educación Media. Bogota: Econometria)

*Affirmative action programs.* Affirmative action, an area of policy directed toward creating differential admission processes to promote equality of opportunity, has received increased attention in many parts of the developing world. India has by far the most elaborate system in the world, with quotas for members of the Scheduled Castes and Scheduled Tribes—the two most disadvantaged groups in society—absorbing half of all the seats in some of its public universities. A recent study examining the effects of quotas for disadvantaged castes and women at 200 engineering colleges found that the affirmative action program had indeed increased college attendance for the targeted students, especially at the prestigious Indian Institutes of Technology (Bagde et al., 2016). Contrary to the widely held belief that affirmative action puts beneficiaries into academic programs for which they are not sufficiently prepared, the targeted students assessed in the study had similar academic results as the other students.

In Brazil, the movement started with a number of public universities establishing their own form of affirmative action program at their own initiative. The most advanced scheme has come from UNICAMP in Campinas, which has designed an affirmative action program providing for easier admission criteria (30 extra points on top of a minimum of 500) for public high school graduates who have successfully passed the first phase of the university admission exam (vestibular). Ten additional points are given to those who declare themselves as black, mixed race or indigenous. A preliminary evaluation of the program revealed that the beneficiaries performed relatively better than high-income students selected through the regular admission, showing that "it is possible to accommodate affirmative action programs and merit criteria when recruiting undergraduate students to a highly selective (research) university" (Pedrosa, 2006).

In recent years, the Brazilian government has sought to integrate affirmative action into the national legal framework. The Law of Social Quotas, enacted in 2012, requires public universities to reserve half of their admission seats for high school graduates coming from the public secondary sector and to vastly increase the enrollment of students of African descent (Romero, 2012).

In setting up affirmative action programs, developing countries governments should heed the lessons from the history of positive discrimination, which has been fraught with controversy and challenges. In-depth research into affirmative action across nations and cultures reveals diversity in the mechanisms and procedures that have proven most effective (Box 15).

*Box 15. Lessons from Preferential Admission Programs*

Even if group preferences and quotas are aimed to be limited in time and scope, in most countries the capacity to control such policies and limit them over time has proven to be illusory, and so has the pretension of eliminating centuries-old inequalities through temporary programs. International experience shows that preferential admission programs tend to have the following negative consequences:

- The reaction of both the preferred and the non-preferred groups are neither controllable nor predicable. Non-preferred group members can redesignate themselves as members of the preferred group creating artificial categories and then distorting the purpose of reestablishing equal opportunities amongst groups and even worsening off the situation of the initial beneficiaries.
- The beneficiaries are not always those initially targeted: preferences can benefit more fortunate members of less fortunate groups, the lowest economic group being left behind.
- The benefits of such programs to the concerned groups or to the society as a whole has often been over-estimated: transfer of benefits from one group to another can change people's mindsets and result in important social, economical and efficiency losses if both groups tend to do less than their best or if the non-preferred groups decide to leave the country.
- Inter-group resentments can appear even when only minor transfers of benefits apply. Group preferences and quotas go against the principle of equality of treatment and can be interpreted as unfair and unjustified privileges even though individuals of the non-preferred groups have not lost anything.
- The concrete results of such policies on the reduction of inequalities are hard to evaluate since pre-existing trends and other social, individual and economical factors simultaneously act on the situation of these groups.

Warning against group preferences or quotas compensation does not mean ignoring that some groups did suffer or are suffering from discrimination; it aims at raising awareness on the concrete, actual and global consequences of such programs. Several country experiences show that the overall results can sometimes be negative for society as a whole. This is particularly important to consider, knowing that once preferred policies are introduced, they can hardly be removed, and often tend to expand over time.

(Source: Sowell, 2004)

In recent years, policy-makers and university leaders in South Africa and Israel have argued that class-based affirmative action could be a better alternative to race-based positive discrimination. However, the initial results of a pilot program launched in Israel in the mid-2000s by four of the country's most selective universities seeking to give better opportunities to disadvantaged applicants through a race-neutral and needs-blind admission system seem to indicate that the most effective approach would be to combine ethnic and social class considerations (Alon, 2016).

*Measures to increase persistence and retention.* Equity promotion policies often emphasize increased access as the main measure of progress. However, it is important to focus also on student success and degree completion, which requires support programs and regular measurement of outcomes such as graduation rates for under-represented groups. To promote student persistence, countries and tertiary education institutions have focused on putting in place dedicated support mechanisms—financial, academic, personal or structural—in order to increase completion rates.

Developing countries governments can rely on a range of retention policies and practices to help the students most in need. The main measures include offering adequate financial aid (needs-based scholarships and student loans – see Chapter 4), to ensure that students will not drop out for lack of resources, and appropriate academic and career counseling (see previous section).

At the institutional level, possible interventions consist of needs-based scholarships or tuition exemption modalities on the financial front, first-year induction, early detection of academic difficulties, academic advising, tutoring and mentoring, and psychological counseling for personal support. Some institutions have a "first-year provost" responsible for closely monitoring the academic results of new students and providing targeted support to students in difficulty, considering that oftentimes the highest proportion of dropouts are first-year students (Box 16).

---

*Box 16. Lessons from Uniminuto – An Inclusive University*

In 1990, a Colombian Eudist priest known for his community development actions, Rafael García Herreros, created an open access private university, Uniminuto, with the explicit purpose of offering good-quality education to young people from low-income families living in disadvantaged areas. After setting up the main campus in the remote outskirts of Bogota, the capital city, Uniminuto established branches in marginalized urban and rural zones all over the country. From the beginning, the curriculum emphasized professional competencies, citizenship values, social innovation and sustainable development.

Uniminuto has experienced a spectacular growth, evolving into a multi-campus university system of 46 branches enrolling close to 100,000 students overall in 2015. About 45,000 are online students. Two-thirds of the students are female; 54% belong to the lowest two income quintiles. Uniminuto's financial model relies essentially on student fees (at a low level) for operational expenditures and loans or donations for capital investment. The University

---

spends about 28% of its revenues on student aid (scholarships, low interest loans and tuition discounts). Altogether, 80% of the students receive some form of financial support.

Uniminuto has put in place a special program of academic support dedicated to at-risk students. Initially, the program specifically targeted first-year students because of their higher propensity for dropping out. However, in recent years, the first-year academic support program evolved into a more comprehensive approach called the Integrated Focus Model (IFM – *Modelo de Atención Integral al Estudiante* in Spanish), which operates during the entire course of studies.

It all started with the First-Semester Initiative, which was launched in 2006 on the main campus in Bogota. The following year, it became the First-Year initiative, with a "first-year vice-dean" assigned to oversee the program. In 2012, Uniminuto decided to transform the First-Year program into a comprehensive academic support model offering a wider range of interventions to accompany students in difficulty and follow them throughout the course of their studies. The Integrated Focus Model involves a sequence of support activities, careful measurement, early warning systems, and impact evaluation. At-risk students have access to five categories of support services: (i) academic counselling, (ii) financial support for temporary difficulties, (iii) psychological counselling, (iv) a life project course, and (v) remedial courses.

In 2012, Uniminuto was the first educational institution to win the G-20's Challenge on Inclusive Business Innovation for its "innovative social model for social inclusion". In 2013, the Financial Times and the International Financial Corporation gave Uniminuto their first Inclusive Business Award.

(Source: Field visits and interviews by Jamil Salmi)

International experience points to the following recommendations in the design of effective persistence and retention programs (Rowan-Kenyon et al., 2010).

- *Connect secondary and tertiary education.* Many of the challenges that students bring with them to institutions of tertiary education result from inadequate secondary education. This is particularly true for students from rural areas and low-income students. Students with inadequate academic preparation are more likely to struggle in tertiary education and are at a higher risk of dropping out before earning a degree. Secondary and tertiary education systems can intervene more purposefully by engaging in coordinated interventions to support academic success and ensure that students are being prepared to continue their education through the highest levels (see previous section on outreach).
- *Support the development of robust institutional research departments.* In addition to enrollment data and grades, universities can benefit greatly from well-developed institutional research departments to track students' background characteristics

and intentions upon enrollment, student engagement, course completion by discipline, and to track the performance of their graduates in the labor market. In addition, institutions should regularly assess student learning and measure student perceptions of learning and campus climate. This information is needed in order to gain an accurate understanding of the student population and student progress, which in turn enables institutions to design and implement effective persistence and retention programs.

- *Develop holistic support mechanisms.* While financial challenges are a primary roadblock to persistence for many students, it is not the only one. Governments and institutions should create programs that combine financial support with academic and personal support services. The most financially disadvantaged students often need academic support to combat inadequate academic preparation, as well as social and structural supports to help in their transition and eventual graduation from tertiary education.
- *Include psychological support services in prevention programming.* While there are numerous examples of financial and academic support programs around the world, there appears to be a lack of emotional support mechanisms available for students at tertiary institutions in developing nations. Tertiary students often face concerns and stresses that can be a barrier to degree completion. For this reason, institutions should further explore psychological support services for students in the form of counseling, mentoring, and advising programs that provide students with the critical emotional support.
- *Consider work-study models.* Institutions could organize work-study programs for their students. These placements are a benefit to the students, not only in terms of providing much needed financial support, but also in promoting engagement with the institution. Students also develop skills in these placements that may be useful after graduation.

*Improving Quality and Relevance*

> *The quality of their learning experiences and the environment in which students learn will shape the future development of our society.* (Hunt Report, Ireland, 2011)

Developing countries governments could consider several measures to bring about improved quality, raise student learning outcomes and increase the relevance of tertiary education programs, including (i) curricular and pedagogical innovations, (ii) reinforced quality assurance, (iii) strengthened links to the productive sectors and the labor market, and (iv) increased internationalization.

*Curricular and pedagogical innovations.* The focus of curricular and pedagogical reforms should be on modernizing program content and making delivery more effective. In their efforts to provide incentives for tertiary education institutions interested and willing to transform their educational approach, the national authorities in developing countries must encourage moving away from traditional teaching methods and making teaching and learning more interactive, collaborative and experiential. Today's cohorts of young students—often described as the e-generation or Renaissance kids—have grown up with the Internet and been learning since their young age from computer screens, websites, and visual media. Traditional ways of teaching have been found increasingly unsuccessful in engaging and motivating the e-generation. Mounting evidence provided by the cognitive and learning sciences indicates that interactive pedagogical approaches facilitate an effective learning experience (Barkley, Cross and Major, 2005; Prince, 2004). As the Institute of Play's mission statement explains, ... "our world is changing so quickly that we can only begin to imagine what the future will hold. But we are failing to teach our kids the skills and knowledge they need to succeed in today's world. So how will we prepare them for jobs that haven't even been invented yet? The real work of a 21st century education is to spark the passion for lifelong learning that our kids will need to navigate their way to a promising tomorrow."[2]

Therefore, the establishment of well resourced Teaching and Learning Centers in all tertiary education institutions should become a priority in support of pedagogical innovations that would facilitate active learning (design-based or problem-based learning, gaming, simulations, peer-to-peer learning, artificial intelligence software for independent learning, etc.). These centers can rely on a range of training activities, including capacity building workshops and mentoring, to support the development of innovative pedagogical approaches among the teaching staff. Box 17 illustrates an innovative approach based on peer learning, pioneered by Professor Eric Mazur, Dean of Applied Physics at Harvard University. Maastricht University, the youngest university in the Netherland, has been a European pioneer in the development of problem-based approaches to teaching and learning in all its programs.

---

*Box 17. Twilight of the Lecture: "Active Learning" Overthrowing the Style of Teaching That Has Ruled Universities for 600 Years*

In 1990, after seven years of teaching at Harvard, Eric Mazur was delivering clear, polished lectures and demonstrations and getting high student evaluations for his introductory Physics 11 course, populated mainly by premed and engineering students who were successfully solving complicated problems. Then he discovered that his success as a teacher "was a complete illusion, a house of cards."

The epiphany came via an article in the American Journal of Physics by Arizona State professor David Hestenes. He had devised a very simple test, couched in everyday language, to check students' understanding of one of the most fundamental concepts of physics—force—and had administered it to thousands of undergraduates in the southwestern United States. Astonishingly, the test showed that their introductory courses had taught them "next to nothing," says Mazur: "After a semester of physics, they still held the same misconceptions as they had at the beginning of the term."

Mazur tried the test on his own students. To Mazur's consternation, the simple test of conceptual understanding showed that his students had not grasped the basic ideas of his physics course: two-thirds of them were modern Aristotelians. "The students did well on textbook-style problems," he explains. "They had a bag of tricks, formulas to apply. But that was solving problems by rote. They floundered on the simple word problems, which demanded a real understanding of the concepts behind the formulas."

Some soul-searching followed. "That was a very discouraging moment," he says. "Was I not such a good teacher after all? Maybe I have dumb students in my class. There's something wrong with the test! How hard it is to accept that the blame lies with yourself."

Serendipity provided the breakthrough he needed. Reviewing the test of conceptual understanding, Mazur twice tried to explain one of its questions to the class, but the students remained obstinately confused. "Then I did something I had never done in my teaching career," he recalls. "I said, 'Why don't you discuss it with each other?'" Immediately, the lecture hall was abuzz as 150 students started talking to each other in one-on-one conversations about the puzzling question. "It was complete chaos," says Mazur. "But within three minutes, they had figured it out. That was very surprising to me—I had just spent 10 minutes trying to explain this. But the class said, 'OK, We've got it, let's move on.'"

"Here's what happened," he continues. "First, when one student has the right answer and the other doesn't, the first one is more likely to convince the second— it's hard to talk someone into the wrong answer when they have the right one. More important, a fellow student is more likely to reach them than Professor Mazur—and this is the crux of the method. You're a student and you've only recently learned this, so you still know where you got hung up, because it's not that long ago that you were hung up on that very same thing. Whereas Professor Mazur got hung up on this point when he was 17, and he no longer remembers how difficult it was back then. He has lost the ability to understand what a beginning learner faces."

This innovative style of learning grew into "peer instruction" or "interactive learning," a pedagogical method that has spread far beyond physics and taken root on campuses nationally. Every year, Mazur gives nearly 100 lectures on the subject at venues all around the world.

Interactive learning triples students' gains in knowledge as measured by the kinds of conceptual tests that had once deflated Mazur's spirits. "In a traditional physics course, two months after taking the final exam, people are back to where they were before taking the course," Mazur notes. "It's shocking." (Concentrators are an exception to this, as subsequent courses reinforce their knowledge base.) Peer-instructed students who've actively argued for and explained their understanding of scientific concepts hold onto their knowledge longer.

Such pedagogical invention isn't just a trial-and-error endeavor. Rigorous evaluations using statistical analysis can help distinguish the most promising innovations. For his part, Mazur has collected reams of data on his students' results. End-of-semester course evaluations he dismisses as nothing more than "popularity contests" that ought to be abolished. "There is zero correlation between course evaluations and the amount learned," he says. "Award-winning teachers with the highest evaluations can produce the same results as teachers who are getting fired." He asserts that he is "far more interested in learning than teaching," and envisions a shift from "teaching" to "helping students learn." The focus moves away from the lectern and toward the physical and imaginative activity of each student in class.

(Source: Lambert, 2012)

Franklin W. Olin College of Engineering, a young private university located in Wellesley, just South of Boston in Massachusetts, is perhaps one of the best example of an institution embodying the radical transformation that interactive, collaborative and experiential learning call for. Olin College opened its doors in 1999 with an audacious charter: offering an experimental laboratory for remaking engineering education. Starting from the observation that STEM education is in crisis in the United States because it fails to attract the right students, because it is teaching the wrong curriculum, and because it is using methods that are known to be largely ineffective, the main purpose of Olin is to train the engineer of the 21st century, "a person who envisions what has never been and does whatever it takes to make it happen" (Buderi, 2014).

Olin College operates with several innovative features. In order to identify future innovators and leaders, it recruits its students not primarily on the basis of their test scores and grades but through face-to-face interviews in multiple settings, including team exercises. Learning is primarily organized around project-based and design-based activities performed by students working in teams. Olin College has no academic departments and does not offer tenure to its faculty members, resulting in an academic culture emphasizing interdisciplinary learning and educational innovation. A typical program will involve several teachers from different disciplines providing integrated courses with interdisciplinary material. The curriculum combines engineering, entrepreneurship and humanities in a unique way. Every Olin student must start and run a business to graduate, and must complete a year-long senior design project sponsored by industry. The students must also acquire leadership and ethical competencies through social sciences and humanities courses. Olin students cross-enroll at Babson College and Wellesley College for entrepreneurships and humanities courses, respectively. To ensure that all Olin graduates are successful at communication in a professional setting, every student is required to present some aspect of their academic work in a public setting at the end of every semester. In the own words of Richard Miller, Olin's founding president:

> Olin had this unique opportunity to rethink education for two years before we taught any classes—this is during the construction of the campus. So one of those years, we dedicated to experimentation with students. We called it the Olin Partner year, because the kids that came that year were not taking courses, but they were actually partners with us in experimentation.
>
> We learned two things from this. The first thing [is] you don't need to have two years of calculus and physics before you can make stuff. Kids are actually capable of learning on their own, particularly when they're motivated. Secondly, and more importantly, the impact of this experience on the students was absolutely transformational. It was now as if they were two feet taller. The kids basically said, "Yes, this is what I want to do for the rest of my life. I know now if I have a few kids around me like this, and a couple of old guys to ask questions of once in a while, I can change the world. I can design anything I can imagine."
>
> Here's basically what happens. If you sat down in the cockpit of a 747 and you don't have a pilot's license, and the challenge is to figure out how to fly this thing and to do it in two days, you probably would get stuck a lot. But what if you had five of you in the room, and what if one of you had had some flight instruction somewhere else, another one had in a played in a flight simulator for a while, some people recognized what a horizon indicator looked like, what the altimeter was. What I'm calling the mean time between failure—the mean time between getting frustrated and stuck, to making progress and then getting frustrated and stuck again—that time distance goes way down if you have a group rather than one person. And kids do this almost intuitively.
>
> And we realized if we could make that happen in everything that happens educationally at this school, these kids will teach themselves and you won't be able to stop them—and when they're finished they'll be ready to take on challenges that change the world.
>
> So, here's one of the realizations: if you look at a catalog of courses and you read the one-paragraph description for what we're going to learn in this class, that is analogous to a recipe for a soufflé in a restaurant. But how the soufflé actually tastes depends on the chef. It depends on how you put those ingredients together and what the interaction is like with the student. So this whole business of separating things into courses and having this one teach the math, and that one teach the physics, and that one teach the engineering, and

assuming that the students are watching how the whole forest is going together just doesn't work.

So now we have courses that have titles that people don't normally see in engineering schools. Principles of Engineering is one. Another is called Design Nature. And what happens is that those subjects are inherently integrated. So the subject itself you can't get through by just learning physics. Physics is embedded in the projects that you do, and every one of those courses is project-oriented. So students actually are formed in teams immediately and the faculty are formed in teams that are teaching them.

One of the [other] things that we discovered, very simple, [is] how do people learn? It turns out people primarily learn from stories—that storytelling is the fundamental skill that all excellent teachers are good at. Furthermore, the stories that work in terms of contributing to education are stories about people. So, Olin is deliberately working to inject people back into the narrative of what engineering is about. Here's an illustration: we have a course called The Stuff of History. It's team taught by a material scientist and a historian of science. They teach the course through the life story of an ancient scientist. The kids actually repeat the discoveries and the experiments that the scientists went through. In this particular course they use Paul Revere. We all learn that Paul Revere rode horses and had something to do with politics. It turns out that the guy was a metallurgist and he invented all kinds of different alloys and metal. So, these kids have a course that's built around the life story of Paul Revere. Rather than having the role of the teacher the omnipotent source of all information—where you're intended to sit there in rows and take notes—they now see essentially a play going on in front of them while these two guys are debating what really happened. And then there's this constant interaction with the students, so it's more like a graduate seminar.

The program continues to evolve—but at this point we have enough data on student outcomes to be convinced that it's working. How do you know if the students in your class are intrinsically motivated? I claim it's very easy. You just have to listen for the questions they ask. If the students ask you, "Will this be on the test?" This is not intrinsic motivation. They're motivated extrinsically by getting a grade. On the other hand, if the students ask you, "I tried over the weekend to make this airplane fly but it failed twice, can you help me figure out how to apply these principles to fix this problem?" That's intrinsically motivated. They will learn that whether they reviewed it or not.

Our approach is essential to deal with our planet's big challenges. At some point the feasibility of having every generation have a better life than the previous one is going to come in to conflict. I have rarely talked to a high school kid who isn't concerned about these issues. Now, those problems are not easily solvable. They're all coupled, they are connected, they are interdisciplinary.

They transcend time zones. They transcend political boundaries. To attack problems like that, it takes a completely different kind of mindset—a different kind of education. Young people are like wet cement. Thinking in a systems way, thinking across disciplines and across political boundaries, is something that will be easier to teach if we start with undergraduates and we do this across the globe. (Buderi, 2014)

Fifteen years after the project was launched, Olin College can boast impressive results. In 2014, Forbes Magazine ranked Olin eight in the United States for highest SAT scores of incoming students. Based on a survey of 130,000 students, Princeton Review placed Olin in the top 20 in 15 categories, including number three for students studying the most, and number 19 for the happiest students in the nation. The testimony of a typical Olin student reflecting on the learning culture of the College would be, "I've never worked this hard in my life and there's nothing else I'd rather be doing" (Buderi, 2014). Olin has been particularly successful in attracting young women into engineering education. While the proportion of women in engineering education is about 20% nationally, it ranges from 40 to 50% at Olin.

*Olin graduates have outstanding career opportunities.* According to a recent survey, 97% of Olin alumni were either employed—in a company or in a business they started themselves—or attending graduate school (22% of those at Harvard, Stanford or MIT). Companies sponsoring senior year projects often recruit the students involved as permanent employees after they graduate.

A few countries have moved to set up a specialized agency dedicated exclusively to the promotion of good teaching and learning practices. Australia's Office for Learning and Teaching, established in 2011 under the authority of the Ministry of Education, is a relevant example in that respect. Operating with an annual budget of about 12 million US$, it main activity consists in offering competitive grants to academics interested in exploring and implementing innovative teaching practices. The Office also contributes to policy and dissemination work on the topic, as well as managing awards to recognize teaching excellence throughout the Australian tertiary education system.

International experience suggests a few lessons regarding the promotion of innovative teaching and learning practices. First, some countries, for example the United Kingdom, have found it convenient to require all PhD candidates to get a teaching certificate before completing their doctorate. This is a first step towards sensitizing future university professors about the importance of good teaching. Along the same lines, a few universities in the United States have begun offering teaching certificates for community college professors.

Second, it is important to offer appropriate incentives that reward teaching excellence on par with outstanding research. Professors must also be allowed the necessary time to work on improving their teaching performance. Finally, early integration of teaching and research is a powerful way of making the educational experience more stimulating and effective. In top US research universities, for instance, "…the co-location of research with education gives rise to large, positive synergies, ensuring that graduates carry with them into industry knowledge of cutting-edge research, techniques, and instrumentation (Executive Office of the President of the USA 2012, p.18).

Developing countries can take advantage of open educational resources to access relevant knowledge and educational material. Box 18 illustrates, through a case study coming from Sierra Leone, how even the poorest universities in the most fragile countries can leverage useful resources to increase educational opportunities and improve the quality of teaching and learning.

---

*Box 18. Leveraging Open Educational Resources*

We hear many stories about the decline of African universities so it was great to hear a story of regeneration and renewal… And it was particularly inspiring that this story came from a county better known in recent years for crisis and tragedy—Sierra Leone.

There's no doubt that the university—and the country's higher education system—faces many challenges. There are crowded classrooms, dilapidated buildings, too few qualified staff, and insufficient IT and library facilities. But there is also a great energy, which has led to the the development of an institutional repository—an online platform to collect and make available research papers and teaching materials within the university and beyond. But at its heart this was a story of ambition and drive to improve the quality of the research and learning environment in the university, and of responding to a grave crisis by pushing even harder to advance the university's mission. As Ebola gripped the country, there were restrictions on movement and of large gatherings of people. University campuses were closed, and education interrupted for thousands of young people.

A few months prior to the Ebola outbreak, INASP had begun a project with the University of Sierra Leone (USL), and with Njala University. The aim was to improve access to essential research and teaching material— online journals and books—coupled with training for librarians and academics, and from this foundation to support academics to publish more of their own work. A team from USL's Institute of Public Administration and Management, led by Miriam Conteh Morgan, had the ambition of transforming the university environment through access to digital information and tools--including an institutional repository. But it was a long-term goal. USL didn't even have an up-to-date website, and certainly no way of hosting a collection of digital materials.

The Ebola shutdown created a new impetus. The university was forced to rethink its teaching model. But how do you 'get to digital with no money?' was

---

the question. The 'worst of times' created 'the best of opportunities'. Faculty members were mobilized, IT staff engaged. Such is the Vice Chancellor's energy for moving things along that he's earnt the nickname 'okada'—after Sierra Leone's motocycle taxis—and his commitment to the project has helped unlock change and engage others.

A university-wide email system was set up so all staff and students had an account. INASP was able to provide an additional small grant, which enabled a server to be purchased, so that materials could be hosted locally. But of course only students with IT access at home would benefit—so the university partnered with NGOs to distribute CDs. With many challenges, and lacking the necessary infrastructure, there was a limit to what the university could do.

But post-Ebola, it was clear that the repository 'had to be done', and it was backed by senior staff. Since then, a team led by USL and Njala colleagues have been working with others to lay the foundations for a Sierra Leone Research and Education Network—a national, broadband network and associated IT services which will underpin academic and research work in the country, and help to connect Sierra Leoneans within and outside of the country.

It's still early days—there's a long way to go before the University of Sierra Leone (and other institutions) will be able to offer the blended approach to teaching that it envisages, combining digital access to study materials with classroom teaching, and assisting faculty to communicate their own work online—and in turn, creating greater impetus for research. But what is notable is that a team of energetic and inspired people not only came together to drive change, but in doing so they have begun to re-imagine how Sierra Leone can offer opportunity to its young people, and strengthen its research base to meet critical local needs.

Fourah Bay College—one of the University's constituent colleges—was once famed as the Athens of Africa. The project supported by INASP is not just about trying to reclaim past glories, but about building for a new present, and imagining a new future. In that way it challenges many of the tales of decline that are commonly heard throughout Sub-Saharan Africa. It is certainly not the only example of that—but it is a particularly striking one.

(Source: http://blog.inasp.info/re-imagining-higher-education-sierra-leone/)

The rapid development of e-learning in general and MOOCs in particular requires targeted policy and technical interventions to help tertiary education institutions in developing countries make the best possible use of these new opportunities for modernizing their curriculum in an accelerated fashion. First, the government agencies responsible for tertiary education development could accompany all interested institutions in the systematic exploration of successful e-learning approaches and the dissemination of lessons learned. Second, these agencies could provide a platform for identifying good practices in the recognition of digital certificates for online courses given by prestigious foreign tertiary education institutions and their integration into the degrees offered by the national universities.

The introduction of innovative teaching and learning practices that promote interactive and collaborative learning also imply remodeling the physical infrastructure and environment of universities. From the flipped classroom, where the professor does not teach but essentially guides and facilitates self-learning and peer learning, to studios and open space classrooms designed to support design-based learning in teams, the new learning facilities represent a flexible learning environment that breaks away from the traditional classroom and lecture hall.

Finally, at a time when many countries put much emphasis on the development of STEM programs, it is important to bear in mind the need for balanced curricula that are not focused exclusively on science and technology disciplines but also include a robust dose of humanities and social sciences. In the words of Steve Jobs, "… technology alone is not enough. It is technology married with liberal arts, married with humanities, that yields the results that make our hearts sing."

*Table 12. Recent Examples of University Closures*

| Countries | Action | Reasons |
| --- | --- | --- |
| Albania | Closure of 18 universities in 2014 | Issuance of fake diplomas |
| Romania | Closure of 6 universities in 2013 and 4 in 2014 | Poor quality |
| Ethiopia | Closure of 5 universities and 11 put on probation in 2011 | Poor quality |
| Kenya | One hundred illegal institutions closed down in 2011. All non-accredited universities to be closed down by 2014 | Lack of authorization to operate and poor quality |
| | Closure of 10 out of 13 campuses of Kisii University in January 2016 | Fraud |
| Nigeria | Closure of 9 institutions | Lack of authorization to operate and poor quality |
| Chile | Closure of a university in 2012 | Poor quality |
| Colombia | Closure of several university programs in 2015 | Poor quality |
| Ecuador | Closure of 12 institutions in 2012 | Poor quality |
| USA | Closure of remaining 28 ground campuses of Corinthian Colleges in 2015 | Fraud and cash shortage |
| Pakistan | Closure of 31 PhD and 26 master's programs at public and private universities | Poor quality |
| Philippines | Closure of an international business school in 2011 | Poor quality |

*Source: Salmi (2015); and various issues of University World News.*

*Reinforced quality assurance.* Considering the large number of poor quality institutions—especially private ones—that operate in the many developing countries that do not have strong quality assurance mechanisms yet, governments should give priority to tightening the licensing system and closing down sub-standard institutions and programs. Table 12 gives a list of countries that have taken action to eliminate poor quality or fraudulent programs.

In parallel, governments should consolidate existing quality assurance mechanisms and align their delivery capacity with the rhythm of creation of new institutions and programs. The larger countries may consider the option of delegating the accreditation responsibility to independent professional associations and organizations, following the model in place in Mexico and the United States. In this new approach, the main role of the national quality assurance agency would be to accredit the professional accreditation bodies.

In addition to strengthening the official quality assurance mechanisms, developing countries governments should also consider offering incentives for the establishment and/or consolidation of internal quality assurance units in all tertiary education institutions, which are essential to the development of a genuine quality assurance culture.

*Strengthened links to the productive sectors and alignment with labor market needs.* Strengthening linkages with industry is an effective way of increasing the relevance of tertiary education programs. Universities can use a large variety of mechanisms, including internships for undergraduate students, in-company placements of research students and academics, practitioners from industry as visiting lecturers. Incorporating training for entrepreneurship into regular university programs can also help bring them closer to the productive sectors. Finally, universities may consider establishing cooperative learning programs that alternate on-campus learning periods and regular in-firm internships (Box 19).

---

### Box 19. Lessons from Co-operative Programs

*Principles and advantages*

Co-operative education is a model that alternates academic studies with relevant work experience in a field directly related to a student's academic or career goals. The advantages of this model are considerable: it allows students to gain relevant work experience, apply theoretical knowledge gained in the classroom and clarify career plans. It also helps students to build contacts with employers and establish networks to facilitate finding employment upon graduation. Working as part of the studies program helps finance education; it is also useful for learning on how to behave on the job and in general to develop the skills which employers want. The advantages for employers are also significant since they have "access to well-prepared short-term workers, flexibility to address human resource needs, cost-effective long-term recruitment and retention, partnerships with Schools, and cost-effective productivity" (The National Commission for Cooperative Education, USA).[3]

*Co-Op at the University of Waterloo in Canada*

Waterloo is home to the world's largest co-op program – 15,800 undergraduate co-op students (more than 56% of the full time undergraduate population at the University and more than twice as many students as the next largest program in the world) and 3,500 partner employers around the world (StudyinCanada. com).[4] A Co-op student at Waterloo graduates with the same number of study/ academic terms as a non-co-op student, plus up to two years of work experience in different professional areas. The student has 4 to 6 work terms (usually four months long each), to try out a variety of careers to find out his/her interests before graduating. On average, by the time the student graduates, he/she has already earned from $25,000 to $74,000, resulting in smaller student loans than other students and a greater capacity at paying them back. Graduates of Waterloo's co-op programs earn about 15% more upon graduation than graduates of non-co-op programs (University of Waterloo).[5] Furthermore, Waterloo University offers the Enterprise Co-Op program where students obtain support (advice of experienced professionals and in some cases economic resources) to develop their own business.

*Experiences at other Tertiary Education Institutions*

Sandwich programs may have existed in the United Kingdom since 1840, and in 1906 the first cooperative education program was launched at the University of Cincinnati in the United States. It was followed by University of Waterloo where a Co-op program was founded in 1957. Other Institutions with co-operative education programs include:

- The Florida Institute of Technology which offers the most condensed cooperative education program ("ProTrack") allowing engineering students to graduate in four years with 3 semester work terms.
- Drexel University in Philadelphia, Pennsylvania and the Northeastern University in Boston, MA, have two of the largest co-operative education programs in the United States. A student graduating from a 5-year degree usually has a total of 18 months of internship with up to three different companies.

- Steinbeis Center of Management and Technology of Steinbeis University, Berlin, offers an international master's program (Master of Business Engineering) that integrates work and academic learning.

(Source: The World Association for Cooperative Education (WACE); The National Commission for Cooperative Education; StudyinCanada.com; University of Waterloo, Canada; and The National Center for Tertiary Teaching Excellence, New Zealand. Singapore: http://www.universityworldnews.com/ article.php?story=20170303182522929)

It is often assumed that efforts to bring universities closer to industry apply only to engineering and applied science programs, not to the social sciences and humanities. But in reality, it is more a matter of mindset than academic discipline. A cooperative program could be set up for a history degree, for instance, whereby students would alternate between formal periods of learning at the university and periods of study/research while attached to a museum or a cultural center, or a company in the creative industries.

Finally, incorporating training for entrepreneurship into regular university programs can also help bring them closer to the productive sectors, thereby boosting their ability to nurture young entrepreneurs. The first ranking looking at what happens to university graduates from the point of view of their success as young entrepreneurs shows that only one developing country, India, appears among the top 50 (Table 13).

*Table 13. Universities with the Highest Proportion of Successful Young Entrepreneurs*

| Country/Region | Number of Universities in Top 50 |
|---|---|
| USA | 41 |
| Canada | 4 |
| Israel | 3 |
| India | 1 |
| United Kingdom | 1 |

*Source: Pitchwork (2014)*

*Increased internationalization.* Internationalization is not a luxury reserved to industrial countries, elite universities or rich students. It is not just one option among many paths open to tertiary education institutions in developing countries. In a world that is becoming every day more interconnected and interdependent,

95

internationalization is one of the key instruments to improve quality and relevance and prepare graduates capable of working as global professionals and living as global citizens.

Internationalization means, among other things, effectively equipping graduates with the wide range of knowledge, skills and competences required in the global economy, conducting internationally competitive research, and attracting international students and professors. Internationalization of tertiary education is more than just signing collaborative agreements with foreign institutions and exchanging students and academics. It involves embedding the international dimension in all aspects of teaching and research, at both the national and institutional levels.

To improve the internationalization dimension, tertiary education institutions need to place more emphasis on preparing globally minded, locally responsible, and internationally competitive students. They need to raise foreign language competencies among their academic staff and graduates. All developing countries would benefit from accelerating the international mobility of students, professors and researchers. Additional resources should be made available to support all these initiatives. Box 20 illustrates what a comprehensive internationalization policy could entail.

---

### Box 20. More Action, Not Just Talk, on Internationalization

For much of tertiary education, internationalization is undergoing a paradigm shift in scale and scope, rather than a fundamental shift in the basic concept. The activity of higher education is increasingly crossing borders with the flow of ideas, students, scholars, and partnerships—both instructional and research. Preparing graduates for a global labor market and economy and helping communities and businesses negotiate a global landscape has increased saliency. Internationalization is not an end, but rather a means to meet these challenges and opportunities.

Comprehensive internationalization is commitment and action to integrate international, global, and comparative content and perspective throughout the teaching, research, and service missions of tertiary education to achieve core learning and discovery outcomes. Although there are regional differences, all appear to share aspects of certain tenets: providing access to international content and perspective to all students, not just a minority; student mobility as a component of internationalization, not a synonym for it; moving internationalization beyond teaching and learning to include research and service missions; expanding the number of faculty and staff members engaged in international efforts.

Treating internationalization as yet another "add on" responsibility can neither be afforded, nor prevent its eventual marginalization in the competition for scarce resources. Sustainability requires its integration into the core missions and involving the campus widely. Lou Anna Simon, president of Michigan State University, champions a reaffirmation of traditional land-grant and public university values of "quality, inclusiveness, and connectivity" for a global environment—or what she refers to as a transition from land-grant to world-grant in orientation and commitment, and integration of the local and the global.

*Institutional Culture.* Comprehensive internationalization needs a culture that defines institutional missions and values in global terms–not just in local or national terms. Needed is a broadly shared culture throughout the institution of a commitment to internationalization and its outcomes.

*Contributors.* While humanities, languages, and social and behavioral sciences remain core elements in international education, professional disciplines take on renewed importance. Problems and opportunities in, for example, public health, environment, food supply, and economies now easily jump boundaries. All disciplines and professions are better informed by global perspective, shaped by it, and capable of contributing globally.

*Leadership for Action.* Clear and frequent messaging from the leaderships is important. The role of academic deans is critical for prompting action in academic programs. Faculty intellectual leadership and commitment is essential for progress. As not everything can be done at once, an important role of leadership is to set priorities for action and hold accountable those who should be contributing?

*Define and Reward What Counts.* What is counted counts. Integration of international dimensions into curricula signals what counts for students. Including international accomplishments into promotion, compensation, and tenure criteria signals what counts for faculty. The allocation of resources to internationalization signals institutional commitment.

*Recruit and Employ for Internationalization.* Institutional capacity is enhanced by recruiting students who have an interest in international learning and by hiring administrators, faculty, and staff members with international backgrounds, experience, or interests.

(Source: Hudzik, 2012)

*Strengthening the Research System*

Universities that do not engage in international collaborations risk disenfranchisement and countries that do not nurture research talent will lose out entirely. (Jonathan Adams)

*Establishment of centers of excellence and/or world-class universities.* As considered in Chapter 2, all developing countries need a minimal research capacity to achieve the SDGs and support their national innovation system. Because of acute resource constraints, few low-income countries may afford a comprehensive research university. They can, however, consider investing in multidisciplinary centers of excellence designed to harness science and technology for the resolution of priority economic and social problems. This is what several African countries are doing with support from the World Bank and other donors (Box 21).

### Box 21. Launch of the African Centers of Excellence

In June 2016, the World Bank approved a US$140 million credit for eight Eastern and Southern African countries to set up 24 centers of excellence in universities to strengthen postgraduate training and research. The Eastern and Southern Africa Higher Education Centers of Excellence Project, or ACE II, follows on ACE I, which was launched in 2014 for Western and Central Africa, with 19 centers of excellence selected across seven countries. The 24 Centers of Excellence (ACEs), which were competitively selected from 108 proposals, will operate in five clusters of regional priorities – industry, agriculture, health, education and applied statistics

The Inter-University Council for East Africa (IUCEA), based in Uganda, is responsible for coordinating and administering the centers. Ethiopia, Rwanda, Tanzania and Uganda will each have four centers; there will be three in Kenya, two each in Malawi and Zambia, and one in Mozambique. Each of the 24 African centers of excellence will be funded by up to US$6 million over the project period of five years. Their mission is to tackle development challenges facing the region through graduate training in masters, PhD and short-term courses, and "applied research in the form of partnerships and collaborations with other institutions and the private sector", said IUCEA.

"Over the project duration of five years, collectively these ACEs are expected to enroll more than 3,500 graduate students in the regional development priority areas, out of which more than 700 will be PhD students and more than 1,000 will be female students, publish almost 1,500 journal articles, launch more than 300 research collaborations with private sector and other institutions, and generate almost US$30 million in external revenue."

The ACEs will help to build the capacity of their host universities to provide quality postgraduate education with relevance to the labor market, and to conduct high quality applied research that seeks innovative solutions to key development priorities. To generate greater impact, they will develop partnerships with other academic institutions, nationally as well as regionally and internationally, and with industry and the private sector. The centers are meant to become role models for other tertiary education institutions by delivering excellent teaching and quality research.

"The Africa Centers of Excellence initiative is creating synergies in higher education across the sub-region by optimizing limited resources and deepening cooperation between countries, while equipping young people with highly relevant skills and knowledge," said Moustapha Ndiaye, World Bank director for regional integration.

(Source: MacGregor, 2016)

The governments of the larger and better-resourced developing countries and emerging economies may consider the desirability and feasibility of establishing one or more world-class university capable of producing leading-edge research and disseminating the results of this research. This could be achieved either by (i) creating a new university from scratch with significant public resources, (ii) selecting among the existing universities those which would be upgraded with additional public funding, and (iii) launching an Excellence Initiative to stimulate the creation or strengthening of centers of excellence within existing universities (Salmi, 2016b). The recent establishment of Nazarbayev University in Kazakhstan is an illustration of the first approach. With respect to the second approach, Thailand is an example of country that selected nine of its public universities as recipients of additional resources to improve their research capacity and output. Similarly the government of Malaysia designed the Science University of Penang as "apex" university and gave it additional funding. Finally Nigeria launched a few years ago an ambitious Excellence Initiative with the goal of having 20 world-class universities by 2020.

These scenarios are not mutually exclusive. It would be possible to combine the first and the second strategies, or the first and the third one, provided the concerned governments are able to mobilize additional resources in a significant way and maintain the higher levels of investment over a long period of time. The results of China's policies in this domain are quite impressive. In the 1990s, the Chinese government launched a series of excellence initiatives—the 211 Program followed by the 985 Program—which have born their fruits. In 2003, when the first edition of the Shanghai ranking was published, only 9 Chinese universities could be counted among the top 500 in the world. The latest ranking, published in September of 2016, includes 54 Chinese universities, including two in the top 100 (Beijing and Tsinghua).

*Training of a critical mass of high-level researchers.* Developing countries cannot live up to their commitment of achieving the SDGs unless they are prepared to accelerate their efforts towards developing a critical mass of high level researchers trained either in the top national universities or overseas. The example of Brazil is very relevant in that respect. In the past three decades, the CAPES Foundation, operating as an arm of the Federal Ministry of Education, has coordinated the country's interventions to improve the quality of Brazil's academic staff through grants and rigorous evaluations programs. More recently, the government stepped up its efforts through the Science without Frontiers initiative, which finances 25,000 annual scholarships for overseas studies at the masters and PhD levels.

To facilitate the insertion of young doctoral graduates into dynamic research teams, developing countries could also fund postdoc schemes. In doing this, they would be emulating government programs operating in other parts of the world, which give the opportunity to accredited universities of hiring promising young researchers for up to two years, at no cost or little cost, as happened for instance in Pakistan in the first decade of the new century.

Finally, it is important to underline that these capacity building efforts will remain fruitless unless developing countries governments are able to significantly increase research budgets, protect the funding allocation process from political considerations and interferences, and maintain stable funding levels over the years.

*Reducing in-breeding.* In many developing and emerging countries, the lack of academic mobility across universities and low degree of internationalization result in excessive academic inbreeding. This is even more visible in those with a relatively small population size and a limited number of universities and their. In Slovenia, for instance, a 2013 survey found that 51% of academics work in the university where they obtained their Ph.D., with a higher share (68%) at the country's flagship institution, the University of Ljubljana (Klemencic and Zgaga, 2015). The situation is even more acute in Macedonia, where 77% of academics are full-time employees of the same university where they obtained their highest degree (Galevski, 2014). The data on Macedonian academics also revealed a high degree of inbreeding at the level of junior researchers, which indicates that the more recently established universities have not managed to diminish this practice engrained in the academic culture of the former Yugoslav republics.

Studies of academic inbreeding have demonstrated that this practice is not conducive to innovation and high performance. In the words of one of the leading researchers on this topic, academic inbreeding promotes "institutional parochialism and intellectual isolation" (Horta et al., 2011, p. 37). Universities that have lower levels of inbreeding tend to have a higher scientific production.

Several measures can be envisaged to reduce academic inbreeding. At the national level, the State can strengthen the quality assurance system by incorporating, among the accreditation criteria, guidelines about the maximum proportion of "inbred academics" in each university, faculty and even academic department, a desirable minimal proportion of foreign academics or foreign-trained academics, and academic mobility more generally. In addition, the State can offer a range of financial incentives to support employment opportunities in other universities for recent PhD graduates and young researchers, promote short term outbound academic mobility for academics without international academic experience, subsidize the recruitment of foreign academics and/or national scholars employed in foreign universities, fund research projects that involve international collaborations, and encourage non-academic institutions (research institutes, state agencies, companies) to hire scientists.

At the institutional level, universities can define rules to limit the number of PhD graduates recruited directly after they finish their research degree, establish promotion criteria that take into consideration the experience in foreign academic settings—including at least a short stay at a good quality foreign

*Table 14. Policy Measures and Good Practices to Reduce Inbreeding*

| Policy Measures | Instruments Policya | Financial Incentive |
|---|:---:|:---:|
| *National Level* | | |
| Accreditation criteria | X | |
| Recruitment of foreign academics/ Macedonian scholars from the Diaspora | X | X |
| Short term outbound academic mobility | X | X |
| Grants for postdoc and young researchers | | X |
| Grants for collaborative research projects | | X |
| Subsidies to encourage non-academic institutions to hire scientists | | X |
| **Institutional Level** | | |
| Transparent, meritocratic recruitment procedures | X | |
| Limits on the recruitment of own PhDs | X | |
| Minimum % of outside academics in each department | X | |
| Promotion criteria | X | |
| Compulsory mobility for PhDs and postdocs | X | X |
| Short term outbound academic mobility | | X |
| Joint doctoral programs among several universities | X | |
| Participation in collaborative research projects | | X |

university—provide guidelines on the maximum proportion of "inbred academics" in each department, set up joint doctoral programs with partner universities. To accompany these policies, universities can set aside funding for academic mobility and collaborative research projects. At the end of the day, the best mechanism to prevent inbreeding is a fully transparent and meritocratic recruitment and promotion process that allows for open competition on the basis of objective measures of academic achievement.

Table 14 shows the full range of possible measures at the national and institutional levels.

*Engagement with clusters and economic sectors.* In the technology underdeveloped economies characterizing many developing countries, the leading universities and other tertiary education institutions can play a critical role as pillars of innovation. Indeed, the presence of universities is important to regional development, through both direct linkages and spillover effects. The successful experiences of technology-intensive poles such as Silicon Valley in California, Bangalore in India's Karnataka State, Shanghai in China, and Campinas in São Paulo State, Brazil, attest to the strongly positive effects that the clustering of advanced human capital alongside leading technology firms can have. In Singapore, the recent establishment by the National University of dedicated research centers on solar energy and logistics—the Solar Energy Research Institute and the Asian Logistics Institute—was instrumental in facilitating the development of a strong economic sector in these two areas. The annual turnover of solar energy companies is close to 3.5 billion dollars, whereas the logistics sector represents 166 billion dollars. The United Kingdom experience is also relevant in this context. Box 22 contrasts the experience of Oxford and Cambridge in the development of linkages between the University and the local economy.

---

### Box 22. Creating Dynamic Clusters: The Cambridge Model

The top two British universities, Oxford and Cambridge, are more than 800 years old. They share a similar history and stem from the same academic culture. They are both considered among the best universities in the world. And yet, when it comes to the impact on their respective city, Oxford and Cambridge have followed divergent paths and achieved strikingly distinct results. Oxford remains an old-fashioned university city, whereas Cambridge has become the "most exciting technology cluster in Europe." What begun in the 1970s with the creation of business parks to welcome entrepreneurial academics and their doctoral students has evolved into a hub of 4,000 knowledge-intensive firms in electronics, pharmaceutics, biotechnology and other frontier domains. It is today the most dynamic place in Europe where professors, Nobel Prize scientists and angel investors plot their next startup.

With a productivity level 30% higher than London's, Cambridge generates more patents that its next six British rivals taken together, it hosts more billion-dollar firms than cities ten times bigger, and it boasts near full employment.

The secret to Cambridge's success seems to lie in a balanced approach combining enlightened policies to provide the right infrastructure and economic environment and a laissez-faire attitude that trusts human ingenuity and serendipity. On the one hand, the university, the city council and the neighboring authorities have worked in a coordinated way to create a favorable ecosystem by setting up science parks and incubators, encouraging the development of business and housing estates, attracting investors and lobbying the government for more open immigration policies. On the other hand, they have kept away from imposing strategic priorities and micromanaging the city's economic development. The city does not decide what type of high-tech industry is more likely to become tomorrow's industry, and the university gives incentives to academics interested in setting up companies, making the membrane between its laboratories and private firms as porous as possible. This has resulted in dynamic partnerships where firms provide advice free of charge and invite students to help them, while academics and angel investors work together to chaperon new companies.

Unlike many universities in the United Kingdom that still work in silos, Cambridge University has been particularly good at stimulating collaboration across academic disciplines. As explained by Jeremy Sanders, one of Cambridge University's pro vice-chancellor, the university's philosophy is to "hire people smarter than you, give them as much freedom and research funding as possible, stand back, and reap the harvest ten years later."

(Source: The Economist, 2015)

In addition to contributing to the local economy through salaries and the purchase of goods and services, the universities can be important economic agents through relevant applied research and the training of highly qualified professionals who can help make the local firms more innovative and productive. Tertiary education institutions can fulfill this role in several ways, not only by participating in new innovations, but perhaps even more importantly by facilitating technology upgrade and absorption.

In supporting the transformation of the existing economic sectors and the creation of new ones, the contribution of universities can take several forms. Table 15 provides a detailed list of the various modalities of collaboration on knowledge transfer and technology commercialization that universities in developing countries could consider. It also indicates what role the national and local authorities could play to facilitate these collaborations.

To strengthen the technology transfer capacity of local universities, which has traditionally been weak in most developing countries, governments should consider establishing support mechanisms to scale up the commercialization of new technologies invented or developed by local universities on a matching grant basis. One of the most successful examples in that respect comes from Germany, where the Fraunhofer Institute operates as a public agency dedicated to financing research projects implemented by universities with a specific industrial application in mind.

Finally, it is important to underline that the contribution of universities to the growth of dynamic local innovation systems does not come only from patents development and startups. The role of graduates with advanced training in catalyzing innovations within firms is equally critical. It is therefore essential to put in place mechanisms and incentives to convince a larger proportion of developing countries scientists to move to the productive sectors rather than staying in universities. In OECD countries, about 70 percent of available researchers are active in firms, and

Table 15. Matrix of Knowledge- and Technology-Transfer Mechanisms

| University-Industry Linkages | Role of National Government | Role of Local Authorities | Comments |
|---|---|---|---|
| **Public space function**<br>Contacts and networking<br>Conferences, fairs and forums<br>Publications and dissemination of findings<br>Alumni associations | | Develop and fund programs to create and support sectoral clusters and networks | With education and training, this function is seen by firms as the most important contribution of universities |
| **Human capital formation**<br>Student participation in firm R&D (internships and co-op programs)<br>Employment of first-level and master graduates<br>Employment of postdoctoral graduates in R&D<br>Participation of industry practitioners in teaching and curriculum development<br>Joint diploma thesis or PhDs<br>University researcher participation in firm<br>Participation of firm employees in university training course (on-campus or on-site) | Priority setting and incentives for establishment of new programs (emerging & inter-disciplinary fields)<br>Targeted scholarships<br>Mobility scholarships<br>Employment flexibility (sabbaticals, leave without pay) | Funding and tax incentives to facilitate insertion of Ph.D. graduates | Primary role of universities in support of innovation |
| **Research**<br>Research contracts<br>Joint R&D projects<br>Research consortia<br>Industry researchers seconded to university labs | Funding (direct/matching)<br>Tax incentives<br>Assessment of research capacity of universities<br>Criteria for evaluating the performance of researchers | Funding<br>Attracting "anchor tenants"<br>Helping cluster formation<br>Targeted support for SMEs<br>Intermediary agencies | Increased returns at the intersection of traditional disciplines |

| | | | |
|---|---|---|---|
| ***Problem-solving and consulting***<br>Consulting contracts<br>Testing, standards, prototypes, and proof of concept designs | Funding | | |
| ***Technical infrastructure***<br>Use of university labs<br>Common lab<br>Common use of machines (on campus or in firm)<br>Science parks | | Funding<br>Serviced land and infrastructure | Need for clear revenue sharing arrangements within universities |
| ***Knowledge commercialization***<br>Licensing of university-held patents<br>Incubators<br>Start-ups<br>Spinoffs | IPR legal framework<br>Financial autonomy of public universities | Funding<br>Technical assistance | More likely to happen in biotechnology and biomedical sciences, also nanotechnology, new materials and IT |

*Source: Based on Yusuf and Nabeshima (2007), and Agrawal and Cockburn (2002)*

less than 25 percent in the university sector. In many developing countries, the opposite situation is usually the norm. To illustrate this contrast, Figure 17 shows the fundamental difference between Brazil and South Korea in the labor market distribution of researchers, thereby revealing the importance of putting in place incentives to encourage scientists to work outside universities.

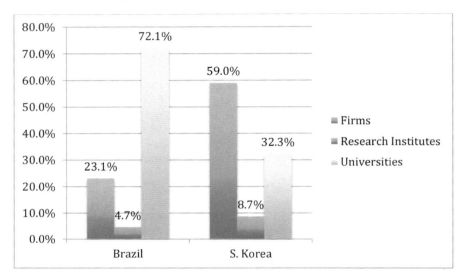

*Figure 17. Distribution of Scientists Active in R& D Activities in Brazil and Korea. Source: Campos (2008)*

## LAUNCH OF THE REFORM

Institutional change always implies conflict, and for it to be positive, it always requires consensus as well. No society can exist without conflict, or mechanisms for producing or resolving conflict through consensus. (Joan Prats, International Institute for Governance, Barcelona)

As Machiavelli wrote in his famous political manifesto, the Prince, "there is nothing more difficult to take in hand, more perilous to conduct, or more uncertain in its success than to take the lead in introducing a new order of things". While this observation is true of any political reform, it is particularly resonant in the case of tertiary education reforms. While primary school children are not known for demonstrating in the streets, university students and professors can often be virulently active in the defense of their interests. In most countries, universities are among the most conservative cultural and organizational institutions, with extremely vocal constituencies, including faculty and the students. These groups can effectively mobilize themselves against policy changes that challenge established practices.

Therefore, one of the most difficult tasks faced by leaders intent on launching a tertiary education reform is to generate sufficient support in favor of the proposed changes. Mark Moore, a political scientist affiliated with Harvard University's Kennedy School of Government, formulated a political management theory that identifies three main conditions for effective implementation of reforms (Moore, 1995). As illustrated in Figure 18, the first dimension is the purpose of the reform. The second one is the operational capacity of the institutions responsible for carrying out the reform. The last one is the degree of political support enjoyed by the leaders and institutions involved in implementing the reform.

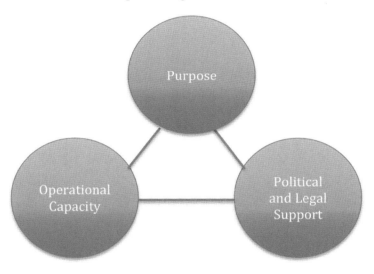

*Figure 18. Political Management Framework.*
*Source: Moore (1995)*

According to Moore, the measure of potential success is the extent to which the promoters of a reform are able to align their goals, the operational capacity and the authorizing environment. This can be achieved by consensus, by building alliances, by forceful imposition, or through a combination of these strategies. Applied to tertiary education reforms, "purpose" would correspond to the vision for the future of tertiary education. "Operational capacity" would represent the technical expertise and institutional capability of the government agencies leading the reform. And "political and legal support" would epitomize the need for ownership by all interested stakeholders in the tertiary education community.

Generating this political and legal support involves three important phases: (i) social assessment, (ii) consensus building, and (iii) appropriate incentives.

Table 16. *Areas of Reform and Likely Opponents*

| Areas of Reform | Stakeholders Likely to Resist |
|---|---|
| Cost Sharing<br>Tuition fees (introduction or substantial increase)<br>Scholarships (stricter targeting)<br>Student loans (increase in interest rate, rising level of indebtedness) | Students |
| Performance-Based Budget Allocation<br>Funding formula<br>Competitive fund<br>Performance contract<br>Vouchers | University leaders |
| Admission Procedures and Criteria (increased selectivity) | Students |
| Structure of Academic Degrees | Academics |
| Institutional Mergers | Academics<br>Students<br>University leaders |
| Increased Accountability<br>Boards with increased responsibilities, Selection of leaders<br>Quality assurance<br>Rankings | University leaders<br>Academics<br>Students |
| Role of Private Sector<br>Expansion of private institutions<br>Existence of for-profit institutions | Leaders of public universities<br>Students |
| Status and Work Conditions of Academics<br>Salaries<br>Elimination of civil servant status of academics<br>Evaluation of performance | Academics |

The first step involves a careful social assessment of the proposed reform in order to review the needs and preoccupations of all major stakeholders. This starts with a scan of the tertiary education landscape with the purpose of identifying who, among the key stakeholders, stands to gain or lose from the proposed reform, and mapping out on that basis who is likely to be indifferent, supportive, or dissenting. This type of political analysis allows for making distinctions between those groups who may be positively impacted by the proposed reforms and those who are likely to lose privileges or be negatively affected. Table 16 seeks to identify the main areas of reform likely to generate resistance or opposition and the stakeholders potentially concerned by these reforms.

Additionally, it is worth distinguishing between two types of reforms: "construction reforms" and "undoing reforms". In the first case, government usually seeks to introduce a new dimension in the tertiary education system, for example an accreditation system in a country without a formal quality assurance system or a student loan scheme to fund low-income students. In the second instance, government is trying to take away acquired privileges that some groups may consider as fundamental rights. For instance, the decision to start charging tuition fees is inevitably seen by students as an attack on their "right to free education". The latter type of reform is obviously more likely to generate opposition than the former.

The second and perhaps more crucial step is the consensus-building phase. Translating a reform program into reality depends, to a large extent, on the ability of decision-makers to utilize the social assessment tool to build consensus among the diverse constituents of the tertiary education community, allowing for a high degree of tolerance for controversies and disagreements. A potentially effective approach for dealing with the political sensitivity of the proposed reforms is to initiate a wide consultation process concerning the need for and content of the envisaged changes, with the purpose of making all stakeholders aware of the linkage between the proposed reforms and the likely improvements in the performance of tertiary education institutions. This effort involves a blend of rational analysis, political maneuvering, and psychological interplay to bring all the concerned stakeholders on board. Achieving consensus on difficult sector policies requires full transparency in discussing the proposed policy measures, as a way of building confidence among all stakeholders. The set of reforms introduced in Mozambique after the end of the civil war, which was mentioned earlier, was successfully implemented because it had been endorsed through effective consensus building under the leadership of the new Minister (Box 23). By contrast, in 2011, the government of Colombia failed to build sufficient consensus around a law proposing measures for the modernization of tertiary education. After street demonstrations by university presidents, academics and students united against the proposed changes, the government had no choice but withdrawing the draft law from Parliament.

*Box 23. Importance of Consensus-Building for Launching Successful Tertiary Education Reforms*

In 2000, Lídia Brito, the Minister in charge of the newly established Ministry of Higher Education, Science, and Technology, initiated a comprehensive tertiary education reform effort. She proceeded to organize countrywide consultations to seek inputs from academics, students, business people, and NGOs. In May and June of that year, the Minister and her colleagues held separate sessions with people from each of Mozambique's ten provinces. About ten persons came from each province, representing existing tertiary education institutions, students, businesses, regional government, and civic associations. Each province was asked to prepare its own development plan, including its training needs. Even though the provinces asked for much more than the country's resources would allow for, the consultations helped the Ministry attain its goal of planning a rational—and equitable—use of available resources.

The consultations built a broad base of support for the reforms and helped the Minister identify "champions" for change. "Champions need to be identified and encouraged at all levels," she says. "Champions are people who are interested in the process, who can bring knowledge to it, and who are able to mobilize others around the vision." The results of the regional consultations were presented in July 2000 to a national seminar with 300 participants from all the provinces, tertiary education institutions, government ministries, and parliament. Out of this gathering came the Strategic Plan for Higher Education in Mozambique 2000-2010, which was approved by the government's Council of Ministers the following month. Several bilateral and multilateral donor agencies offered significant financial and technical assistance in support of the national plan.

(Source: Bollag, 2003)

A third, key ingredient for facilitating acceptance of reforms that challenge the status quo is the availability of additional resources that can be channeled towards tertiary education institutions and other concerned groups such as the students. The extent to which governments rely on positive incentives to encourage change rather than mandatory edicts to impose reforms has a positive influence on outcomes, as tertiary education institutions and actors tend to respond more readily to constructive stimuli. The impressive reforms introduced in Pakistan between 2002 and 2010—notably the new tenure track scheme linking academic performance and salaries, the new quality assurance system and the scholarship program for overseas PhDs—are due, to a large extent, to the fact that the Higher Education Commission, the public authority in charge of tertiary education development, convinced the government to triple the budget distributed to the university sector. Another, related way of increasing political acceptability and avoiding disruptions is to introduce 'grandfathering' provisions and transitory funding arrangements that guarantee, for all institutions and beneficiary groups, amounts of resources equal to those they would have received under the previous system, at least for some period of time.

The voluntary nature of the competitive funds that some countries use (see Chapter 4) is an important factor to accompany reforms. The availability of additional resources can encourage tertiary education institutions to embrace proposed changes and be innovative, while leaving out those not willing or ready to transform themselves.

In addition, it is important to think carefully about the timing and proper sequencing of reforms. When the Ghanaian vice-chancellors agreed on a plan for raising tuition fees in public universities in January 2005, they presented it in the form of a ten-year graduated increase program, which facilitated acceptance from the students. Oftentimes, it is more effective to delay a key decision by a few weeks or even months to allow sufficient time to build a consensus (Salmi, 2010).

Ultimately, tertiary education reform is most feasible within a supportive policy environment in which all participants are in fundamental agreement on the scope, pace, and direction of reform. While having a political road map to guide the reform efforts is neither a magic formula nor a guarantee of success, ignoring potential opponents and failing to engage them in a dialogue about the proposed reforms is a recipe for failure.

## ENSURING THE SUSTAINABILITY OF THE REFORM

The successful launch of a tertiary education reform is not sufficient in itself. It is equally important to put in place the conditions that can guarantee a sustained positive impact in the long run. This involves two dimensions, one linked to the reform process itself, and one related to the content of the reforms.

In the first instance, the reform packages should be presented and adopted as national programs, not as partisan initiatives of a single political party or of the governing majority. This is the only way of ensuring that the consensus achieved when launching a reform has a durable effect. In Denmark, for example, when the 2002-2003 governance and financing reforms were passed by the Parliament, they were clearly endorsed by all political parties, who unanimously recognized the need for substantial transformation of the tertiary education system as an integral part of the country's knowledge economy strategy. In a February 2013 article ("*let's go Denmark*"), *The Economist* analyzed the strength of the political culture in the Nordic countries involving a tradition of negotiated compromises and the ability to undertake audacious change at the same time, which has allowed these nations to evolve smoothly into dynamic knowledge-based economies without eroding their social fabric characterized by a high degree of cohesion and inclusion (The Economist, 2013). Being able to undertake reforms consensually designed and accepted as long-term State policies, rather than as the program of a given government driven by short-term electoral considerations, may be the biggest challenge in countries with little tradition of bi-partisan politics.

In the second instance, the set of reforms must include "enabling" measures that can facilitate the long-term durability of the proposed changes. Appropriate governance and sustainable financing are the most important enabling conditions. While the rest of this section explores what favorable governance arrangements entail, the next chapter will be entirely devoted to a detailed analysis of the main dimensions of a sustainable funding strategy.

*Principles of Good Governance*

Efforts to improve the quality of teaching and learning and raise the research output in public universities in developing countries cannot succeed without the modernization of governance structures and processes. This modernization is needed to give them more flexibility and help develop a forward-looking thinking approach that could translate into a transformational vision and a solid strategic plan to implement the vision.

Worldwide, the governance of universities ranges from strong state regulation to academic or managerial self-governance, with various degrees of stakeholder guidance. Despite these differences, universities in many countries have been converging in their structure and practice toward a stronger role for the president/ vice-chancellor/rector and the leadership team, while becoming more autonomous and accountable (Fielden, 2008; Salmi, 2013c). In that perspective, developing countries should consider moving towards (i) more empowered university boards, (ii) the appointment of university leaders through a managed process based on professional criteria, and (iii) clear rules of engagement for increased autonomy and accountability.

*Role of university boards.* Clear decision-making responsibilities and accountabilities should be granted to strengthened boards, which would be responsible for appointing the university leader, endorsing the strategic plan, and approving the budget. International experience shows that, to function effectively, boards should have no more than 20 members, including a significant number of independent external members (Salmi, 2013c). Box 24 describes good practices for monitoring the effectiveness of Boards.

---

*Box 24. Effectiveness and Performance Review of University Boards*

Governing bodies should regularly monitor their own effectiveness and the performance of their institution against its planned strategies and operational targets and their primary accountabilities. Governing bodies should further review their effectiveness regularly. Not less than every five years they should undertake a formal and rigorous evaluation of their own effectiveness, and that of the committees, and ensure that a parallel review is undertaken of other internal boards and committees. The governing body shall revise its structure or processes accordingly.

In reviewing its performance, the governing body shall reflect on the performance of the institution as a whole in meeting long-term strategic objectives and short-term key performance indicators. Any such review of performance should take into account the views of the academic board, and should be reported upon appropriately within the institution and outside. Where

---

possible, the governing body should benchmark institutional performance against the performance of other institutions (at home and abroad). In considering their own effectiveness, governing bodies may wish to engage persons independent to the institution to assist in the process.

The results of effectiveness reviews, as well as of the institution's annual performance against appropriate indicators of performance, should be published widely, including on the Internet and in its annual report.

(Source: Good Practice Guide for Governing Bodies of Indian Technical Institutions, World Bank-NPYU/Ministry of HR Development and States Governments of India, 2011)

*Selection of university leaders.* In quite a few countries countries, notably Asian and African, governments appoint university leaders. Political considerations often come into play, as illustrated by the recent mass firing of university vice-chancellors in Nigeria (Fatunde, 2016). At the other end of the spectrum, for example in many Eastern European and Latin American countries, the academic community elects the university leader through a popular vote.

In recent years, however, a growing number of countries have transferred this responsibility to the university board. In this new approach, the Board conducts a competitive search to appoint, on purely professional considerations, the most suitable candidate from a pool of candidates from within and outside the institution. Denmark is one example of a thorough governance reform, which has helped propel its universities onto the global scene (Box 25). Finland moved in a similar direction a few years ago.

*Box 25. Tertiary Education Reform in Denmark: The University Act of 2003*

Through reforms in key areas—management autonomy, funding and institutional leadership—Denmark transformed its university system into a dynamic independent sector contributing to broad national and global success.

It all started with the establishment by the Ministry of Higher Education and Research of an independent Commission in 2000, the *Forskningskommissionen*, consisting of 12 individuals from academia, business associations, industry, unions, funding organizations and civil society. It was widely recognized among politicians, university leaders, employers and in society at large that Denmark's position as a leading welfare state could be challenged when moving from the industrial society towards a knowledge society.

The Commission recommended to improve and strengthen the tertiary education system and provided guidelines for a national reform strategy based on the following principles: institutional capacity for change within a framework of autonomy and accountability, search for academic talent through an open labor market, introduction of quality assurance at all levels, independence of the research advisory and financing system, and increase in research funding. The Commission's recommendations became to a very large extent the blue print for the Government's and the Parliament's subsequent reform agenda for the sector.

The 2003 University Act changed university leadership from collegiate structures into a system of empowered line management, introduced new programs to stimulate public-private research partnerships, modernized the research council structure to include strategic funding channels in addition to traditional discipline based research councils, consolidated the tertiary education and research system through mergers in order to create internationally competitive institutions, developed a new performance-based core funding system, doubled research training programs and, finally, to called for the intensification of international engagement.

*Institutional Autonomy.* As of 2003, all universities in Denmark were considered as independent subsidiaries of the Ministry of Science, Technology, and Innovation. Funds are distributed based on established rates for research and on per student enrollments and completion, to establish more objective criteria for funding. Institutions are allowed to use their budget as they deem necessary, may also seek outside sources of funding to complement the state contributions, and may establish profit-making activities. Performance contracts serve as an agreement between the government and individual institutions regarding how each institution seeks to maximize its knowledge assets. Institutions work to their strengths, as defined by themselves, and seek successes at points where they are most competitive. They are free to define their internal organization.

*Institutional Leadership.* Governance of the institution is primarily in the purview of an independent university board with a majority of external members. The board itself selects its ten external members, who are outstanding individuals knowledgeable about the role of universities. The five internal members (two academics, one representative of the administrative staff, two students) are elected by faculty, staff and students, respectively. The board selects and appoints the rector, based on the recommendations of a search committee made of members of the board, the academic councils and the university management team. Each university's rector serves at the will of the board.

The rector is the university's external face and the top line manager, responsible for the leadership of the university and for day-to-day management, as well as for the appointment of academic leaders and managers. Deans are hired and supervised by the rector and in turn hire and supervise department heads. The principle is that the first in line manager selects the candidate for a position and the second in line manager oversees the process. For example the dean selects the heads of departments and the rector appoints them. Academic councils have no formal role in this process. Open academic and managerial leadership positions are always advertised widely in the national and sometimes international media. In summary, the reform resulted in additional degrees of autonomy and the adoption of a professional governance model intended to enhance the capacity for decision-making, and for the development of distinct institutional profiles. (Source: Aagaard and Mejlgaard, 2012; Holm-Nielsen, 2016; Salmi, 2009a)

Some countries have even moved to opening the position of university leaders to distinguished academics from other countries, instead of limiting the eligibility of candidates to academics of the recruiting university, as still happens in many if not most developing countries.[6] In Portugal, for instance, the universities that have volunteered for a special autonomous status in 2007 conduct an international search to recruit their rector, as illustrated by Box 26.

*Box 26. Advertisement in the Economist for the International Recruitment of the Rector of a Public University in Portugal*

· U ︎ C ·

UNIVERSITY OF COIMBRA

**PUBLIC NOTICE**

FOR THE POST OF RECTOR OF THE UNIVERSITY OF COIMBRA

In accordance with article 86 of Law n.° 62/2007 of the 10th September, article 45 of the University of Coimbra Statutes, and the Regulations approved by the General Council of the University, public notice is hereby given to start the process of application for the post of Rector.

**1.** The Rector is the highest body of University governance and external representation. H/she has a four year mandate that must be served on a full time basis.
**2.** The application process for the post of Rector of the University of Coimbra is open to professors and researchers of the University of Coimbra and of other national and foreign universities or research institutions, provided that they hold a doctorate and are not yet retired or otherwise made ineligible by the provisions of the law.
**3.** Applications, in print and digital form, should be submitted by the applicants themselves and addressed to the President of the General Council along with the following documents:
a) a cover letter giving the applicant's personal data and contact information, including an email address or fax number for the sole purpose of being notified on matters pertaining to the electoral process;
b) a detailed, signed and dated curriculum vitae and any other documents deemed relevant to the application;
c) a declaration by the applicant stating, on his/her honour, that s/he is not ineligible under the provisions of the law;
d) an action programme, written in Portuguese, for the four year mandate.
**4.** Applications may be submitted by email to conselhogeral@uc.pt. Only complete applications actually received before 5:30 PM on 10th January 2011 will be considered.
**5.** Further information pertaining to the electoral process – specifically the date, time and place of the public hearing for presenting and discussing the action programmes before the General Council and the election date – can be obtained by following the link below: http://www.uc.pt/reitoria/governo/cons_geral/eleicaoreitor

Coimbra, 26th November 2010
The President of the University of Coimbra's General Council
(Artur Santos Silva)

The philosophy behind the appointment of university leaders is that this approach can be more effective for universities interested in bringing on board change-oriented mindsets rather than academics or administrators with conservative outlooks, essentially interested in maintaining the status quo. The following recent announcements for the recruitment of a new dean at King's College, London and a new director at the London School of Economics illustrate how the search for exceptional talent is now taking place beyond national boundaries.

*Increased autonomy and accountability.* International trends in governance patterns in OECD countries reveal that, in order to improve their performance and become more innovative, tertiary education must enjoy the ability to make decisions in an autonomous manner and manage their academic and financial resources with flexibility. Institutional autonomy is a key element in the successful transformation of public tertiary education institutions (OECD, 2007). Autonomous institutions are more responsive to incentives for quality improvement, resource diversification, and efficient use of available resources (Salmi, 2013c).

Tertiary education institutions must therefore be in a position to exercise meaningful control over the principal factors affecting the quality and costs of their programs. Autonomy includes, among its many dimensions, the ability of each institution to set its own admission requirements, determine the size of its student body, and establish new programs and courses (academic autonomy). Staffing autonomy means that tertiary education institutions are free to determine their employment conditions, such as hiring and staff remuneration, without which it is difficult to be responsive to new and rapidly changing labor market demands. Finally, institutions must have financial autonomy, including the ability to assess tuition fees, establish eligibility criteria for financial assistance to needy students, and reallocate resources internally according to self-determined criteria. Independent fiscal control is necessary so that institutions can strengthen weak academic units, cross-subsidize programs, and fund new initiatives quickly and flexibly in response to evolving needs.

Increased institutional autonomy would need to be accompanied by a well-defined accountability framework for public universities. International experience indicates that good accountability practices involve at least two types of yearly reports at the very minimum: (i) a financial audit report according to private practice law and international accounting standards; and (ii) an annual performance report showing progress against each university's own strategic objectives and yearly plan. Table 17 presents the range of accountability instruments that developing countries governments could consider in relation to desirable policy objectives.

*Table 17. Principal Instruments of Accountability*[7]

| Instruments \ Dimensions | Academic integrity | Fiscal integrity | Effective use of resources | Quality and relevance | Equity |
|---|---|---|---|---|---|
| Strategic plan | | | | X | X |
| Key performance indicators | | | X | X | X |
| Budget | | | X | | |
| Financial audit | | X | X | | |
| Public reporting | | | X | X | X |
| Licensing | X | | | | |
| Accreditation/ academic audit/ evaluation | X | | | X | |
| Performance contracts | | | X | X | X |
| Scholarships/ student loans/ vouchers | | | X | X | |
| Rankings/ benchmarking | | | | X | |

## NOTES

[1] An earlier version of this framework was developed in a policy note prepared for the former Australian Aid Agency, AusAID (Salmi, 2013b).

[2] http://www.instituteofplay.org/about/

[3] The National Commission for Cooperative Education (NCCE) is dedicated to advancing cooperative education throughout the United States. At: http://www.co-op.edu/aboutcoop2.html

[4] StudyinCanada.com. "University of Waterloo". At: http://www.studyincanada.com/english/schools/profile.asp?SchoolCode=uwatl08&ProfileType=University&URL=index

[5] University of Waterloo, Canada. "Co-op at Waterloo". At: http://findoutmore.uwaterloo.ca/coop/

[6] It is ironic to observe that, while half of the national football teams that competed in the last World Cup in Rio de Janeiro in 2014 had recruited a foreign trainer to increase their winning prospects, the notion of selecting a foreign academic to lead a university is hardly acceptable to the large majority of academics in developing countries.

[7] This table draws on the recommendations made by the author in the context of the joint OECD/World Bank reviews of tertiary education in Chile (2009) and Colombia (2011) as principal writer of the financing chapters.

# ENSURING FINANCIAL SUSTAINABILITY

## *What is at Stake?*

Nothing will matter more to Europe's future than the ability of countries, governments, workers and companies to innovate – a process which will depend in no small degree on the efficiency of our decision-making and the quality of our human capital.

(Ederer, 2006)

Even though most countries recognize that their long term prosperity is dependent on their ability to train the qualified professionals, scientists and technicians needed to run the economy and conduct relevant research to spearhead innovations—making the development of a solid tertiary education system a high order priority—, very few countries, rich or poor, have managed to define and implement a sustainable financing strategy. Therefore, the success of any country's vision and plans for developing its tertiary education system will hinge, to a large extent, on the availability of sufficient financial resources and the ability to rely on allocation methods that encourage innovation and effective use of resources among tertiary education institutions.

The urgency of designing and implementing a sustainable financing strategy for the development of tertiary education is strongly felt in all the countries affected by the demographic bulge resulting from rapid population growth and steady progress in reaching the Education for All goals, especially since the launch of the Fast-Track Initiative in 2004. The potential for further expansion is therefore enormous, particularly in Sub-Saharan Africa and South Asia. For instance, between 1999 and 2008, secondary education enrollment grew by 66% in Southeast and East Asia and by 51% in South Asia. The Asian Development Bank projects that the 17-25 year-old age cohort will grow in the lower double digits over the next 20 years (ADB, 2012). Data from Pakistan, for example, illustrate the immense challenge faced by countries confronted with the rising demand for tertiary education. Table 18 projects the number of students under two scenarios. In the first case, even if the enrollment rate stays stable at 2.9%, the number of students would almost double by 2018. In the second case, if Pakistan succeeds in reaching an enrollment rate of 8% by 2018, it would mean tripling the number of students.

*Table 18. The Demographic Challenge in Pakistan*

| Year | 17-23 years age-group | Number of students with fixed enrollment rate at 2.9% | Number of students if enrollment rate increases to 8% |
|------|----------------------|------------------------------------------------------|-------------------------------------------------------|
| 2002 | 19.3 million | 560,000 | 560,000 |
| 2006 | 22.1 million | 640,000 | 880,000 |
| 2010 | 25.4 million | 740,000 | 1,270,000 |
| 2014 | 29.1 million | 840,000 | 1,750,000 |
| 2018 | 33.4 million | 970,000 | 2,340,000 |

*Source: Higher Education Commission, Islamabad*

## ELEMENTS OF A SUSTAINABLE FINANCING STRATEGY

When it comes to the main characteristics of their resource mobilization strategies, tertiary education systems all over the world can be divided roughly into four main groups:

1. A small number (about 10 countries) of well-funded systems that rely almost exclusively on public funding (more than 1.5% of GDP) and public provision (more than 90% of enrollment). These include the Gulf countries, the Nordic countries, Saudi Arabia, Scotland,[1] Singapore, and Switzerland;
2. A small number (less than 10 countries) of predominantly public systems that are relatively well funded through a combination of public resources and a significant level of cost sharing with appropriate student aid. Examples in this category are Australia, Canada, England, Hong-Kong (China), Iceland, the Netherlands, and New Zealand;
3. Mixed provision systems (more than 25% private enrolment), relatively well funded through public resources and relatively high levels of cost sharing in both public and private institutions. These include Chile, China, Japan, Jordan, Malaysia, South Korea, and the US; and
4. Public and mixed provision systems that tend to be insufficiently funded overall (most countries in the rest of the world).

For the great majority of countries that are in the last category, elaborating a sustainable funding strategy would involve careful consideration of the following three elements:

- *Strategic decisions that influence the medium and long-term financing needs:* what institutional configuration would allow for a balanced expansion of the tertiary education system?

- *Resource mobilization options:* how can public and private funding sources be mobilized in the most effective manner? What are efficient and equitable student aid mechanisms?
- *Resource allocation approaches:* what are appropriate mechanisms to distribute public resources in a manner that encourages innovation and rewards performance?

### STRATEGIC DECISIONS INFLUENCING FINANCING REQUIREMENTS

In most developing countries, rapid growth of enrollment cannot be achieved only in the traditional mode of building and funding new public universities with government budgetary resources, considering the prevailing restrictions on public funding. Therefore, even though it is not a financial measure per se, the configuration of the tertiary education system has crucial financing implications. Spreading enrollment growth across a variety of tertiary education institutions—universities and non-universities, public and private—, instead of simply expanding the public university sub-sector, can be an effective strategy for reaching the country's enrollment targets in a more financially manageable way from a public resources perspective. Countries seeking to achieve a balanced enrollment growth must consider a three-pronged strategy: (i) developing dynamic non-university tertiary institutions, (ii) scaling up cost-effective distance education modalities, and (iii) stimulating the expansion of a vibrant, good-quality private tertiary education sub-sector.

Indeed, the conventional model of the European research university has proven too expensive to sustain mass tertiary education enrollment and not appropriate to meet the range of learning needs of a more diverse student body. Increased differentiation in tertiary education, through the development of a whole range of non-university institutions along traditional universities, can help meet the growing social demand and make tertiary education systems more responsive to changing labor market needs. Developing countries governments should therefore include, in their expansion strategy, support for the development of an institutionally differentiated tertiary education system. In this way, it is more feasible to provide a large array of relevant education and training opportunities in a more financially sustainable way.

The South African example is relevant in that respect. In the late 1990s, the democratic government set up a task force charged with elaborating a vision of the size and shape of the post-apartheid tertiary education system. The task force developed a comprehensive plan for diversifying tertiary education opportunities in South Africa,. Box 27 discusses how South Africa approached the need for balanced development of its tertiary education system in the transition years after the end of apartheid.

*Box 27. Shape and Size Task Force on Higher Education in South Africa*

The Shape and Size Task force of the Council on Higher Education "made the case for higher education as a potentially powerful contributor to, and necessary condition for, achieving the goals of social equity, economic and social development and democracy" and acknowledged that "(h)igher education's primary role is to develop the intellectual and skills capabilities of our society to address and resolve the range of economic (including labor market), social, cultural, political and other challenges faced by society. It must do so at a national, regional and local level as well as contribute to the development of the continent. Higher education must also play a central role in meeting the difficult realities of international competition under the new conditions of globalization."

To meet such broad demands, the higher education system needed to be differentiated and diversified, and the Task Force recognized five significant areas of South Africa's higher education system that, together, provide a comprehensive system to meet the needs of society.

1. Institutions dedicated to high-quality undergraduate teaching and learning ("bedrock institutions"), with locations around the country, providing access to urban and rural students alike. These institutions would have the broadest impact, educating the largest percentage of undergraduate students.
2. Comprehensive post-graduate and research institutions, providing undergraduate education as well as graduate-level degrees, to develop "high-level knowledge producers of national and international standing" across all disciplines.
3. Specifically focused Master's and Doctoral level institutions, providing graduate level opportunities for study and research in three specific areas: Humanities and Social Science; Commerce; and Science, Engineering, and Technology (SET).
4. Distance education, allowing innovations at both existing as campus-based institutions and potential distance focused institution(s) to reach more students. Such institutions should be maintained, expanded, and encouraged as a means of diversifying and modernizing the South African higher education system. These institutions could provide undergraduate and graduate training, depending upon their capacity and ability to meet national accreditation standards.
5. Private higher education, newly accepted in South Africa through the South African constitution and the Higher Education Act of 1997, meeting growing demand for higher education that the public sector cannot expand to serve. Private higher education would, however, have to be subject to accreditation and regulation to assure quality and to minimize any detrimental effects it may have on the public system of higher education.

(Source: Task Force, 2000, Chapter 3, Retrieved 12/22/05 from http://www.polity.org.za/html/govdocs/reports/education/chereport3.html)

## Development of the Non-University Sub-Sector

Several categories of institutions have evolved across the five continents, including polytechnics, universities of applied sciences, community colleges, further education colleges, technical and technology institutes, post-secondary vocational training institutes, and distance education institutions (World Bank, 2002). In diversified systems, while universities continue to be the main locus of advanced research, non-university institutions perform essential complementary roles by providing relevant and more cost-effective education and training programs.

Table 19, which shows the share of enrolment in non-university institutions in the various regions of the world, reveals that Latin America and East Asia are the leading regions when it comes to institutional differentiation.

*Table 19. Enrolment in Non-University Institutions by Region (2011)*

| Region | Proportion |
|---|---|
| East Asia and the Pacific | 26,1 |
| Eastern Europe and Central Asia | 16,8 |
| Latin America and the Caribbean | 25.0 |
| Middle East and North Africa | 13,8 |
| South Asia | 9,1 |
| Sub-Saharan Africa | 22,4 |

*Source: Based on available data at Edstats, not all countries are represented. Retrieved on October 2013.*

Community colleges occupy an important place within differentiated systems, as the US experience reveals. In 2012, community colleges enrolled 44 percent of the total undergraduate student population, playing a key role in the preparation of middle-level workers and employees (Box 28). In South Korea, the number of junior colleges is almost as high as the number of universities (152 versus 178).

*Box 28. Importance of Community Colleges in Preparing for Middle-Skills Jobs*

According to labor economist Carnevale, executive director of Georgetown University's Center on Education and the Workforce, almost a third—17 million out of 55 million—new job openings between 2010 and 2020 are going to require middle skills, as baby boomers retire and new jobs are created.

Today, the US largely relies on community colleges to provide entry-level training for the sub-baccalaureate workforce, not only in factories and foundries, but in healthcare institutions and white-collar offices. Middle-skill jobs now require more formal workforce preparation in order to make entry-level workers "training ready" as they begin their careers.

Community colleges are ideally situated to provide practical career and technical preparation as well as general learning. The mix of general academic learning and workforce preparation that is the unique signature of the nation's community colleges can lead to both further education and learning on the job. Moreover, the community colleges' mix of general competencies and workforce development allows students to live more fully in their time by becoming more active citizens and successful workers.

Community colleges have for decades been doing what middle-skill workers need now: retraining the long-term unemployed, matching new graduates' skill sets to job opportunities through internships and mentoring, serving regional geographic localities and training-up nontraditional students. These things form the backbone of the community college mandate.

(Source: Carnevale and Smith, 2013)

Vocationally oriented tertiary-level institutions are also able to offer training opportunities that respond flexibly to the labour market demand to young people who are not prepared or motivated to undertake a long academic career. In Brazil for example, the technical training centres operated by SENAI (National Industrial Training Services) successfully operate multi-disciplinary programs in a large number of professional fields. Its Colombian equivalent, SENA, enrols close to 40% of all post-secondary students. The success of such institutions hinges on their ability to forge and maintain close linkages with employers to guarantee the relevance of the training provided. This is best achieved by welcoming representatives from the productive sectors into the governance bodies of the institutions and involving them in curriculum design and updating.

Universities of applied sciences and technical institutes, such as the German *Fachhochschulen*, the Dutch HBOs and the French IUTs, are other examples of undergraduate professional institutions that are successful at preparing well-trained graduates at a lower cost than regular universities. A number of African countries, including Madagascar, Morocco and Tunisia, have effectively adapted this model as a viable alternative to the more expensive traditional universities.

Asia is perhaps the region that has the greatest degree of institutional diversification, as illustrated by Table 20, which shows the distribution of tertiary education institutions by categories in South East and East Asia.

*Distance Education Institutions and Virtual Education*

For countries with low enrollment rates, open universities and distance education programs can be a cost-effective approach for increasing enrolment. The British experience shows that the judicious use of new technologies can be a source of major savings. At the United Kingdom Open University, the cost of producing a graduate is about one-third that at a regular university (Salmi, 2009b).

*Table 20. Types and Numbers of Tertiary Institutions with Distance Education Programs*

| Country | 3-4 Year Degree and Post-Graduate Program | 2-4 Year Under-graduate Degree | 2 and 3 Year Diploma | Short Certificate | Professional and Technical |
|---|---|---|---|---|---|
| Cambodia | U & C 69 | Institutes 9 | | | |
| PRC | U 1,237 | U 1,264 | U & C 1,878 | | |
| India | U 504 | C 25,951 EC 2,388 | | | MS 1,231 PC 2,237 TI 65 |
| Indonesia | U 460 | Acad. 1,034 | Poly 162 | | |
| Lao PDR | U 34 | | Poly 11 | | |
| Malaysia | U & UC 1,710 | C 488 | Poly 24 | CC 37 | |
| Philippines | U & UC 1,710 | | C 114 | TI 30 | |
| Korea Rep. of. | U 178 Cyber 19 | C 152 | | | |
| Sri Lanka | U 15 | PG Inst 7 Pr Inst 9 | | | |
| Thailand | U 102 | C 26 PG Inst 6 | CC 19 | | |
| Vietnam | U 239 | C 197 | | | PC 408 |

*Notes: Acad = academies, C = colleges, CC = community colleges, Cyber = cyber universities, EC = engineering colleges, Inst = institutes, Lao PDR = Lao People's Democratic Republic, MS = management schools, PC = professional colleges, PG Inst. = postgraduate institutes, Poly = polytechnics, PRC = People's Republic of China, Pr Inst = private institutes, TI = technical institutes, U = universities, UC = university colleges.*
*Source: ADB (2012)*

Distance education has benefited large segments of population in many parts of the world, in countries as diverse as India, South Africa and Thailand. Thailand's two Open Universities, for instance, have been the principal instrument for expanding access and reaching out to students from rural areas and the poorest social stratum. Today, they enroll about 40% of the total student population. Table 21 gives the list of the largest open universities in Asia.

In addition, China has 16 open universities with enrolment ranging from 50,000 to 270,000 students, whereas India has 8 open universities in the 55,000 to 95,000 students range.

On the African continent, the South African Open University, UNISA, caters to 400,000 students, producing the largest numbers of graduates among all South African universities every year.

*Table 21. Asian Open Universities by Country and Size*

| Size | Country | Name of Institution | Enrolment |
|---|---|---|---|
| Mega Open Universities (500,000 students and above) | China | Open University | 2,663,500 |
| | India | Indira Gandhi National Open University | 2,468,208 |
| | Pakistan | Allam Iqubal Open University | 1,565,783 |
| | Indonesia | Universitas TerbukaIndonesia | 646,647 |
| Big Open Universities (100,000–499,999 students) | China | Jiangsu Open University | Jiangsu Open University 157,088 |
| | | Guangdong Open University | 158,271 |
| | | Zhejiang Open University | 139,974 |
| | | Beijing Open University | 110,084 |
| | | Sichuan Open University | 102,917 |
| | | Hunan Open University | 100,421 |
| | | Anhui Open University | 100,277 |
| | Korea | Korea National OpenUniversity | 182,000 |
| | India | Yashwantrao Chavan | 342,862 |
| | | Maharashtra Open | 176,048 |
| | Thailand | Sukhothai Thammathirat Open University | 400,000 |
| | | Ramkhamhaeng University | 400,000 |
| | Japan | Open University, Japan | 80,000 |
| | Bangladesh | Bangladesh Open University | 271,630 |

*Source: ADB (2012)*

## Development of the Private Sector

Faced with a rapidly growing demand for tertiary education, many nations throughout the world have encouraged the growth of private universities and institutes to complement public investment as part of their expansion strategy. In several cases, the growth of private tertiary education has been so significant that more students are enrolled in private institutions than public ones, as can be seen in several Latin American countries (Brazil, Chile, Costa Rica, Dominican Republic, El Salvador, Paraguay) and East Asian economies (Cambodia, Indonesia, Korea, the Philippines). In Sub-Saharan Africa, Côte d'Ivoire has the highest proportion (80%). Table 22 presents the average proportion of private sector enrolment in various regions of the planet, showing that this is a worldwide phenomenon.

*Table 22. Private Enrolment as a Share of Total Tertiary*
*Education Enrollment by Region (2011)*

| Region | Proportion |
|---|---|
| East Asia and the Pacific | 42,2 |
| Eastern Europe and Central Asia | 29,2 |
| Latin America and the Caribbean | 50,2 |
| Middle East and North Africa | 39.0 |
| South Asia | 47.0 |
| Sub-Saharan Africa | 32.0 |

*Source: Based on available data at the World Bank's Edstats database;*
*not all countries are represented.*

Africa was the last region to witness private sector development in tertiary education, starting in the late 1980s. But the increase has been spectacular in the past two decades. Between 1990 and 2014, the number of private institutions rose from 30 to about 1,000, compared to a growth of 100 to 500 for public universities (Bloom, Canning, Chan, and Luca, 2014). In Chad, Congo, Côte d'Ivoire and Uganda, private sector enrolment has tripled or quadrupled in the past decade.

Private tertiary education institutions come in many sizes and shapes. Using the two dimensions of degree of selectivity in admission and legal status, it is possible to distinguish among at least ten categories of such institutions, as illustrated by Table 23. Several Asian, Latin American and Middle Eastern countries have highly selective private universities—secular and/or religious—that can often be found among the best institutions in these countries. The second tier of private tertiary education institutions is made of less academically and socially selective institutions. The third tier consists of open access private institutions that are frequently of dubious quality (see Chapter 2).

*Table 23. Types of Private Tertiary Education Institutions*

| Legal Status \ Degree of Selectivity | Elite | Semi-Elite | Non Elite |
|---|---|---|---|
| Secular Non Profit | X | X | X |
| Religious Non Profit | X | X | |
| For-Profit | | X | X |
| Public-Private Partnerships | X | | |

In most of the countries where they are allowed to operate, for-profit institutions tend to be the biggest and fastest growing group among private providers. Brazil is the country with the largest number of students enrolled in for-profit institutions, around 1.5 million, representing close to half of all private sector students.

There are few examples of private institutions resulting from a partnership with the State, but where they exist they represent an innovative funding approach. The best known cases can be found in Malaysia, where three public corporations sponsored the establishment of a private university each (Universiti Teknologi Petronas – UTP, Kuala Lumpur Infrastructure University College – KLIUC, and Multimedia University – MMU). In each case, the public corporation financed all the initial investment costs and the first three years of running expenditures. Afterwards the new universities have continued to operate as independent private entities.

In addition to relieving the pressure on government financial resources, the participation of private providers has often introduced a positive dimension of institutional differentiation and has brought about healthy competition. To ensure that their programs meet acceptable standards of quality and relevance, private tertiary institutions are often closely attuned to labor market needs and tend to respond more flexibly to the evolving demand. They are also well placed to launch curricular and pedagogical innovations. This, in turn, can induce public institutions to be less change adverse and more prone to strategic transformation in order to improve the quality and relevance of their program offerings.

The successful development of private tertiary education as a substantial pillar of developing countries' expansion strategy is dependent on two important preconditions to ensure that quality and equity are not negatively affected by the growth of the private sector. In the first place, the existence of many poor quality providers, documented in Chapter 2, makes it imperative to put in place effective quality assurance mechanisms (licensing and accreditation) and to weed out programs and institutions that do not meet minimal quality standards. The Ghanaian Ministry of Education recently announced that new private tertiary institutions should give priority to science and technology programs in line with the government's determination to implement a 60:40 policy guidelines regarding the distribution of university enrolment, that is 60% in STEM disciplines and no more than 40% in the social sciences and humanities. Promoting quality in the private sectors is all the more important as private institutions in many countries tend to receive a high share of low-income students, as recently documented for example in Chile, Japan, and Poland, as well as in for-profit institutions in the United States (Hunt et al., 2016).

Second, an important consideration that affects the quality of private tertiary education is the need for a clear legal framework to distinguish between for-profit and nonprofit institutions. In many countries—notably in Latin America, Asia and Africa—the absence of such legislation results in the operation of commercial enterprises barely disguised as non-profit universities. This situation has serious implications. First, the owners of private institutions may be more inclined to maximize their profit share than reinvesting any surplus in the education side of the institution. Second, realizing profits under the guise of a non-profit status may be seen as a form of tax evasion, representing a social loss to the country. Third, some countries—Colombia for example—are concerned about money laundering through private tertiary education institutions.

Legislation allowing private universities to be for-profit, if properly designed, could bring these questionable practices into the open, and allow the profits to be properly taxed. Even when private universities do not get direct subsidies, they may benefit from public contributions indirectly, via student aid and research funding. Therefore all their financial transactions need to be transparent to demonstrate that resources, both public and private, are being properly used. To facilitate a more objective discussion of the pros and cons of allowing for-profit institutions to operate, Figure 19 outlines the main differences between non-profit and for-profit institutions that need to be taken into account by the regulatory framework.

In the second place, governments must monitor carefully the socio-economic distribution of the students enrolled in and graduating from private tertiary education institutions. Some countries, Malaysia and Mexico for example, have mandated a minimal proportion of low-income students to whom private providers should provide financial support. In addition, many countries have put in place a student loan system that allows economically challenged students to access sufficient funding to cover the cost of attending a private institution. A later section of this chapter looks at financial aid specifically.

Governments may also consider two further sets of measures to help achieve the policy goal of increasing enrolments in private institutions. First, in terms of regulatory framework, it would be desirable to remove the unnecessary legal and administrative hurdles that sometimes constrain the establishment or development of private tertiary education institutions. In Azerbaijan, for example, the Ministry of Education controls the number of students that each private university is allowed to recruit and the type of programs that they are allowed to offer. Allowing flexibility for private tertiary education institutions in terms of faculty hiring and remuneration practices, level of tuition fees, and program and curriculum development would go a long way towards providing a favorable operational environment for these institutions, as long as they abide by existing quality assurance norms.

Second, some governments have found it useful to offer limited subsidies to the private sector as an incentive for stimulating its growth. For example, private institutions might be given the opportunity to apply for government financial support in areas of high priority, such as engineering or health sciences, should investors be willing to set up this kind of expensive programs. Subsidies for teacher salaries could also be considered, as happens in several Sub-Saharan African countries. Another support mechanism could be to grant or lease land to private tertiary education institutions. Finally, needy students enrolled in quality private institutions should be eligible for financial aid, as will be discussed later on.

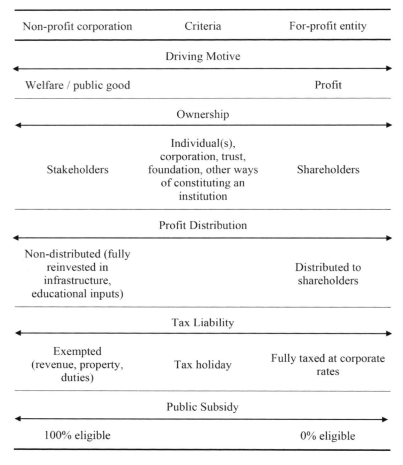

| Non-profit corporation | Criteria | For-profit entity |
|---|---|---|
| | **Driving Motive** | |
| Welfare / public good | | Profit |
| | **Ownership** | |
| Stakeholders | Individual(s), corporation, trust, foundation, other ways of constituting an institution | Shareholders |
| | **Profit Distribution** | |
| Non-distributed (fully reinvested in infrastructure, educational inputs) | | Distributed to shareholders |
| | **Tax Liability** | |
| Exempted (revenue, property, duties) | Tax holiday | Fully taxed at corporate rates |
| | **Public Subsidy** | |
| 100% eligible | | 0% eligible |

*Figure 19. Key Areas of Differentiation between Non-Profit and*
*For-Profit Private Tertiary Education Institutions.*
*Source: Jamil Salmi, Richard Hopper and Svava Bjarnson*

Legal and financial incentives to stimulate the development of quality private tertiary education institutions can of course be justified only on the grounds that they represent a channel for expanding enrolments at a lower public cost than by expanding public universities.

*Removing Systemic Barriers and Achieving Synergies*

For this type of institutional diversification strategy to work in the long term, it is important to define clear policies supporting the respective roles of the various types of institutions to avoid the proliferation of dead-end institutions and programs. One of the challenges that many countries face is to dispel the perception that non-university institutions and programs are second rate compared to the regular universities. An OECD evaluation revealed that it was very much the case in Chile, for example, where the network of professional institutes (IPs) and technical training centers (CFTs) enroll around 30% of the total student population. These institutions are not well considered and their graduates find it difficult to move to the university sub-sector (OECD/World Bank, 2009).

> ...the tertiary education system is so segmented, and success in entry tests so strongly correlated with socio-economic characteristics, that students have significantly different academic and career opportunities depending on their secondary education background, family income level, gender and geographical location. The lack of articulation and pathways between technical training centers, professional institutes and universities compounds these issues and makes upward professional mobility extremely difficult for those entering non-university tertiary education.

Similarly, in Colombia, the OECD/World Bank review of tertiary education found that "progress up through the tertiary levels is limited by lack of a National Qualifications Framework, credit transfer, and collaborative arrangements between different tertiary institutions" (OECD/World Bank, 2012).

By contrast, one of the strengths of the Canadian and US tertiary education systems is the flexible articulation between community colleges and universities, allowing for easy transfer from one type of institution to the other and, thereby, offering multiple paths and increased opportunities for students starting in non-university institutions, especially students from under-privileged backgrounds (Brand et al., 2012). This flexibility is especially important in a lifelong learning perspective as tertiary education institutions are increasingly expected to provide relevant training and retraining options to individuals in all stages of their professional life.

A very innovative example of flexible platform can be found in South Korea. The Academic Credit Bank System (ACBS) gives the opportunity to students taking classes from different institutions to acquire an actual degree issued and validated by he Ministry of Education (Box 29).

---

### Box 29. *The Korean Academic Credit Bank*

South Korea's Academic Credit Bank System (ACBS) allows students to earn a degree by combining credits from different sources. Although the ACBS was formed to give students a path towards a degree without requiring post-secondary institutes to recognize transfer credits, it is also useful for students who have nearly enough qualifications to graduate, but are deterred from finishing by the difficulty of registering in a new institution with the risk of needing to repeat classes. A particularly pressing problem came from students who had obtained academic credits from more than one institution but did not possess enough credits from any single institution to obtain a degree. The government's solution to the problem of universities and colleges refusing to deliver greater system flexibility through transfer credits was to create a new system that would, in effect, circumvent the universities on credit transfer.

The easiest way to understand ACBS is to think of it as a degree-granting agency of last resort. What ACBS allows people to do is to pool the credits they have earned from various sources, and package those into a degree, or a plan of study that leads to a degree. Although at first glance this may make ACBS seem like a kind of Prior Learning Assessment and Recognition system, it is in fact nothing of the kind. When the ACBS certifies that someone has a degree, and asks the Ministry of Education to issue the degree, it is not certifying that the degree-recipient possesses the knowledge and skills equivalent to someone who holds that same degree from an institution. Rather, it is actually certifying that students have followed an ABCS-designed curriculum and accumulated the relevant number of core, general, and elective credits for that program. To do this, ACBS has, with the assistance of numerous subject matter experts, developed its own standard curriculum for each of its 218 degree programs (109 majors and 24 degrees at the Bachelor's level, and 109 majors and 13 degrees at the Associate's level).

Students wishing to obtain a degree from ACBS begin by registering in a particular program. The registration may occur at any point in the credit accumulation period: some students register before getting a single credit, others do not bother to register until they have all their credits. ACBS verifies that the courses match program requirements and that they have been issued by accredited programs. If the accumulated credits meet the curriculum, then the ACBS recommends that the ministry issue a degree to the student.

ACBS has grown rapidly over the years. In 2006, 12,376 students registered to pursue an associate degree, and 39,146 to seek a bachelor's degree. By 2011, the number of registered students had reached 62,087 at the associate degree level and 59,336 at the bachelor level. ACBS awarded 5,084 associate degrees and 14,009 bachelor degrees in 2006. In 2011, the numbers were 29,585 and 22,769, respectively.

The main challenge confronting ACBS at the moment is the issue of quality control. An increasing percentage of credits are coming from online providers whose quality is difficult to monitor. Already, the ACBS takes extra measures to counter potential fraud, most notably by requiring private online providers to get accredited every two years instead of the usual four. ACBS officials are aware that the possibility of fraud will remain a reputational threat into the indefinite future. The worry is that if abuses are uncovered at a few ACBS-accredited institutions, it will taint all ACBS degrees, past and present.

(Source: Usher, 2014b)

Overcoming this challenge of lack of connection between the university and non-university sub-sectors requires establishing functional linkages among the various types of tertiary education institutions. Universities and non-university institutions should not operate as parallel, unrelated sub-sectors, but rather as complementary parts of a well-articulated system that offers multiple learning paths. Student mobility must be encouraged by removing all the barriers among the segments of the tertiary education system, among institutions within each segment, and among disciplines and programs within institutions. The promotion of open systems can be achieved through recognition of relevant prior professional and academic experience, degree equivalencies, credit transfer, tuition exchange schemes, access to national scholarships and student loans, and creation of a comprehensive qualifications framework.

To bring about the needed flexibility and ensure a coordinated approach to all education and training institutions and modalities, a growing number of countries have put in place a National Qualifications Framework that defines a variety of entry points and pathways for people seeking to gain new skills and qualifications at any age and at any stage in their careers. A well designed and functioning National Qualifications Framework can give all citizens the opportunity to receive national recognition for their skills and qualifications. Skills learned on the job can be acknowledged officially without the individual's having to attend a formal training course. National Qualifications Frameworks are meant to offer greater flexibility for the learner and remove barriers to learning. Unit standards and qualifications span academic, vocational, and industry-based education and training, and each is registered at an appropriate level on the qualifications framework. The Scottish and Australian national qualifications frameworks are widely recognized as among the most successful experiences in this area (Box 30).

---

*Box 30. Salient Features of the Australian National Qualifications Framework*

Australia was one of first generation of national qualifications frameworks, with New Zealand, South Africa, Scotland, and separate frameworks in the rest of Britain. It shares three characteristics with the Scottish credit and qualifications framework, the other relatively successful national qualifications framework.

First, the Australian framework was established in 1995 by incorporating qualifications structures and agreements that had been developed separately for senior secondary certificates, vocational education and higher education over the previous two decades. The current framework, like its Scottish counterpart, is effectively a federation of sub frameworks.

Second, the Australian and Scottish frameworks are relatively loose federations, allowing each sector's qualifications to develop in relative isolation from each other, notwithstanding their formal location in the same framework. Over the same period, Australian governments allowed senior secondary and

---

higher education qualifications to evolve with benign neglect. In contrast to Australia's loose arrangement, the New Zealand government sought to incorporate senior secondary and university qualifications within a more tightly regulated framework, which provoked substantial resistance.

Thirdly, even in vocational education Australia's qualifications framework has served an important role within a broader qualifications system that includes quality assurance and mechanisms for assessing, awarding and transferring credit. The South African government and many countries that have developed qualifications frameworks more recently have imposed on them understandable but excessive expectations.

(Source: Moodie, 2009)

Finally, given the important resource constraints faced by most developing countries, governments should aim, as much as possible, to achieve synergies by focusing investment on projects that can benefit the entire system. Several countries, for instance Sri Lanka, have established a dedicated national Internet network linking all tertiary education and research institutions. Others have set up a national digital library with open access education resources serving the entire tertiary education system. A few years ago, the World Bank facilitated a process of technology transfer between Pakistan and Madagascar for the establishment of a digital library in the latter country. Other nations could benefit from similar South-South collaborative initiatives. In the late 1990s, Argentina was a pioneer in designing and implementing an integrated Management Information System (MIS) for all tertiary education institutions.

## RESOURCE MOBILIZATION OPTIONS

Besides the institutional and program diversification options analyzed in the previous section, developing countries can rely on the following four principal sources of revenue to fund the expansion and improvement of their tertiary education system:

- Public budget
- Cost sharing
- Income generation
- Donor support

Before analyzing each of the first three options, it is important to observe that, considering the resource-constrained environment of most developing countries, the scope for mobilizing significantly higher levels of resources and the likely balance among the four potential sources of revenue will depend greatly on the specific situation and characteristics of each country. Table 24 illustrates the diversity of situations and tries to assess the range of funding options available to various groups of countries, also taking into account the potential role of the private sector along the lines discussed earlier in this chapter.

*Table 24. Potential for Resource Mobilization*

| Funding Source | Low-Income Countries | Middle-Income Countries | Upper Middle-Income Countries |
|---|---|---|---|
| Public Budget | X | XX | XXX |
| Cost Sharing | X | XX | XX |
| Income Generation | X | XX | XXX |
| Private Sector Development | XX | XXX | XXX |
| Donor Support | XX | X | – |

Comparing Brazil and China provides interesting lessons on the differential impact of funding strategies. By the end of the Cultural Revolution in the early 1980s, China's tertiary education system had been crippled and the enrolment rate was around 2%. Since then, the country's leadership has invested steadily in the reconstruction and development of a strong tertiary education system. In 1997, aware that it would be difficult if not impossible to keep expanding while, at the same time, improving quality and building up a strong research capacity, China introduced universal cost sharing at the undergraduate level. Brazil's tertiary education expansion strategy, by contrast, combines tuition-free public universities and a large private sector. Table 25 presents the main features of each country's funding approach and assesses the relative importance of each funding source.

*Table 25. Brazil and China's Funding Strategies*

| Funding Source | Brazil | China |
|---|---|---|
| Public Budget | XX | XXX |
| Cost Sharing | – | XX |
| Income Generation | X | X |
| Private Sector Development | XXX | X |

Figure 20, which compares the evolution of tertiary level enrolment in both countries in the past two decades, shows that China's funding strategy has been more effective than Brazil's.

Besides looking at the quantitative growth dimension, it is also relevant to assess the evolution of the research capacity of universities in both countries. The number of universities included in the Shanghai ranking is a useful proxy in that respect. In 2004, Brazil and China had 4 and 16 universities among the top 500, respectively. Ten years later, the number was 6 for Brazil and 44 for China. In 2015, Brazil placed only the University of São Paulo in the top 200, compared to 10 Chinese universities.

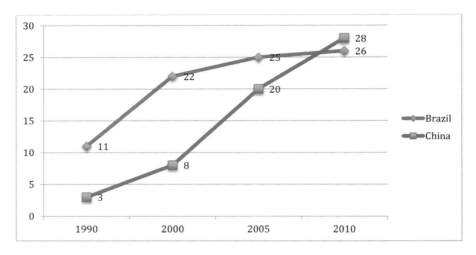

*Figure 20. Evolution of Tertiary Enrolment Rate in Brazil and China (%) (1990–2010).*
*Source: UIS*

### Increasing Public Resources

Considering the substantial social benefits of tertiary education analyzed in Chapter 2, developing countries with low levels of public funding must consider carefully the feasibility of significantly increasing public spending to be able to translate their vision for the future of tertiary education into reality. The purpose would not only be to cover the quantitative expansion and qualitative improvement needs of the sub-sector, but also to invest in university research in carefully selected areas of high priority.

While it is difficult to ascertain a universal rule to set the ideal proportion of GDP that should go to tertiary education, developing countries can combine a rigorous assessment of their financing needs with a methodical benchmarking of other economies at similar levels of development to define a reasonable level of resource commitment. In Eastern Europe and Central Asia, for instance, several countries— especially among the former Yugoslav republics and former members of the Soviet Union—spend no more than 0.3% of GDP, which makes them outliers compared to the European average of 1.1% of GDP.

In Latin America, where the average public spending is 0.6% of GDP, several countries invest much less, as illustrated by Table 26, which compares the resource mobilization efforts of a number of Latin American and East Asian nations.

In Sub-Saharan Africa, several countries spend less than 0.5%% of GDP, compared to the average proportion of 0.8% allocated between 1998 and 2012. Angola, Benin, Cameroon, Congo, the Gambia, Liberia, Mauritius, Mozambique and Swaziland all devote less than 10% of their education budget to tertiary education,

*Table 26. Resource Mobilization in Selected Latin American and East Asian Countries (2012)*

| | | Public Funding as a Share of GDP | | |
|---|---|---|---|---|
| **Tuition fees as** | | ≤ 0.5 | 0.5 – 1 | ≥ 1 |
| **share** | ≥ **40** | | Chile | |
| **of unit cost in** | | | | |
| **public** | **20 – 40** | | South Korea, Thailand | China, Indonesia, Jamaica, Malaysia |
| **institutions** | ≤ **20** | Dominican Rep., El Salvador, Guatemala, Guyana, Myanmar, Peru | Argentina, Brazil, Colombia, Honduras, Mexico, Paraguay | Bolivia, Barbados Costa Rica, Cuba, Ecuador, Nicaragua Venezuela |

*Source: Salmi (2013d)*

compared to the regional average of 18.5% (Darvas et al., 2016). It is on the basis of this kind of analysis that the Ministry of Higher Education could negotiate with the Ministry of Finance a funding formula that would provide increased financing to meet the development needs of the sub-sector.

At the same time, the financial needs of the tertiary education sub-sector cannot be considered without adopting a comprehensive resource allocation approach for the entire education system. While there is no magic formula determining the "correct" share of resources to be devoted to tertiary education within the overall education envelope, certain principles and guidelines can be followed to ensure a balanced distribution of budgetary resources and an appropriate sequencing of investment across the various subsectors of the education system, considering a country's level and pattern of educational development, pace of economic growth, and fiscal situation.

International data show that expenditures on tertiary education usually range between 15 and 25 percent of public education expenditures. As observed by the World Bank (2002), developing countries that devote more than 20 percent of their education budget to tertiary education, especially those countries that have not achieved universal primary education coverage, usually show a distorted pattern of resource allocation. In these economies, a disproportionate share of resources goes to supporting an elitist university system while the budget allocated to preschool, basic and secondary education remains insufficient. In addition, as observed in Chapter 2, many tertiary education systems are wasteful because of the high proportion of dropouts and, in the case of Francophone Sub-Saharan Africa and North Africa, the high proportion of non-educational expenditures such as untargeted student subsidies at the expense of non-salary pedagogical inputs that are crucial for quality learning.

The time dimension is also important to consider. Careful attention to sequencing is an integral part of the resource allocation decision-making process. Most developing countries do not have sufficient resources to invest heavily in all education sub-sectors at the same time. The example of Korea, which was able to raise its tertiary education enrollment from 2% at the time of independence in 1945 to one of the highest levels in the world today, contains useful lessons in this respect. The development of tertiary education took place in five distinct phases. It started in the 1950s with the slow expansion of public institutions and the introduction, from the beginning, of cost sharing at a level equivalent to 30 percent of recurrent expenditures. The second phase, in the 1960s, consisted in encouraging the establishment of private institutions, with some public funding support for capital costs and scholarships. Then, in the 1970s and 1980s, the government focused on the expansion of engineering and technical education to meet new manpower requirements as the country industrialized, emphasizing the development of both universities and junior colleges to train all levels of human capital needed by the economy. During the fourth phase, throughout the 1990s, government efforts focused on quality, accountability, and R&D capacity. Finally, in the past fifteen years, Korea has invested a lot to strengthen the competitiveness of its top universities, notably through the Brain 21 program. Figure 21 shows clearly how the sequencing of investment in tertiary education followed the expansion of enrolment at the lower levels of the education system.

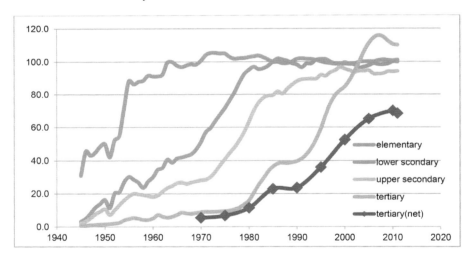

*Figure 21. Evolution of Enrolment Rates in Korea (1945–2010).*
*Source: MOE, Yearbook of Educational Statistics; UIS*

Finally, governments can facilitate public-private partnerships to finance some of the costs of quantitative expansion. In many countries, the construction and management of student residences is taking place under public-private partnership arrangements. A recent experience in Senegal has showed that public-private partnerships can also be leveraged to build new universities. Commercial banks from Senegal and China worked together to finance the construction of two new public universities, at a slightly subsidized interest rate.

## Cost Sharing and Student Aid

If in some states of the (United States) higher education institutions are also "free", that only means in fact defraying the cost of education of the upper classes from the general tax receipts. (Karl Marx and Friedrich Engels[2])

Even though tuition fees are an important element of any resource mobilization strategy—representing a significant source of potential income—, it is one of the most difficult topics in the tertiary education policy agenda. Indeed, very few countries have been able to conduct a rational debate on tuition fees in tertiary education. As many governments have found out the hard way, any attempt to introduce fees in a democratic setting is fraught with ideological battles and carries high political risks.

In fact, after a period of relative calm on university campuses all over the world during the first decade of the new century, since 2011 strong student against the high cost of university education have happened in places as diverse as Berkeley, Bogota, Johannesburg, Khartoum, Lilongwe, London, Madrid, Montreal, Santiago and Seoul. The general mood against cost-sharing explains why the few Western European governments that had introduced fees in the 2000s—for instance Austria, Germany (in several states – *Länder*), Slovenia (for parallel track students) —have rescinded them.

A similar trend can be observed in other parts of the world. In Canada, the provincial government of Quebec acceded to the protesting students' demand not to increase fees in 2012. The same thing happened in South Africa in 2015. In South Korea, the government cut fees by 15% in 2013. In Chile, after the student riots in 2011 and 2012, the abolition of tuition fees in both public and private universities was one of the main pledges of the new president during her electoral campaign in the fall of 2013. Finding ways of implementing this promise, in a country where 70% of the students are enrolled in private institutions, has been a major preoccupation of the Bachelet government.

However, notwithstanding the strong political opposition against cost sharing, the reality of many countries' fiscal situation and the acute needs for increased tertiary education investment make it difficult to avoid looking seriously at introducing or raising tuition fees. Ireland, which had abolished fees in the late 1990s, had to reintroduce them in 2013 to the tune of 3,000 Euros a year under the pressure of the financial crisis. A recent report prepared by an expert committee in Denmark calls for a serious look at the introduction of tuition fees for all students, which would be a first in a Nordic country.

If this is the case in industrial economies, it is even truer in the developing world. While public funding remains the main source of funding for tertiary education in most countries in the world, the fact is that few developing countries have been able to significantly expand their tertiary education system, while at the same time improving its quality, without relying on a growing financial contribution from students and their families to cover the cost of studies. One of the most emblematic cases is China, which in 1997 introduced fees equivalent to 20% of the cost of undergraduate studies. In the Middle East, the Jordanian and Palestinian public universities get most of their resources from student contributions. Until the recent political problem caused by the student upheaval, Chile was the only country in Latin America with significant tuition fees in its public universities, amounting to about 30% of unit costs. Since the fall of the Berlin Wall and the disappearance of the Soviet Union, most newly independent nations of Eastern Europe and Central Asia have followed a dual-fee approach to generate resources to compensate for their falling public budgets. Many Sub-Saharan African governments have allowed their public universities to adopt a similar funding strategy, whereby the most academically qualified students are able to study free of charge while the next group of students can enroll into fee-paying programs. In Jordan, the students who get the best grades at the end of high school pay a subsidized annual tuition fee of $1,650 while the others must pay about $4,000 a year.

The first element in any policy move towards greater cost sharing consists in establishing with clarity the purpose of seeking an increased financial contribution from students and their family. It is possible to identify four categories of reasons that, separately or together, justify the need to raise tuition fees: (i) pressure to expand access, (ii) the modernization agenda, (iii) efficiency considerations, and (iv) the equity imperative. First of all, many developing countries face strong pressure to increase tertiary education opportunities because of the demographic bulge combined with progress in meeting the Education for All goals. These countries require additional resources to raise the enrolment rate in response to growing demand from high school graduates. Furthermore, as analyzed in Chapter 2, most tertiary education systems in the developing world find themselves under-resourced to the point of compromising the quality of teaching and learning, reducing the relevance of programs and constraining the research output. Third, not only do these countries suffer from the resources constraint, but in addition available resources are not used efficiently. In open-access and tuition-free tertiary education systems, many incoming students are not sufficiently well prepared academically. This translates into high dropout rates, especially during the first year of studies. Moreover, students have little incentives to graduate on time because of the perceived low cost of study. Available data indicate that students who are aware of the cost of their education are more likely to have good academic results and graduate on time. In Colombia, for example, which has the oldest and one of the most comprehensive student loan systems in the world, the completion rate of loan beneficiaries is 64%, compared to only 48% on average for the general student population (OECD/World Bank, 2012).

Finally, there is a strong equity rationale for increased cost sharing. Even though, intuitively, keeping tertiary education free of charge for all is seen as the best way of promoting equity, evidence shows that free tertiary education is in reality highly inequitable, unless the country has a highly progressive income tax system, as is the case in the Nordic countries. Experience in many parts of the world indicates that there is a strongly regressive element in most publicly funded tertiary education systems whereby students from advantaged backgrounds tend to access tertiary education disproportionately at no personal cost and obtain higher remuneration after graduating, yet rely on less-advantaged general taxpayers to fund their education. Independently from the need for additional resources, financing of tertiary education would be much more equitable if students from high and middle-income families would contribute a larger share of the cost of their education. In addition, in countries with a significant private sector, many low-income students, who are unable to gain access to public universities, pay for high cost private tertiary education.

A few examples can illustrate this general phenomenon. In Colombia, an estimate of the benefits incidence of public subsidies in tertiary education reveals that the richer two quintiles receive a disproportionately high share of resources, almost three quarters of the total amount of subsidies going to public universities (Table 27).

*Table 27. Benefits Incidence of Public Subsidies in Public Universities (2008)*

| Quintile 1 | Quintile 2 | Quintile 3 | Quintile 4 | Quintile 5 |
|---|---|---|---|---|
| 3.7% | 6.7% | 15.4% | 28.4% | 45.8% |

*Source: Méndez (2009)*

Still in the Latin American region—which has the highest degree of inequality in the world—, the comparison of Argentina, Brazil and Chile sheds light on the relative impact of different access and funding policies. Argentina has an open access and free tuition policy; Brazil has a restricted access and free tuition policy; and Chile has both restricted access and high tuition fees. The natural expectation would be that Chile would display the highest degree of inequality. But, in reality, Brazil is the most regressive country, followed by Argentina, and then Chile. As revealed by Table 28, which shows the enrolment rate in each country for the various socio-economic groups, Chile has the highest enrolment rate for the poorest two quintiles.

Looking at data on access to the University of São Paulo—Brazil's most prestigious public university—, helps to understand the mechanisms at play. The great majority of candidates (86%) who take the entrance examination (*vestibular*) come from public high schools; only 14% of the candidates went to a private high school. But, based on the results of the highly competitive examination (admission rate of 1 to 15), 70% of the students admitted come from private secondary schools,

*Table 28. Enrolment Rates by Income Quintile in*
*Argentina, Brazil and Chile*

| Quintile | Argentina | Brazil | Chile |
|----------|-----------|--------|-------|
| Q1 | 18.0% | 5.0% | 21.2% |
| Q2 | 25.3% | 6.3% | 26.4% |
| Q3 | 29.5% | 11.6% | 26.0% |
| Q4 | 38.2% | 20.7% | 37.5% |
| Q5 | 56.6% | 47.0% | 61.6% |

*Source: SEDLAC database at http://sedlac.econo.unlp.edu.ar/*
*eng/statistics-detalle.php?idE=37*

versus 30% from public schools. Thus, the sons and daughters of high-income families with strong cultural capital, who can afford to study in the expensive good quality private secondary schools, are better prepared to get access to the top public universities of the country, which are tuition-free (Rodriguez et al., 2008). This fundamental dimension of inequality was perfectly captured by Brazil's best known weekly magazine, *Veja*, which run an article on 2 October 2006 with the following title: "Poor people pay to study in private faculties whereas rich people study for free in public universities."

In the case of Chile, the better results from an equity viewpoint stem from the fact that, even though all students must pay high tuition fees in both public and private universities, the country has a comprehensive system of well-targeted grants and student loans to protect low-income students. In fact, a benefit incidence analysis of public expenditures in Chile's tertiary education system clearly demonstrated that the student aid subsidies are distributed in a progressive way, whereas the public funds allocated directly to the universities are highly regressive. Table 29 displays the share of public resources benefiting each income quintile group for each funding mechanism. If the share of resources is equal to or larger than the share of that group in the overall student population, the funding mechanism is neutral or has a positive distributive effect. A smaller share means that the mechanism is regressive.

The data clearly show that, in spite of the high level of tuition fees in the Chilean public universities, the tertiary education financing system allocates a larger share of resources (38%) to students from the poorest two quintiles, who represent 24% of the total student population. This is essentially due to the prominence of student aid mechanisms (scholarships and student loans) in the funding system. The scholarships and the guaranteed student loan program for students enrolled in private institutions (CAE) are the most progressive mechanisms. The subsidized loan programme aimed at students in the most prestigious public and private universities (*Fondo Solidario*), however, is not well targeted from an equity perspective, since students

*Table 29. Benefits Incidence Analysis of Public Spending in Tertiary Education*

|  | Q1 | Q2 | Q3 | Q4 | Q5 | Total |
|---|---|---|---|---|---|---|
| Direct budgetary transfer | 10.8% | 14.1% | 18.3% | 25.9% | 30.9% | 100.0% |
| Indirect budgetary transfer | 7.6% | 13.9% | 18.2% | 27.6% | 32.7% | 100.0% |
| Scholarships | 53.8% | 32.3% | 6.2% | 7.4% | 0.3% | 100.0% |
| Fondo Solidario | 21.5% | 14.3% | 35.7% | 28.5% | 0.0% | 100.0% |
| INGRESA/CAE | 39.7% | 24.1% | 22.7% | 13.5% | 0.0% | 100.0% |
| MECESUP/FDI | 11.2% | 15.0% | 19.6% | 26.6% | 27.5% | 100.0% |
| CONICYT | 7.2% | 13.0% | 16.1% | 24.3% | 39.4% | 100.0% |
| Share of public subsidies received by each quintile | 20.7% | 17.3% | 21.0% | 22.9% | 18.1% | 100.0% |
| Share of each quintile in total enrolment | 10.0% | 14.1% | 18.7% | 26.6% | 30.5% | 100.0% |

*Source: Prepared by Jamil Salmi in the context of the 2009 OECD Review of Tertiary Education in Chile (OECD/World Bank, 2009)*

from Quintiles 3 and 4 are over-represented. Figure 22 illustrates this distribution pattern in a striking way.

Available data on Sub-Saharan African countries show a similar pattern of regressive distribution of public expenditures on tertiary education in the absence of tuition fees. Figure 23, which shows the Lorenz Curve for six countries, demonstrates a high degree of inequality among income groups. In Malawi, for instance, the richest top 20 percent of the population enjoys as much as 92 percent of government spending on tertiary education. In Mali the richest income quintile receives 86 percent and in Tanzania the share is 82 percent. As recently observed by a team of African researchers:

> Overall, free higher education in Africa was built on inequitable social structures. As a result, it reproduced and reinforced these inequalities. To state the obvious, free higher education in highly unequal societies mainly benefits the already privileged, who have the significant social, cultural and economic capital required to access, participate and succeed in education. ... Equally, free higher education was an expensive project that the poor political economies could hardly afford in the long run. As enrolments grew, more resources were required to support a meaningful university experience. These resources were simply not available. ... Consequently, free higher education eventually spawned ideal conditions for prolonged protests and mediocre higher education. (Langa et al., 2016)

The same situation can be observed in most North African and Middle Eastern countries, where public tertiary education continues to be tuition-free. A few years

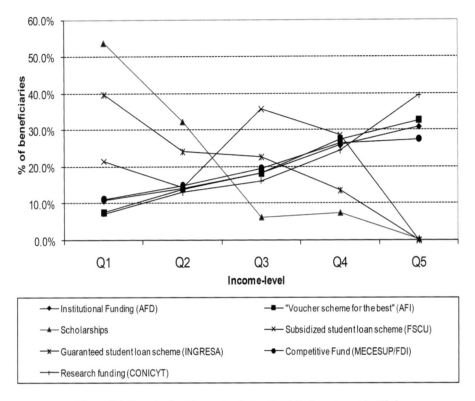

*Figure 22. Benefits Incidence Analysis of Public Investment in Chile.*
*Source: OECD/World Bank (2009)*

ago, Egypt's Prime Minister made a statement in the press to the effect that "free education is not a right for everyone but only for the needy".

One of the important policy implications of this analysis is that looking at tuition fees in isolation shows only half of the picture. To be complete, any analysis of funding patterns should focus on the net cost to students, representing the actual cost to students once scholarships and loans are deducted from the cost of tuition fees. This gives a different picture than just looking at tuition fees, as illustrated by Figure 24, which shows the level of tuition fees in a number of OECD countries, together with the proportion of students who benefit from a scholarship or a loan for their studies. Countries that have a comprehensive student aid program can afford significantly higher fees than those where students have limited access to scholarships and loans.

The Canadian Province of Ontario recently took the positive initiative of merging its various scholarships and loan remission programs into a large up-front grants

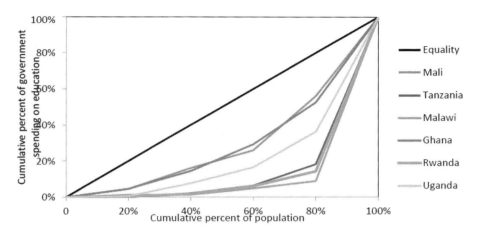

*Figure 23. Concentration Curves for Tertiary Education Public Expenditures in Selected SSA Countries.*
*Source: LMS data*

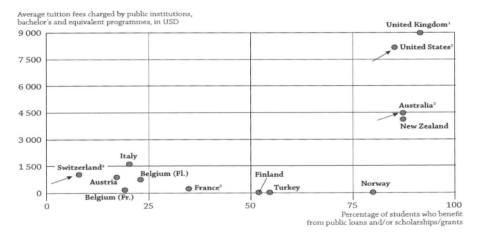

*Figure 24. Tuition Fees and Student Aid in Selected OECD Countries.*
*Source: Education at a Glance (2015)*

package. This amounts to offering tuition-free to all low-income students in net terms (Usher, 2016).

In designing and implementing any cost sharing scheme, policy makers should ensure that all students have equal opportunities to access and complete tertiary education, for both fairness and efficiency reasons. From an equity viewpoint,

145

modern theories of redistributive justice all converge in moving the traditional focus of social justice from outcomes—such as welfare or utilities—to opportunities. For example, Roemer (1998) recognized that, while individual bear some responsibility for their own welfare, they also face situations over which they have no control, which influence how much effort they can invest and the level of welfare that they are eventually able to achieve. Equity, therefore, demands an "equal opportunity policy" to equalize "advantages" among individuals from groups with different circumstances.

The economic efficiency argument in favor of equity is just as strong. A talented, low-income and/or minority high school graduate who is denied entry into tertiary education represents an absolute loss of human capital for the individual person and for society as a whole. The lack of opportunities for access and success in tertiary education leads to under-developed human resources and a resulting shortfall in the capacity to capture economic and social benefits (Harbison, 1964; Bowen and Bok, 1998; Ramcharan, 2004).

Bearing all the aspects analyzed so far into mind, an effective and equitable cost-sharing policy would require consideration of the following principles:

- *Universality*. When cost sharing is introduced, tuition fees should apply to all students. No distinction should be made among eligible students, based on their grades or the type of institution they enroll into.
- *Elimination of economic barriers*. No academically qualified student should be denied the opportunity to access and complete tertiary education for economic reasons.
- *Sequencing*. Tuition fees should be introduced only after a well-functioning and targeted student aid system is in place. Policy-makers should judiciously consider the net cost to students when allocating student aid.
- *Overcoming political opposition*. The political economy of cost sharing is as important as its technical aspects. Any policy change aiming at increasing cost sharing should carefully address the political dimensions.

Having these in mind, international experience points to the following three key technical dimensions of cost-sharing policies: (i) level of tuition fees, (ii) financial aid package, and (iii) policy monitoring and evaluation.

The first element that policy-makers and university leaders need to pay attention to is to set cost sharing at an appropriate level. It is essential to ensure that the resources that would be mobilized by introducing tuition fees and/or reducing related subsidies (food, lodging, transportation, etc.) are substantial enough to justify the high political cost of putting in motion this kind of financial reform. Policy-makers looking at the option of increasing cost sharing should base their decisions about the level of fees and subsidies on detailed financial scenarios. These scenarios, which would seek to balance financing needs and additional resources brought in through cost sharing, should factor in the likely impact of the country's demographic trends and the quantitative expansion needs. Together with setting the level of tuition fees, policy-makers ought to propose a clear and transparent mechanism for determining the yearly increase in relation to the official cost of living index.

The second set of considerations is related to the configuration and scope of the financial aid package that must accompany the planned increases in cost sharing. Junor and Usher (2004) defined three main categories of monetary barriers to accessing tertiary education: the cost-benefit barrier, the liquidity (cash-constraint) barrier, and the debt aversion (internalized liquidity constraint) barrier. The cost-benefit barrier occurs when an individual decides that the costs of attending university (including tuition and living expenses as well as the opportunity cost of not working during the duration of the study program) outweigh the returns to their education. The accuracy of a cost-benefit analysis depends on the correctness of the information used in the calculations of both costs and benefits. Research has shown that low-income students are less likely to have access to and use accurate information (Usher, 2005).

Liquidity barriers refer to a student's inability to gather the necessary resources to pursue tertiary education after having decided that the benefits do outweigh the costs. The amount of personal resources, resources from family and friends, scholarships, grants and/or loans are not enough to cover tertiary education costs, and they either do not have access to or are unaware of financing alternatives to supplement their existing resources.

Finally, debt aversion constraints exist when a student values the benefits of tertiary education relative to its costs, can borrow to access to sufficient financial resources, but chooses not to enroll because the financial resources available to him/her include loans. Prospective students with debt aversion simply do not wish to or are afraid to incur debt that must be repaid at some point in time.

In recognition of these constraints, the financial aid package should be sufficiently substantial to protect economically vulnerable students against cost increases, in the form of either tuition fees or living expenditures. In addition, it is important to achieve a proper balance between scholarships and student loans. Scholarships and grants should preferably be limited to the neediest students; otherwise it would defeat the purpose of greater cost sharing. At the same time, adequate information should be available to reach low-income students with debt aversion.

In theory, going the student loan route is preferable because of the sustainability dimension. If the program operates with reasonably high levels of repayment, it allows for inter-generational transfers that make it much more financially sustainable than scholarships, which are pure grants. But by their very nature, student loan institutions are faced with a constant dilemma. As instruments of equity promotion, they have an important social responsibility and need to be designed in such a way as to serve the funding needs of students from low-income groups. As financial institutions, they are required to respect basic principles of financial viability to be able to continue to operate in a sustainable fashion and serve generation after generation of students. These two inherently antagonistic objectives are difficult to reconcile and represent the fundamental challenge faced by any student loan scheme.

Few student loan institutions have managed to overcome this challenge. However, the Colombian Student Loan Agency, ICETEX, stands out as a success story, at least as far as mortgage-type loan systems are concerned (Box 31).

### Box 31. ICETEX, a Success Story

In 1950, Colombia created the first student loan institution in the world, called ICETEX (*Instituto Colombiano de Crédito Educativo y Estudios Técnicos en el Exterior*). It is still one of the best of its kind.

Between 2002 and 2011, the total number of annual ICETEX student loans (new and renewed) increased from 53,969 to 155,199, reaching 20% of the student population (one of the highest share in the developing world). The institution provides subsidized loans to students from the poorest families, ethnic and racial minorities, and students with disability. For instance, the poorest students have a zero real interest rate during the loan period.

ICETEX provides different payment options available to borrowers in order to ease repayment burdens by having payments grow as income grows. The repayment schedule is related to the evolution of the salaries of young graduates helping borrowers to pay.

Since the mid-2000s, ICETEX has benefited from a strong and innovative leadership team, who has been able to mobilize additional resources from government and multilateral donors. As a result, it has extended coverage to about 20 percent of the total student population, focusing on students from the lowest socioeconomic groups. This is the highest student loan coverage rate in Latin America and one of the best in the developing world. ICETEX has also improved its collection record—reducing overdue loans from 22 percent in 2007 to 13 percent in 2009— and modernized its management practices, bringing operating costs from 12 percent in 2002 to 3 percent in 2010. It has also entered into partnerships with participating universities to provide not only financial but also academic and psychological support to loan beneficiaries, which has greatly reduced dropout rates among loan beneficiaries, compared to students without a loan. To help students from the lowest income groups, ICETEX also supplements its student loans with scholarships to cover living expenses.

Today, ICETEX's main challenge is to continue increasing resources to finance more and poorer students. Evidence suggests that most dropouts for financial reasons could be avoided if there were more ICETEX loans and subsidies available.

(Source: OECD/World Bank, 2012)

Many factors explain the relative success or failure of any student loan scheme, including design considerations relative to the interest rate and administrative costs, the strength of its leadership, the quality of management practices and systems, and the ability to react rapidly and flexibly whenever problems arise. But loan collection is certainly the most important element. At the end of the day, no matter what type of student-loan system operates in a country, it is doomed unless its collection mechanism is designed and operates in an effective manner.

Traditional, mortgage-type student-loan schemes are vulnerable by design. Without an income-contingent provision, times of economic crisis are bound to cause repayment difficulties, as unemployment rises and incomes stagnate. Obviously, income-contingent loan systems have a higher probability of success. International experience shows that income-contingent loans, designed after the Australian and New Zealand HECS model, tend to have higher repayment rates. Not only are they more efficient in terms of loan recovery through the national tax system, but also they are more equitable since graduates pay a fixed proportion of their income and are exempted from repaying if they are unemployed or their income is below a pre-determined ceiling (Box 32). Econometric calculations have showed that the repayment burden with mortgage loans can be very high for low-income graduates—as much as 80 per cent for those in the lowest parts of the income distribution (Chapman et al., 2014). The student protest movement that erupted in Chile in 2011 was partly triggered by the growing loan burden of students benefitting from a CAE loan, which did not have an income-contingent provision.

---

### Box 32. Income Contingent Loans in Australia and New Zealand

Australia and New Zealand, which both charged little or no fees at their public institutions until the late 1980s, adopted similar strategies to increase cost sharing. They raised fees while introducing student loan programs that would allow students to pay for these higher fees over an extended period of time based on their incomes once they completed their education. But the two countries took somewhat divergent approaches in the characteristics of the income contingent repayment schedules they adopted.

In 1988, Australia chose a very innovative approach to cost sharing through its Higher Education Contribution Scheme (HECS). Faced with prospective widespread student opposition to tuition fees, Australian policy makers decided to use public funds to pay the fees while students were enrolled. All students participating in HECS were then obligated to repay these fees after completing their tertiary education as a percentage of their incomes, although students with below average incomes were exempted from repayment. HECS applies only to fees, not living expenses.

Beginning in 1990, New Zealand took the somewhat more traditional approach of imposing fees at their public institutions that students and their families would be required to pay upfront when they enrolled. Beginning in 1992, students could borrow to cover the cost of these fees as well as a substantial amount of living expenses. Repayment of these loans would then occur through the income tax system based on a percentage of students' income once they completed their education.

New Zealand and Australia have moved in different directions since they first adopted their income contingent student loan schemes. New Zealand began with a more market-based approach in which virtually all borrowers (who then constituted a small share of students) repaid on the basis of their income, with interest rates slightly below market levels. Over time, New Zealand has moved away from market-based principles by increasing subsidies, including exempting more low-income students from making repayments and forgiving interest on most loans. As a result, borrowing has grown substantially over time. The overriding policy concern now is that high debt levels are leading an increasing number of graduates to emigrate from New Zealand to avoid their loan repayment obligations. The government has responded by making repayments for borrowers who remain in New Zealand interest-free beginning in 2006.

Australia's HECS system, on the other hand, created a public expenditure challenge at first as a growing number of students enrolled in higher education without having to pay fees upfront. To reduce pressure on the budget, Australia moved in 1997 toward the market by reducing HECS subsidies and introducing three bands of HECS tuition fees as well as reducing the level of income exempted from HECS repayment. In addition, more market-based loan programs have been developed for the more than one-quarter of students who do not participate in HECS, including growing numbers of foreign students and domestic students enrolling in fields of study not covered by HECS. In 2016, the government closed the loophole that allowed Australians living abroad to leave their debt unpaid while being away from Australia. Estimates indicate that, as a result of that loophole, as much as A$800 million have remained unpaid since the launch of the student loan program in 1989.

So as Australia has moved to a more market-based student loan system, New Zealand has moved away from a market-oriented approach. But in both cases, the income-contingent loan system has contributed to significant increases in coverage and improved equity.

(Source: Chapman et al., 2014; Salmi and Hauptman, 2006)

The third and last technical consideration concerns the requirement to put in place a solid monitoring and evaluation system, with appropriate results indicators and baseline data, to follow up on the equity and efficiency impact of increased cost-sharing and watch out for possible unanticipated consequences. In Australia, the introduction of a uniform income-contingent loan system in 1988—the Higher Education Contribution Scheme (HECS)—was accompanied by a carefully designed monitoring system that allowed the government to verify that low-income students would not be adversely affected (Chapman, 2006). The Colombian student loan agency has been able to improve its repayment levels drastically in the past decade thanks to its institutional research program. Careful study of the academic trajectory of loan beneficiaries helped realize that the default cases were, in their majority, linked to economic difficulties faced by dropouts. ICETEX has moved to an integrated financial and academic approach that includes not only giving out loans to low-income students but also working collaboratively with their universities to ensure the availability of appropriate academic and psychological support for the most vulnerable students. This has greatly reduced dropout rates among loan beneficiaries, compared to students without a loan (Salmi, 2014).

Besides the technical elements of cost sharing policies, the political sensitivity of introducing tuition fees should be carefully taken into consideration to avoid any strong backlash. Not only do governments ensure that low-income students are protected against adverse equity effects through a comprehensive student aid system, but in addition they need to create ownership among the various stakeholders and mobilize support for the proposed measures through the kinds of consensus-building efforts described in Chapter 3. The main purpose of these consensus-building activities would be to establish a clear linkage between increased cost sharing and the expected improvements that additional financial resources would bring about. Sometimes university leaders are better placed to initiate this kind of dialogue at the institutional level rather than having the government authorities imposing cost sharing nationally. Box 33 documents a positive experience at the University of Sonora in Northern Mexico, where the rector was able to convince the students to start paying tuition fees. The public University of Trujillo in Peru went through a similar process a few years ago.

---

*Box 33. Consensus Building and Cost Sharing in Northern Mexico*

The Mexican constitution provides for free public education at all levels, and cost sharing has always been fiercely resisted by the professors and students of the country's largest public university, the National Autonomous University of Mexico (UNAM). By the late 1990s, the only payment the students would make was a symbolic contribution equivalent to 2 US Cents a year. In 1999 the university was closed for almost a year by a strike supported by the majority of its 270,000 students, after the rector suggested that middle income and high income students would pay tuition fees of about 140 US$. Part of the money raised in that manner was to be used to give grants to students from low income families.

In Northern Mexico, by contrast, the rector of the public University of Sonora was successful in introducing cost-sharing after initiating, in 1993, a consensus-building process to explain to the academic staff and the students the need for supplementary resources to maintain the quality of teaching and learning. In doing this, the rector took advantage of an ambiguous clause in the Mexican Constitution, which allows autonomous public universities to make all the necessary decisions to manage their financial resources notwithstanding the "free education" mandate.

After strong initial resistance, including a widely publicized 2,000-kilometer march by protesters from Hermosillo to Mexico City, the students accepted the principle of a yearly payment to generate supplementary resources coupled with a participatory mechanism to allocate these resources to equity and quality-improvement initiatives. Since 1994, the students have paid an annual contribution of about US$500. A joint student-faculty committee administers the funds, which are used to provide scholarships for low-income students, renovate classrooms, upgrade computer labs, and purchase scientific textbooks and journals. A poster is prepared every year to disseminate information on the use of the money collected at the beginning of the academic year.

*Income Generation*

Income generation at the institutional level is the third resource mobilization pillar that developing countries can rely on. Governments ought to actively encourage public tertiary education institutions to diversify their income sources beyond the collection of tuition fees. While the potential for resource mobilization is much more limited in low-income countries than in middle- and upper-middle income nations, tertiary education institutions could actively seek additional resources through donations, contract research, consultancies, continuing education and other fund-raising activities. Appendix 1 presents the range of income generation practices that can be found throughout the world.

Not all sources of income have the same potential. Contrarily to what is commonly assumed, technology transfer is not a highly productive activity from an income generation viewpoint, and very few institutions hit the jackpot with path-breaking innovations that can be successfully commercialized. Even at Harvard University, income from technology transfer licenses is equivalent to only 1% of annual fund raising receipts. Experience suggests that providing continuing education, undertaking productive activities and raising funds from alumni and corporations are the most important income generation sources.

Fund raising is not seen as a priority area in most developing countries, especially in low-income countries, based on the assumption that resources are limited throughout the economy and that philanthropy is not part of the culture. However, experience shows that, even in resource-constrained countries, there are always a few rich firms and persons to be found, who are likely to make financial contributions to universities if they are approached and presented with good reasons to make a donation. Box 34 summarizes the experience with fund raising in Europe. Even though, the economic conditions may be substantially different from those prevailing in developing countries, the fact that European universities are new to fund raising makes it likely that some lessons may be relevant to developing countries that have also little if any experience in this area.

> ## Box 34. Lessons from Fund-Raising Efforts in Europe
>
> A 2011 European Commission survey on the fund raising efforts of European universities found that success was related to three main factors. The first is what is defined as institutional privilege, i.e. the wealth and reputation of the university, as well as pre-existing relationships with potential donors. The second is the level of commitment of senior academic leaders and other research staff in this regard. The third and final factor has to do with the environmental of a university, namely its location and the geo-political context in which it operates.
>
> With regards to the type of donors, the survey showed that European universities raise money mostly from private corporations, while contributions from alumni are much less frequent.
>
> Experience indicates that successful fund-raising involves the following dimensions:
>
> • Commitment of management and governing bodies.
> • Full participation of academic staff.
> • Financial and human investment in fund-raising activities.
> • Rewards for staff successful in attracting philanthropic donations.
> • Production and dissemination of materials for fund-raising purposes, such as a website, leaflets and brochures.
> • Use of a database to maintain and update records on interactions with donors.
> • Reporting on philanthropy in universities' annual financial reports.
>
> One of the successful cases of effective fund-raising efforts came from the United Kingdom, where a government-sponsored matching funding scheme was set up in 2008 following similar positive experiences in Singapore and Hong Kong. Between 2008 and 2011, the government matched any eligible gift made to a participating tertiary education institution.
>
> (Sources: European Commission (2011), *Giving in Evidence: Fundraising from Philanthropy in European Universities*, Brussels. http://ec.europa.eu/research/era/docs/en/fundraising-from-philanthropy.pdf. Universities UK (3 April 2008), "Information for Members: Formal Launch of the Matched Funding Scheme for English HE institutions", *Investor in People*, London.)

To facilitate resource diversification at the institutional level, developing countries governments must make sure that two conditions are fulfilled. First, it is important to give the clear signal that success in fund raising will be rewarded rather than punished. A few industrial countries—for example Canada, Hong Kong,

Singapore and the United States—have designed effective matching grant programs as an incentive for fund-raising. While the lack of public resources will most likely make it difficult for developing countries to put in place similar matching programs, at the very least they should not penalize the most enterprising tertiary education institutions. Too often, Ministries of Finance are tempted to cut down the budget allocation to universities that are perceived as successful in raising funds from the private sector or from philanthropists, or to require that they transfer to the Treasury any surplus money that they raise by themselves. Practices that reduce government budget allocations to offset the incremental resources raised by the institutions and regulations that seek to recuperate the resources obtained by public tertiary institutions are self-defeating as they remove the incentive to generate additional income.

Second, it is important to put in place tax deductions that make it advantageous for firms and individuals to donate money to tertiary education institutions. Favorable tax incentives have been found to be crucial for stimulating philanthropic and charitable gifts to tertiary education institutions. In the United States, 2015 was a record year in terms of fund raising, with tertiary education institutions bringing in a total of $40 billion. Stanford University alone pulled in $1.6 billion, ahead of Harvard with $1.1 billion. Canada, Hong Kong, several Continental European countries and the United Kingdom also offer generous tax incentives to encourage donations to universities. In Latin America, Brazil, Colombia and Chile permit income tax deductions. Among developing countries, India has one of the most generous tax concession schemes, as all individual and corporate donations to universities are fully exempt from taxation (World Bank, 2002).

*Innovative Models: Social Innovation and Tertiary Education Funding*

"Hi there. My name is Ron Steen. I am selling 2% of my future earnings for a chance to go to college." This provocative invitation, posted on eBay in August 2006 by an incoming freshman at California State University, Fullerton, stirred up a controversial debate on the financing challenges faced by US tertiary education (Hess, 2008). Even though eBay did not allow Mr. Steen to keep his ad, his creative initiative illustrated at the time the need to explore new funding solutions. The estimated $1.2 trillion student debt in the United States today attests to the fact that the funding problem has not gone away, if anything it has grown more serious. And if this is true in one of the richest countries in the world, the urgency is even greater in many if not most middle- and low-income nations, where the rapidly growing demand for tertiary education opportunities against a background of constrained fiscal situation threatens to blow into a severe financial crisis.

Thus, in addition to the traditional forms of resource mobilization analyzed so far in this chapter, developing countries governments may want to challenge tertiary education stakeholders to think boldly and set up innovative partnerships that could generate additional funding in a direct or indirect way. In October 2015, the design firm OpenIDEO launched an online challenge to invite the global community to come up with novel ideas to address the financing crisis in tertiary education (McNeal, 2016). The competition yielded many innovative projects that could well be applied to a developing country context, or that could in turn spark other audacious income generation initiatives for tertiary education. The six most promising crowd-sourced solutions are featured below:

- *Tuition Heroes.* The company monitors the annual growth rate of tuition fees and grants a "tuition hero" status to colleges and universities that keep their tuition in line with normal inflation rates. "Tuition hero" institutions receive a badge to display on their websites and in marketing materials. The concept is similar to the way the Energy Star badge gives efficient appliances brand recognition. In this case, tertiary education institutions are recognized for their efforts to remain accessible to academically qualified low-income students.
- *PelotonU.* This project matches working adults who seek a college degree to online programs, and provides an office where they can study and receive additional tutoring and mentorship. It guarantees that students will graduate debt-free. To achieve this, PelotonU helps the students obtain a government scholarship for low-income students (Pell Grants), employers pay for student support, and local donors provide gap funding.
- *One Day Experience.* The company helps 15- to 24-year-olds with career counseling. It connects young adults who are not yet ready to choose a career and professionals who can give them a sense of what working in their industry would be like. The Barcelona-based company connects the indecisive young people with professionals in their fields of interest and gives them the opportunity of shadowing these mentors on the job for a day. The company provides "vouchers" that young adults use to cash in for one day on the job with experts in industries that they are interested in knowing better.
- *ALEX—Anyone's Learning Experience.* Based on the observation that colleges and universities have many empty seats in courses each year, Anyone's Learning Experience operates as a marketplace for online and in-person individual courses. People who want to take college courses, whether they are pursuing a degree for the first time or they are changing careers, log into the platform and can find university courses that have extra places. Students pay for individual classes at institutions and ALEX takes a commission of the sale.
- *Brighter Investment.* Inspired by Kiva, the online micro-lending organization, Brighter Investment provides a platform for potential donors who want to support university education for high-potential students in developing countries who face financial barriers to getting their degree. Aspiring students sign up with the platform and apply to the university of their choice. Vancouver-based Brighter Investment pools together funds from individual donors to cover the cost of tuition and living expenses. Students repay a share of their income for a set period of time after graduation.

- *1Gen2Fund.* This is a crowd-funding platform that helps first-generation students successfully complete a four-year college degree. The platform gives first generation students who meet certain criteria a place to ask for financial help, receive e-coaching and access additional support resources. Rather than competing for individual scholarships, students ask directly for funds, while alumni and other donors sign up to provide financial support and mentorship. 1Gen2Fund is a nonprofit organization that operates on a percentage of donations.

Other innovative financial technology initiatives have seen the light since the 2015 OpenIDEO challenge. Based on the same principles as ALEX, Bludesks.com has a more systematic concentration on low-income students and students in developing countries. Low-income students register at bludesks.com for discounted prices in on-campus courses in a large network of high-quality tertiary education institutions. Students receive academic credit for their completed courses and benefit from an on-campus experience. The participating institutions receive additional income by using their capacity more efficiently and get recognition for reaching out to a more diverse student population that otherwise could not afford them.

Climb Credit is a startup providing student loans that take into consideration the value of the courses financed and the expected returns. It focuses on sizeable, quantifiable increases in earnings. With an average loan size of $10,000, it tends to finance programs and courses less than a year in duration in about 70 carefully vetted institutions, ranging from coding to web design to programming robots for carmakers—the program with the highest return (The Economist, 2017).

Monash University's recent issuing of a green bond is also worth mentioning in this respect. The Australian university became the first education institution in the world to issue a "climate bond" in the US private placement market (SI, 2016). The university is planning to use the US$ 158 million raised to finance several green projects, such as environmentally-friendly buildings and solar panels.

## RESOURCE ALLOCATION MECHANISMS

To encourage an effective use of public resources and stimulate healthy competition among tertiary education institutions—both public and private ones—, developing countries governments could introduce a combination of performance-based budget allocation mechanisms that would provide financial incentives for improved institutional results and better alignment with national policy goals (OECD, 2007; Salmi and Hauptman, 2006). Policy-makers may consider four main types of innovative allocation mechanisms, separately or combined, to achieve this purpose:

- Output-based funding formulas: output or outcome measures are used to determine all or a portion of a funding formula, for example universities are paid for the number of students they graduate, sometimes with higher prices for graduates in certain fields of study or with specific skills.

- Performance contracts: governments enter into regulatory agreements with institutions on the basis of set performance-based objectives.
- Competitive funds: financing is awarded to peer-reviewed proposals designed to achieve institutional improvement or national policy objectives.
- Vouchers: students receive coupons representing a given financial value that allows them to pay for their studies at any tertiary education institution of their choice.

*Formula Funding*

A transparent and objective way of distributing funds for recurrent expenditures is to use a formula linking the amount of resources allocated to some indicator of institutional performance such as the number of graduates. Examples of countries that have built performance into their funding formulas include:

- Denmark, which has a "taximeter model" in which 30 to 50 percent of recurrent funds are paid in relation to the number of students who successfully pass exams every academic year;
- The Netherlands, where half of recurrent funding is based on the number of degrees awarded as an incentive to improve internal efficiency;
- South Africa, where the funding formula takes both the number of students enrolled and the number of graduates into consideration;
- Australia, where funding for doctoral student places is based on a formula comprising graduates (40%), research outputs (10%) and research income, including competitive winnings (50%).

A 2004 feasibility study in Malaysia calculated that the country could save between 10 and 30 percent of the operating budget of the public universities if resources were allocated on the basis of a funding formula using unit costs benchmarked against the better performing institutions in the tertiary education system (Innovation Associates, 2004).

*Performance Contracts*

Performance contracts are non-binding regulatory agreements negotiated between governments and tertiary education institutions, which define a set of mutual obligations. In return for the participating universities' commitment to meeting the performance targets established in the agreement, the government provides additional funding. The agreements may be with several or all institutions in a given tertiary education system, or with a single institution. All or a portion of the funding may be conditional upon the participating institutions meeting the requirements in the contracts. The agreements can be prospectively funded or reviewed and acted upon retrospectively.

Examples of countries or sub-national jurisdictions with performance contracts include:

- Chile, which introduced "performance agreements" on a pilot basis in the late 2000s, whereby four public universities volunteered to receive additional resources to implement a carefully negotiated institutional improvement plan with clear progress and outcome indicators. The scheme has since been extended to a large number of public and private universities.
- Denmark, which uses "development contracts" setting long-term improvement goals for the institutions.
- Finland, which has contracts that set out general goals for the entire tertiary education system as well as specific goals for each institution.
- France, which since 1989 has allocated about one third of the recurrent budget through four-year performance contracts. Payments are made when the contracts are signed, with a post-evaluation to assess the degree and effectiveness of implementation.
- Several US States, for example Louisiana, Maryland, Michigan, North Dakota, South Carolina, Tennessee, and Virginia, use some kinds of postsecondary education "compacts".

*Competitive Funds*

Competitive funds have proven their strength and value as an effective and flexible resource allocation mechanism for investment purposes (Box 35). With this mechanism, institutions are generally invited to formulate project proposals that are reviewed and selected by committees of peers according to transparent procedures and criteria. Positive experience in countries as diverse as Chile, Egypt and Indonesia has shown the ability of competitive funds to help improve quality and relevance, promote pedagogical innovation, and foster better management, objectives that are difficult to achieve through funding formulas. Developing countries governments could seriously consider piloting a competitive fund as a channel for allocating public investment funds to tertiary education institutions.

The actual eligibility criteria vary from country to country and depend on the specific policy changes sought. In Argentina and Indonesia, for instance, proposals could be submitted by entire universities or by individual faculties or departments. In Chile, both public and private institutions were allowed to compete. In Egypt a fund was set up in the early 1990s specifically to stimulate reforms in engineering education.

One of competitive funds' principal benefits is the practice of transparency and fair play through the establishment of clear criteria and procedures and the creation of an independent monitoring committee. An additional benefit of competitive funding mechanisms is that they encourage universities to undertake strategic planning activities, which help them formulate proposals based on a solid identification of needs and a rigorous action plan.

### Box 35. Effectiveness of Competitive Funds

Well-designed competitive funds can greatly stimulate the performance of tertiary education institutions and can be powerful vehicles for transformation and innovation. One of the first such funds, Argentina's Quality Improvement Fund (FOMEC), which was supported by the World Bank, was instrumental in encouraging universities to engage in strategic planning for the strengthening of existing programs and the creation of new interdisciplinary graduate programs. Within universities, faculties that had never worked together started cooperating in the design and implementation of joint projects. In Egypt, the Engineering Education Fund helped introduce the notion of competitive bidding and peer evaluation in the allocation of public investment resources. The fund promoted, in an effective manner, the transformation of traditional engineering degrees into more applied programs with close linkages with industry.

A fundamental prerequisite for the effective operation of competitive funds—and one of their significant benefits—is the practice of transparency and fair play through the establishment of clear procedures and selection criteria, as well as the creation of an independent monitoring committee. In Chile, a second wave of tertiary education reforms was supported by a competitive fund for diversification (development of technical institutes in the non-university sector) and quality improvement of all public universities. Brazil, Mexico, and Uganda have encouraged the formation of advanced human capital in science and technology through competitive funding mechanisms. In all these cases, the participation of international peer review experts has figured prominently.

In countries with a diversified tertiary education system with unequally developed types of institutions, there may be a compelling argument for offering several financing windows with different criteria, or for setting up compensatory mechanisms to create a level playing field between strong and weak institutions. In a project supported by the World Bank in Indonesia during the 1990s, three different windows were designed to serve universities according to their actual institutional capacity. In the last tertiary education project financed by the World Bank in China in the early 2000s, the top universities were required to form a partnership with a university in a poor province as a condition for competing. In Egypt the competitive fund in the Engineering Education Reform project in the late 1980s had a special window for technical assistance to help less experienced engineering schools prepare well-formulated proposals. In Chile, a special window was opened to provide preparation funds for universities requiring assistance in strategic planning and subproject formulation.

(Source: World Bank, 2002)

*Vouchers*

A few governments keen on introducing more competition in their tertiary education system have also considered using grants, student loans and vouchers as a possible funding approach based on student demand, following the recent examples of several Eastern European and Central Asian countries, such as the former Soviet Republics of Kazakhstan, Georgia and Azerbaijan, and Lithuania. The purpose of demand-based funding is to promote greater competition among tertiary education providers in response to student interests by giving public support indirectly through the users rather than directly to the tertiary education providers (Salmi and Hauptman, 2006). While many countries use voucher-type arrangements to pay institutions for enrolments driven by student preferences, there are few that rely on grants or demand-side vouchers in the form of coupons provided to students to pay for recurrent expenses. The most prominent example can be found in Kazakhstan, where about 20% of the students receive voucher-like education grants that they carry with them to the public or private university of their choice, so long as they opt for studying a grant-carrying program aligned with the country's development priorities. The eligibility of beneficiary students is determined by their score in the highly competitive Unified National Test and their expressed choice of program of study. As far as the participating tertiary education institutions are concerned, eligibility is a function of their standing with the quality assurance unit of the Ministry of Education and Science, and the subjects they offer.

Even after only a few years of operation, the Kazakh voucher system appears to be functioning as an effective allocation instrument to reward those institutions that are perceived as better performing and offer national priority subjects. All tertiary education institutions, public and private alike, are very attentive to their ability to attract education grant beneficiaries. The voucher scheme also seems to be a powerful tool for promoting the growth of the better quality private institutions, which have been able to multiply the number of grant beneficiaries whom they attract within the first three years of implementation of the vouchers scheme (OECD/World Bank, 2007).

The Universities for All program (ProUni) launched in 2006 in Brazil constitutes an interesting variation of a voucher scheme. Under that program, the Brazilian government uses tax incentives to "buy" places in private universities for deserving, academically qualified low income students who were not admitted in the top public universities because of the limited number of places. In Colombia, a similar scheme operates in the Department of Antioquia. A public-private partnership bringing together the local authorities, a group of private universities and a number of private sector employers offers qualified low income students who could not find a place in a public university the opportunity to study at one of the local private universities. The students get a scholarship equivalent to 75% of the tuition costs and receive a loan from the National Student Loan Agency (ICETEX) for the remaining 25%.

Another example of student demand-based funding was put in place in 2015 in Colombia. The Government introduced a new scholarship scheme at the national level, called *Ser Pila Paga* ("It pays to be a good student"), whereby the top high school graduates from low-income families could get funding to study at any accredited university, public or private.

CONCLUSION

*My interest is in the future*
*because I am going to spend the rest of my life there.*

Charles Kettering

Financing reform is not an end in itself. Its primary purpose is ensuring medium and long-term funding sustainability in order to expand tertiary education opportunities, improve the quality and relevance of existing programs, and build research capacity. This is why it is an essential part of the national vision about the future of tertiary education and the reform plans of any country keen on strengthening the contribution of its tertiary education system to economic and social development.

The reality on the ground is that most developing countries face serious financial tensions and difficult funding trade-offs as they attempt to reconcile the three fundamental objectives of quantitative expansion, quality improvements and R&D strengthening, as illustrated by Figure 25.

Quantitative
Expansion in an
Equitable Manner

Improved Quality
and Relevance of
Teaching &
Learning

Strengthened
Research Capacity

*Figure 25. Fundamental Tensions among Financing Needs*

In this context, the elaboration of a sustainable financing strategy for the development of tertiary education in any country can be guided by the following six principles.
- plan the shape and institutional configuration of the tertiary education system strategically, bearing in mind that this determines, to a large extent, the cost of expanding coverage and operating tertiary education institutions;
- mobilize sufficient resources, public and private, to meet the needs for quantitative expansion and quality improvement on an equitable basis;

- guarantee that cost-sharing is always accompanied by adequate and sufficient student aid;
- rely on funding mechanisms that are performance-based and, when appropriate, allocated in a competitive manner;
- ensure full compatibility and consistency among the various funding instruments used; and
- offer objectivity and transparency in the design and operation of all funding mechanisms (policy objectives sought, rules and procedures for resource allocation).

## NOTES

[1] While it is true that Scotland does not charge fees for Scottish students, 45% of the Scottish universities teaching income is financed by the tuition fees paid by foreign students and non-Scottish UK students, up from 39% in 2010. To a certain extent, the fee-paying students are cross-subsidizing the Scottish students.

[2] Critique of the Gotha Program, chapter IV (1875).

# ROLE OF THE DONORS

## WHAT WORKS: LESSONS OF EXPERIENCE FROM DONOR INTERVENTIONS

Even though bilateral and multilateral donors have traditionally given priority to basic education as part of the global Education for All commitment (Fast Track Initiative and Global Education Partnership), donor support for investment in tertiary education has continued in many developing countries, even in low-income economies. Experience shows that, to have a robust and durable impact, donor programs and projects in support of tertiary education development must be guided by the following principles:

- Holistic design
- Reliance on incentives
- Attention to sustainability

### Holistic Project Design

The theory of change and capacity development proposed in this document to guide the interventions of donor agencies rests on the premise that, in complex tertiary education environments, better quality research and teaching outcomes cannot be obtained without the proper alignment of all the key factors contributing to these outcomes. It is not sufficient to focus on one aspect, for example just injecting large amounts of additional financial resources or financing scholarships to train professors, while neglecting the other drivers of performance of tertiary education institutions.[1]

Theories of change in basic education point to a large number of factors affecting educational outcomes, such as the quality of teaching, time spent on tasks, the quality of educational facilities, the curriculum, or language of instruction. The complexity is likely to be even greater in the case of tertiary education institutions, considering their multiple missions of teaching, research and service to the community and the local economy.

The appreciation of these elements of complexity is consistent with the findings of a recent review of theories of change in development. "In tension with the drive for more assurance of results, there is a growing recognition of the complexities, ambiguities and uncertainties of development work, involving complex political and social change in dynamic country contexts. Theory of change thinking is viewed as one approach to help people deal positively with the challenges of complexity" (Vogel, 2012, p. 11).

Unlike what happens at the lower levels of education, the interaction between research and teaching adds a dimension of complication to the measurement of results in tertiary education. Besides inculcating appropriate values and attitudes to young people, the main purpose of primary and secondary education is to transmit existing knowledge. By contrast, a core mission of universities is to create new knowledge, in addition to teaching existing knowledge. As a matter of fact, the synergy between the production and dissemination of knowledge is one of the characteristics and strengths of universities (Boyer, 1990; Clark, 1995).

The joint production of education and research makes the separation of results between research output and graduates somehow artificial. The quality of research influences, to a large extent, the quality of teaching and learning. Some studies argue that teaching can also positively influence the direction and quality of research (Becker and Kennedy, 2004). This feature of academic life needs to be taken into consideration when examining the determinants of the quality of graduates. For these reasons, the proposed theory of change looks at the causal chain leading to improved research and graduates within a single framework.

Furthermore, the range of monetary and prestige incentives that countries and higher education institutions use to reward good research and teaching affect directly the behavior of academics and the likelihood of a strong link between the two activities. For example, under the influence of the global rankings, a growing number of universities are offering special monetary incentives for publications in prestigious international journals, which can result in excessive recognition of research contributions compared to teaching.

Figure 26 represents the general theory of change for increasing the supply and quality of graduates and improving the production and quality of research by strengthening the capacities that affect these two outcomes. After identifying two sets of context factors—system-level and institutional level dimensions—that affect the performance of tertiary education institutions by directly influencing their mode of operation, the figure shows a sequence of inputs and intermediary results that, according to the literature, lead to better graduates and research.

The main implication of this framework is that donor programs and projects must take these dimensions of complexity into account in the design of their programs and projects in support of tertiary education development. A related, important lesson from international experience is that interventions at both the national and institutional levels are best designed and implemented hand in hand as they are mutually reinforcing and cannot operate in isolation. For example, establishing a national quality assurance agency (evaluation, accreditation, quality audits, etc.) without empowering and supporting individual tertiary education institutions to build up their own internal quality assurance procedures and capability is unlikely to make a significant impact on the quality and relevance of teaching and learning. A Swedish SIDA program to enhance the scientific research capacity of Bolivia in the early 2000s included both support to the Research Council at the national level and assistance to individual universities.

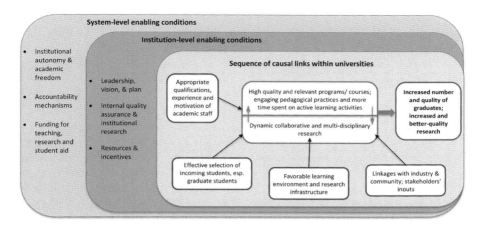

*Figure 26. General Theory of Change for Producing More/Better-Qualified Graduates and More/Higher Quality Research*

Similarly, several tertiary education projects supported by bilateral or multilateral donors have facilitated the introduction of integrated management information systems (MIS) at both the national and institutional levels, on the assumption that neither the state nor individual institutions can formulate and implement reforms without effective monitoring and management tools. Governments need reliable data from the tertiary education institutions to design national policies and individual institutions must use data from the rest of the system to be able to do benchmarking to guide their strategic planning. In the late 1990s, in Argentina, a World Bank-financed project helped put in place Intranet and Internet networks among all the public universities as well as between the universities and the outside world. Software for all dimensions of academic management was developed and combined into an integrated MIS that provides information at the level of each individual institution and consolidates this information into a program run by the national tertiary education authorities for monitoring and planning purposes. Many universities were at first cautious or even hostile, but ended up enthusiastically embracing these innovations because the adaptations helped them invest in modern information and communication technologies and provided them with useful management tools.

Thinking holistically applies not only to the scope of the donor programs and projects, but also to the time dimension involved in carrying out interventions that seek to transform tertiary education systems and institutions. Improvements in research and teaching do not happen instantly or even quickly. Institutional change and capacity development are long-term processes that require many years of sustained interventions. For example, to start a new program at the master's level would require, in addition to designing an appropriate curriculum, sending a few promising young academics overseas to obtain a PhD, which would take four to

165

five years. Then it would take another two years to graduate a first cohort of master students. Similarly, to build up the research capacity of a university department in a partner country, one would need to set up new labs and train a minimum core of researchers. Once the new team is in place, it would take several years to see the results of the new research activities.

Oftentimes, donor agencies supporting tertiary education institutions in developing countries are not always able to factor into the design and organization of their programs the fact that it takes a long time to bring about meaningful change. Their support is often embedded in projects whose duration does not exceed four or five years, reflecting regular budget cycles and common restrictions affecting the length of financial commitments to aid programs and projects. It is therefore important to sequence donor activities in accordance with the time requirements and the institutional capacity of the implementation agencies in developing countries.

The time factor does not have implications only for the design and duration of donor interventions but also for the measurement of results and impact. Donor agencies must integrate this important variable into their evaluation framework, being aware in particular that the effects of their capacity development interventions may not become visible until many years after the end of the program or project.

*Incentives*

Relying on positive incentives to induce change, rather than mandatory edicts and externally defined investments, has a positive influence on outcomes, as tertiary education institutions and actors tend to respond more readily to constructive incitements (World Bank, 2002). Several donors, both multilateral and bilateral, have had positive experience with the use of competitive funds as an effective vehicle of change. Well-designed and flexibly managed competitive funds can greatly encourage tertiary education institutions to transform themselves, thus acting as powerful vehicles for innovation and enhanced performance. Argentina's Quality Improvement Fund (FOMEC), set up in the mid-1990s with World Bank financial support, was instrumental in inducing universities to engage in strategic planning as the first step towards identifying which existing programs would be consolidated and which new interdisciplinary graduate programs would be established. Within universities, faculties that had never collaborated started cooperating in the design and implementation of joint projects (World Bank, 2002).

The voluntary nature of participation in programs financed competitive funds is an important aspect. The availability of additional resources can encourage tertiary education institutions to embrace reforms and innovations, while leaving out those not willing or ready to transform themselves. Sometimes several policy interventions can be mutually reinforcing. In Argentina, Chile, Indonesia and Romania, for instance, only universities participating in the accreditation process defined by the national quality assurance system were eligible to compete for the competitive innovation and quality enhancement grants funded by the World Bank.

*Sustainability*

More effective results can be achieved if the impact of donor intervention is not limited to the project period but continues beyond the availability of donor-supported technical and financial assistance. Several design features can contribute to increased sustainability of donor investment. First, the likelihood of smooth project implementation and increased longer-term sustainability is much bigger if the beneficiary tertiary education institutions can contribute at least part of the funding. Using a sliding scale—diminishing the donor contribution and increasing the counterpart contribution every year—can be a practical approach for ensuring sustainability beyond the project life (Salmi, 2012b).

Second, generic governance and management constraints that might negatively affect the implementation of project activities should be addressed as part of the preparation process. This reinforces the importance of undertaking a thorough diagnosis of sectorial issues ahead of project preparation that can help identify critical governance bottlenecks that can affect the ability of achieving project objectives. In the same vein, support for tertiary education operations should not involve only the national authorities in charge of tertiary education but also the Ministry of Finance and the Ministry of Economic Development, to ensure full integration of the project in the country's economic and social development priorities.

Finally, implementation can be smoother if the project is developed with, rather than for the beneficiary institutions. Ideally, the tertiary education themselves should spell out the specific objectives and targets, as they must have primary implementation responsibilities. Project design should therefore provide for an appropriate balance between decentralization of responsibilities to universities and central coordination.

## ROADMAP FOR DONOR SUPPORT IN TERTIARY EDUCATION

This section proposes a roadmap for donor assistance in support of tertiary education reform, starting with the exploration of possible roles for donor agencies, considering the need to adapt to specific country conditions, and underlining the importance of donor coordination.

*The Role of Donor Agencies*

Notwithstanding the fact that the success of tertiary education reforms is predicated upon the willingness of concerned stakeholders to take full ownership of the proposed changes, the international donors community could also play a useful role in support of the reform and development process in tertiary education. First, they could offer technical and financial assistance to help with the consensus building part during the vision development and strategic planning phases preceding the design and implementation of comprehensive reforms.

Another useful contribution that some of the donors could make in this context is to play the role of "honest broker" by convening meetings that would bring together stakeholders who would not normally collaborate, thus creating a safe space where the various stakeholders could start a policy dialogue about possible reforms.

The third important type of collaborative activities that the donors could usefully support would be the preparation of analytical reports to provide an objective diagnosis of the challenges faced by the tertiary education system in a given country and explore reform options based on relevant international experience. This could include putting in place effective monitoring systems to measure progress towards attaining the SDGs.

Finally, the donors could help partner countries ensure the sustainability of reforms through co-financing of investments to accompany the initial period of the reform, focusing donor funding on the most vulnerable elements of the program. For example, rather than offering scholarships for doctoral studies in OECD countries without any concern for possible brain drain, support for PhD programs in the strongest local universities can go a long way towards building the research capacity of developing countries. Similarly, instead of just financing advanced equipment for scientific laboratories, the donors could enter into an agreement whereby they would finance maintenance and equipment renewal expenses using a sliding down schedule, while the counterpart agency or institution would cover a progressively larger share of expenses over the duration of the project, thus guarantying the availability of national funds once the external funding stops.

*Adapting donor support to country conditions.* Table 30 provides a summary of the range and categories of reforms and capacity building interventions that donor agencies could support in developing countries.

Donor agencies will need to define priorities and a mix of interventions appropriate to the specific conditions of each country. The factors to be taken into consideration for that purpose will be the political and macroeconomic circumstances, the state of development of the tertiary education system, the urgency of policy changes needed, and the country's readiness and appetite for undertaking meaningful reforms. In selecting its areas of interventions, the donors must carefully weigh the balance of financial cost, technical complexity and political difficulty of any possible reform.

In determining priorities for the type of policy reforms that donors can support, it is worthwhile discriminating between first- and second-generation reforms.[2] First-generation reforms, which address core problems of tertiary education systems (equity, quality, efficiency, governance, financing), are the first steps in moving from one way of doing things toward a more appropriate approach. These reforms include, for instance, setting up an accreditation agency in previously unregulated systems, adopting an academic credit system, moving from open-ended admissions to selective access, creating non-university institutions alongside traditional

168

*Table 30. Matrix of Possible Donor-Supported Interventions*

| Modality / Objective | Policy Reform | Capacity Building |
|---|---|---|
| Increasing Coverage and Equity | Affirmative action programs<br>Lifelong Learning framework (recognition of prior learning, pathways, credit transfer) | Development of non-university institutions (polytechnics, community colleges)<br>Outreach and retention programs<br>Student services |
| Improved Quality & Relevance | Quality assurance law and agency<br>Regulatory framework for private providers | Faculty development<br>Curriculum development<br>Modernization of pedagogical practices<br>Library development<br>Internal quality assurance systems<br>University-industry linkages |
| Increased Research Output & Impact | Innovation policy framework<br>Career paths for young researchers<br>Digital infrastructure | Development of postgraduate education<br>Research infrastructure<br>Centers of excellence |
| Improved Stewardship and Governance | Vision for the future of tertiary education<br>Creation of buffer agency<br>Labor market observatories | Strengthening of planning and monitoring capacity at national level<br>Institutional MIS |
| More Sustainable Financing | Cost sharing<br>Performance-based allocation (funding formula, performance contracts) | Targeting and effectiveness of student aid<br>Financial management at institutional level |

universities, allowing private providers to operate, making public tertiary institutions autonomous, introducing cost sharing through fees and reduced subsidies in public institutions, transforming scholarships into student loans, or starting to rely on formula funding.

Second-generation reforms are those undertaken by countries that have already addressed many of their basic problems but need to fine-tune existing arrangements to take first-generation reforms a step farther or to correct unintended effects. These second-generation reforms would include, for instance, strengthening the quality assurance system, clarifying the distinction between for-profit and non profit private institutions, extending the eligibility of a student loan program to all tertiary education institutions in a diversified system, introducing flexible mechanisms of articulation and credit transfer among institutions, and setting up competency-based evaluation mechanisms for online courses.

Finally, in low-income countries emerging from an armed conflict or a large-scale natural catastrophe—such as the 2010 earthquake that killed 200,000 people in Haiti—, donors should distinguish between support for immediate reconstruction needs and long-term development efforts. In the first instance, the priority would go to facilities, digital infrastructure, educational material, textbooks, and short-term capacity building. At the same time, it would be important to pave the way for preparing a sustainable development strategy (vision and plan) for the long term and strategic plans for the leading institutions in the country. The donors could also provide assistance for North-South and South-South strategic partnerships between institutions, and for use of the Diaspora.

*Importance of donor coordination*   An important lesson from low-income countries, especially the fragile nations emerging from conflicts or large-scale natural catastrophes, is the need for close coordination among donors. Lack of coordination has two potentially negative effects. First, the assistance components offered by the various donors may not be always related to the priority needs of the system and/or institutions targeted. Second, the programs and projects supported by the donors may not be fully consistent or even compatible among themselves, which could lead to serious dysfunctions in the system.

To mitigate these risks, the Ministry of Higher Education needs to play a proactive role in orchestrating donor coordination. This is important in order to ensure that the various donor programs and projects fit coherently in the Government's own list of development priorities. Having a well-crafted vision and a credible strategic plan will help significantly in this respect. The impact of development aid on the sustainability of tertiary education reforms in partner countries could be even stronger and more lasting if the entire donor community would agree to work together and coordinate its financial contributions in support of the government's tertiary education strategic plan, as has happened quite successfully over the past 15 years with the Education for All plans and the Fast-Track Initiative in many countries throughout the developing world. This support could be organized around key projects prepared by the government or around an entire slice of the national reform program.

## NOTES

[1]   This section draws on a theory of change developed by the author in the context of a recent evaluation of NORHED, the Norwegian Government's program in support of partnerships with developing countries universities (DPMG, 2014).

[2]   This concept was introduced by the author in Constructing Knowledge Societies (World Bank, 2002).

# CONCLUSION

## *The Reform Imperative*

The sea is dangerous and its storms are terrible, but these obstacles have never been sufficient reason to remain ashore.

(Ferdinand Magellan, 1520)

Many developing nations can take pride in the impressive growth of tertiary level enrollment attained in the past two decades. Coverage has significantly increased on all continents and pockets of high quality teaching and leading edge research are found in several developing economies. Some of the countries have also pioneered innovative features, such as student loan agencies, national assessments of student learning outcomes, labor market observatories and risk-based quality assurance approaches. But despite these achievements, the overall situation of tertiary education systems in developing nations is one of severe access and completion disparities, poor quality of teaching and learning, lack of relevance, low research production, inadequate governance and insufficient funding.

In a recent visit to the United States, the Prime Minister of the Canadian province of Ontario observed that, increasingly, the main source of comparative advantage on which economies can rely on is not capital, technology or raw materials anymore, but the talent of their educated population. Similarly, in one of her first speeches, the new Prime Minister of Norway emphasized in early 2015 the need for her country to move away from oil and gas dependence and build its future on knowledge. Developing countries keen on accelerating economic progress and achieving the Sustainable Development Goals should display the same conviction and recognize that tertiary education is essential for the creation, dissemination and application of knowledge. Tertiary education institutions can play a crucial role in fostering the knowledge, insights, innovative abilities and creative thinking needed for designing and implementing effective poverty alleviation strategies. Countries must therefore place tertiary education capacity building at the center of their development agenda.

For this purpose, the governments of developing economies must develop a long-term vision of the future of their tertiary education system and set in motion an appropriate set of structural reforms and investments that would help raise access and reduce disparities, improve quality and relevance, strengthen research capacities, modernize governance practices and promote increased accountability, and achieve financial sustainability.

In the process, developing countries must find sustainable solutions to address two critical trade-offs. First, they must be able to meet the increasing demand with appropriately good quality and relevant programs. Second, they need to alleviate the pressure that the growing number of graduates puts on relatively weak labor markets to avoid growing unemployment among educated youths. This can be achieved only by encouraging students to seek the types of institutions and programs that have high returns because they are closely linked to the needs of the economy and society and offer a modern curriculum and innovative pedagogical practices.

The reforms should induce tertiary education institutions to leave their comfort zone and become more innovative in responding to the evolving needs of students and the regional economy. Moving away from a "business as usual" mindset requires courageous initiatives to cultivate the uniqueness of each tertiary education institution through programs and curricula focused on relevant niche areas, interactive pedagogical approaches, quality enhancement practices that incorporate the measurement of student learning and labor market outcomes, and closer links to employers, the community and the region.

Among all the areas of reform, changes in the way tertiary education institutions are financed and public resources are allocated are the most difficult to introduce. Being able to undertake reforms consensually designed and accepted as long-term national State policies, rather than as the program of a given government driven by short-term electoral considerations, may be the biggest challenge in many developing countries where there is little tradition of democratic reform based on bi-partisan politics.

And yet, without a sustainable funding strategy in the long term, no tertiary education system can experience notable improvements in its performance. It is doubtful that any country can successfully balance the quantitative growth imperative and the need for improved quality and relevance in the absence of sufficient resources and appropriate financial incentives to encourage innovative approaches in the pursuit of better results. At the same time, the financing reforms aimed at transforming and developing tertiary education in a sustainable manner must preserve the public good mission of universities and protect the equity imperative that should permeate government policies in support of tertiary education development.

Against this background, the donor community could use its convening influence to support policy dialogue and knowledge sharing around critical tertiary education reform issues in partner countries, and mobilize multilateral and bilateral aid resources to finance priority investments in tertiary education development. Lessons about the relative impact of different forms and types of support for tertiary education reveal that external contributions are more likely to be successful if they are appropriate to the specific circumstances and challenges of each developing country, based on a careful study of sector issues, and predicated on strategic planning at the national, local, and institutional levels. Perhaps most important in ensuring the effectiveness of their inputs will be the donors' willingness and ability to work in a coordinated manner in supporting the partner countries' own vision and reform program.

Finally, the rapidly changing world in which tertiary education institutions function today generates disruptive effects that create a whole range of opportunities and challenges influencing the role, mission, mode of operation and performance of these institutions. How these forces in the tertiary education ecosystem play out in each country will determine the new "perils" and "promises" that are likely to shape the development and contribution of tertiary education in the years to come.

# REFERENCES

Aagaard, K., & Mejlgaard, N. (Eds.). (2012). *Dansk forskningspolitik efter årtusindskiftet*. Aarhus: Aarhus University Press.

Adams, J. (2013). Collaboration: The fourth age of research. *Nature, 497*(7451), 557–560.

Aghion, P., & Howitt, P. (2006). Appropriate growth policy: A unifying framework. *Journal of the European Economic Association, 4*, 269–314.

Agrawal, A., & Cockburn, I. M. (2002). *University research, industrial R&D, and the anchor tenant hypothesis* (NBER Working Paper 9212). Cambridge, MA: National Bureau of Economic Research.

Alon, S. (2016, April). Is class-based or race-based affirmative action best? *University World News, 410*.

Altbach, P. (2001). Academic freedom: International realities and challenges. *Higher Education, 41*, 205–219.

Association of Pacific Rim Universities (APRU). (2016). *APRU impact report*. Hong Kong: APRU. Retrieved from http://apru.org/news/item/660-apru-impact-report-2016

Asian Development Bank (ADB). (2012). *Access without equity? Finding a better balance in higher education in Asia*. Manila: The Asian Development Bank.

Aspiring Minds. (2015). *National employability report: Engineers*. Retrieved from www.aspiringminds.com

Bagde, S., Epple, D., & Taylor, L. (2016). Does affirmative action work? Caste, gender, college quality, and academic success in India. *American Economic Review, 106*(6), 1495–1521. Retrieved from http://dx.doi.org/10.1257/aer.20140783

Barbaro, B., & Eder, S. (2016, May 31). Former trump university workers call the school a 'Lie' and a 'Scheme' in testimony. *New York Times*. Retrieved from http://www.nytimes.com/2016/06/01/us/politics/donald-trump-university.html

Barber, M., & Mourshed, M. (2007). *How the world's best-performing school systems come out on top*. New York, NY: McKinsey & Company.

Barber, M., Donnelly, K., & Rizvi, S. (2013). *An avalanche is coming: Higher education and the revolution ahead*. London: IPPR. Retrieved from http://med.stanford.edu/smili/support/FINAL%20Avalanche%20Paper%20110313%20(2).pdf

Barceló, B. (2015, November 5). Educación universitaria, ¿camino hacia el progreso? *Este País* (online newspaper). Retrieved from http://estepais.com/articulo.php?id=313&t=educacion-universitariacamino-hacia-el-progreso

Barkley, E. F., Cross, K. P., & Major, C. H. (2005). *Collaborative learning techniques: A handbook for college faculty*. San Francisco, CA: Jossey-Bass.

Becker, W. E., & Kennedy, P. E. (2005). *Does teaching enhance esearch in Economics?* Retrieved from http://www.aeaweb.org/annual_mtg_papers/2005/0107_1430_0901.pdf

Benedict, L. (2009). Academic freedom at the crossroads in the United States. *International Higher Education, 57*. Retrieved from http://ejournals.bc.edu/ojs/index.php/ihe/issue/view/833

Birdsall, N. (1996). Public spending on higher education in developing countries: Too much or too little? *Economics of Education Review, 15*(4), 407–419.

Bloom, D. E., Canning, D., Chan, K., & Luca, D. L. (2014). Higher education and economic growth in Africa. *International Journal of African Higher Education, 1*(1), 22–57.

Blumenstyk, G. (2014, December 2). Blowing off class? We know. *New York Times*.

Bollag, B. (2003). *Improving tertiary education in Africa: Things that work*. Washington, DC: The World Bank, Africa Region Working Paper Series.

Bowen, W. G., & Bok, D. (1998). *The shape of the river*. Princeton, NJ: Princeton University Press.

Boyer, E. L. (1990). *Scholarship reconsidered: Priorities of the professoriate*. Princeton, NJ: Carnegie Foundation for the Advancement of Teaching.

Brand, J. E., Pfeffer, F. T., & Goldrick-Rab, S. (2012). *Interpreting community college effects in the presence of heterogeneity and complex counterfactuals*. Wisescape Working Paper. Retrieved from http://wiscape.wisc.edu/uploads/media/c8d24231-d12e-403c-adab-848cb1321e13.pdf

Buderi, R. (2014). Olin College President Rick Miller on reengineering engineering. *Xeconomy*. Retrieved from http://www.xconomy.com/boston/2014/09/24/olin-college-president-rick-miller-on-reengineering-engineering/?single_page=tru

Burridge, N., Payne, A. M., & Rahmani, N. (2016). Education is as important for me as water is to sustaining life: Perspectives on the higher education of women in Afghanistan. *Gender and Education, 28*(1), 128–147. doi: Retrieved from http://dx.doi.org/10.1080/09540253.2015.1096922

Burton, R. C. (1995). *Places of inquiry: Research and advanced education in modern universities.* Berkeley, CA: University of California Press.

Business Insider. (2016, April 2). Cash-hungry university changed its admission standards. *University World News, 407.* Retrieved from http://www.universityworldnews.com/article.php?story=20160402140827924

Campos, I. M., & Valadares, E. C. (2008). *Inovação Tecnológica e Desenvolvimento Econômico.* (Unpublished paper). Retrieved from http://www.schwartzman.org.br/simon/blog/inovacaomg.pdf

Carey, K. (2006). *College rankings reformed: The case for a new order in higher education.* Washington, DC: Education Sector.

Carnevale, A., & Smith, N. (2013, January). Preparing America for middle-skill work. *The Community College Journal.*

Chapman, B. (2006). Income related student loans: Concepts, international reforms and administrative challenges. In P. N. Teixeira, D. B. Johnstone, M. Rosa, & H. Vossensteyn (Eds.), *Cost-sharing and accessibility in higher education: A fairer deal?* (pp. 79–104). Dordrecht: Springer.

Chapman, B., Higgins, T., & Stiglitz, J. (Eds.). (2014). *Income contingent loans: Theory, practice and prospects.* London: Palgrave MacMillan.

Chiose, S. (2016, September 16). The big data revolution: Will it help university students graduate? *The Globe and Mail.* Retrieved from http://www.theglobeandmail.com/news/national/can-big-data-analysis-stop-students-from-dropping-out-of-university/article31939870/

Darvas, P., Gao, S., Shen, Y., & Bawany, B. (2016). *Sharing higher education's promise beyond the few in Sub-Saharan Africa.* Washington, DC: The World Bank.

D'Hombres, B. (2010). *Inequity in tertiary education systems: Which metric should we use for measuring and benchmarking?* Washington, DC: The World Bank. (Unpublished paper).

DPMG. (2014, June). *Theory of change and methods for evaluating NORHED.* Washington, DC: Development Portfolio Management Group. .(Unpublished).

Ederer, P. (2006). *Innovation at work: The European human capital index* (p. 4). Brussels: Lisbon Council Policy Brief.

Ederer, P., Schuller, P., & Willms, P. (2011). *Human capital leading indicators: How Europe's regions and cities can drive growth and foster social inclusion.* Brussels: The Lisbon Council, Policy Brief.

Ekowo, M., & Palmer, I. (2016). *The promise and peril of predictive analytics in higher education: A landscape analysis.* Washington, DC: New America.

El Mundo. (2016, January 30). *Profesiones que desaparecen y otras que son el futuro pero aún no existen.* Retrieved from http://www.elmundo.es/economia/2016/01/30/56aba00222601d457c8b465f.html

Executive Office of the President. (EOP). (2016). *Artificial intelligence, automation and the economy.* Charleston, SC: Createspace Independent Publishing Platform.

Fain, P. (2014, November 14). Standardized tests for the job market. *Inside Higher Education.* Retrieved from https://www.insidehighered.com/news/2014/11/14/indian-companys-skills-test-college-graduates

Fatunde, T. (2016, April 2). President apologises for sacking of 13 vice-chancellors. *University World News, 170.* Retrieved from http://www.universityworldnews.com/article.php?story=20160401170932437

Fielden, J. (2008). *Global trends in university governance* (Education Working Paper Series No. 9). Washington, DC: Education Sector, Human Development Network, World Bank.

Floc'h, B. (2008, August 6). Pauvres universités françaises. *Le Monde.*

Florida, R. (2008). *Who's your city.* New York, NY: Basic Books.

Frey, C. B., & Osborne, M. A. (2013). *The future of employment: How susceptible are jobs to computerisation?* Oxford: Oxford Martin School, Oxford University.

Galevski, M. (2014). *The academic profession in Macedonia: Conditions and challenges* (Unpublished master's thesis). Danube University Krems, Austria.

Gallagher, J. (2016, November 17). Dementia game 'shows lifelong navigational decline'. *BBC World News*. Retrieved from http://www.bbc.com/news/health-37988197

Gardner, H. (2009). *Five minds for the future*. Cambridge, MA: Harvard Business Review Press.

Goos, M., & Manning, A. (2007). Lousy and lovely jobs: The rising polarization of work in Britain. *The Review of Economics and Statistics, 89*(1), 118–133.

Harbison, F. H. (1964). *The strategy of human resource development in modernizing economies: Policy conference on economic growth and investment in education*. Paris: OECD.

Harris, G. (2016, May 21). Veterans groups seek a crackdown on deceptive colleges. *The New York Times*. Retrieved from http://www.nytimes.com/2016/05/22/us/politics/veterans-groups-seek-a-crackdown-on-deceptive-colleges.html?emc=edit_th_20160522&nl=todaysheadlines&nlid=67135616&_r=0

Hess, F. M., & Carey, K. (2008, June 18). Popping the tuition bubble. *AEI Online*. Retrieved from http://www.aei.org/publications/pubID.28160/pub_detail.asp

Holdsworth, N. (2016, March 11). Calls for prosecution over PhD thesis on Soviet traitor. *University World News, 404.* Retrieved from http://www.universityworldnews.com/article.php?story=2016030721405948

Holm-Nielsen, L. (2017). Opportunities for change: University reforms in Denmark. *CYD Foundation Study, 1.*

Horta, H., Sato, M., & Yonezawa, A. (2011). Academic inbreeding: Exploring its characteristics and rationale in Japanese universities using a qualitative perspective. *Asia Pacific Education Review, 12*, 35–44.

Hristov, D. (2016, April 1). How to produce future-proof graduates using big data. *University World News, 407.*

Hudzik, J. (2011). *Comprehensive internationalization: From concept to action*. Washington, DC: NAFSA.

Hunt, S., Callender, C., & Parry, G. (2016). *The entry and experience of private providers of higher education in six countries*. London: University College London, Centre for Global Higher Education. Retrieved from http://www.researchcghe.org/wp-content/uploads/2016/08/PPreport.pdf

ILO (International Labour Organisation). (2015). *Key indicators of the labour market KILM* (KILM 14). Retrieved from http://www.ilo.org/global/statistics-and-databases/research-and-databases/kilm/WCMS_422454/lang--en/index.htm

Innovation Associates. (2004). *Development of a new funding methodology for Malaysian public institutions of higher education*. (Report commissioned by the Ministry of Higher Education).

Jongsma, A. (2014, September 26). African higher education space another step closer. *University World News, 336).* Retrieved from http://www.universityworldnews.com/article.php?story=20140925091428577&query=African+higher+education+space+another+step+closer

Junor, S., & Usher, A. (2004). *The price of knowledge: Access and student finance in Canada*. Montreal: Canada Millennium Scholarship Foundation.

Kamenetz, A. (2016, October 30). How one university used big data to boost graduation rates. *NPR Higher Education*. Retrieved from http://www.npr.org/sections/ed/2016/10/30/499200614/how-one-university-used-big-data-to-boost-graduation-rates

Kelderman, E. (2012, March 2). To raise completion rates, states dig deeper for data. *Chronicle of Higher Education*. Retrieved from http://chronicle.com/article/To-Raise-Completion-Rates/131037/

Kinser, K. (2009). How the for-profit sector contributes to access in U.S. higher education. *Enrollment Management Journal, 3*(4), 23–44.

Klemencic, M., & Chirikov, I. (2014). *How do we know the effects of higher education on students? On the use of student surveys*. Communication at the Second Bologna Researchers Conference, Bucharest, December.

Klemencic, M., & Zgaga, P. (2015). Slovenia: Gradual phasing out of academic inbreeding and short-term mobility. In M. Yudkevich, P. Altbach, & L. Rumbley (Eds.), *Academic inbreeding and mobility in higher education: Global perspectives*. London: Palgrave Macmillan.

Lambert, C. (2012, March–April). "Active learning" may overthrow the style of teaching that has ruled universities for 600 years. *Harvard Crimson.*

Langa, P., Wangenge-Ouma, G., Jungblut, J., & Cloete, N. (2016, February 26). South Africa and the illusion of free higher education. *University World News, 402.* Retrieved from http://www.universityworldnews.com/article.php?story=20160223145336908

Levy, F., & Murnane, R. J. (2013). *Dancing with robots: Human skills for computerized work.* Washington, DC: Third Way NEXT.

Levy, F., & Murnane, R. J. (2005). *The new division of labor: How computers are creating the next job market.* Princeton, NJ: Princeton University Press.

MacGregor, K. (2016, June 18). 24 centres of excellence for East and Southern Africa. *University World News, 418.* Retrieved from http://www.universityworldnews.com/article.php?story=20160618095557616&query=African+Centres+of+Excellence.

McNeil, M. (2016). Innovative approaches (IDEO). *Edsurge.* Retrieved from https://www.edsurge.com/news/2016-02-12-ideo-challenges-innovators-to-reimagine-the-cost-of-college

Mohamedbhai, G. (2016, May 15). Quality in Africa: New initiatives. *Inside Higher Education.* Retrieved from https://www.insidehighered.com/blogs/world-view/quality-africa-new-initiatives?utm_source=Inside+Higher+Ed&utm_campaign=c4453f2951-DNU20160516&utm_medium=email&utm_term=0_1fcbc04421-c4453f2951-197561345

Moodie, G. (2009, July 12). Australia: National qualifications frameworks. *University World News, 84).* Retrieved from http://www.universityworldnews.com/article.php?story=20090710112537701

Moore, M. H. (1995). *Creating public value: Strategic management in government.* Cambridge, MA: Harvard University Press.

Mourshed, M., Chijioke, C., & Barber, M. (2010). *How the world's most improved systems keep getting better.* London: McKinsey and Company. Retrieved from http://mckinseyonsociety.com/how-the-worlds-most-improved-school-systems-keep-getting-better/

NACIQI (National Advisory Committee on Institutional Quality and Integrity). (2007). *Secretary spellings encourages greater transparency and accountability in higher education at national accreditation meeting.* Washington, DC: NACIQI.

Naicker, S., Plange-Rhule, J., Tutt, R. C., & Eastwood, J. B. (2009). Shortage of healthcare workers in developing countries: Africa. *Ethnicity and Disease, 19*(1 Suppl 1), S1-60–S1-64.

Núñez, M. J. (2009). *Incidencia del Gasto Público social en la distribución del Ingreso, la Pobreza y la Indigencia.* Archivos de Economía, Dirección de Estudios Económicos, Departamento Nacional de Planeación (DNP), República de Colombia. Retrieved from http://www.dnp.gov.co/LinkClick.aspx?fileticket=6f2t5lJ7yIU%3D&tabid=897

OECD. (2007). *Tertiary education for the knowledge society, OECD thematic review of tertiary education: Synthesis report* (Vol. 1). Paris: OECD.

OECD. (2011). *Higher education in regional and city development: Southern Arizona, United States.* Paris: OECD.

OECD. (2012). *Education at a glance: OECD indicators.* Paris: The OECD.

OECD. (2013). *Assessment of higher education learning outcomes AHELO: Feasibility study report volume 3 further insights.* Paris: OECD.OECD. (2015a). *The innovation imperative: Contributing to productivity, growth and well-being.* Paris: OECD.

OECD. (2015b). *Education at a glance.* Paris: OECD.

OECD. (2015c). *Open educational resources: A catalyst for innovation.* Paris: OECD.

OECD. (2016). Measuring what counts in education: Monitoring the sustainable development goal for education:. In *Education at a glance 2016* (pp. 13–16). Paris: OECD. Retrieved from http://www.oecd.org/edu/skills-beyond-school/AHELOFSReportVolume3.pdf

OECD & World Bank. (2009). *Review of the Chilean tertiary education system.* Paris & Washington, DC: The OECD and The World Bank.

OECD & World Bank. (2010). *Reviews of national policies for education: Higher education in Egypt.* Paris & Washington, DC: The OECD and The World Bank.

OECD & World Bank. (2012). *Review of the Colombian tertiary education system.* Paris & Washington, DC: The OECD and The World Bank.

Ohmae, K. (1995). *The end of the nation state: The rise of regional economies.* New York, NY: Simon and Schuster.

Oketch, M., McCowan, T., & Schendel, R. (2014). *The impact of tertiary education on development: A rigorous literature review.* London: Department for International Development. Retrieved from http://r4d.dfid.gov.uk/

O'Malley, B. (2016, November 4). Violent attacks shrink the space for higher education. *University World News, 435.* Retrieved from http://www.universityworldnews.com/article.php?story= 20161104235804433

Onishi, N. (2016, February 18). Nigeria's booming film industry redefines African life. *The New York Times.* Retrieved from http://www.nytimes.com/2016/02/19/world/africa/with-a-boom-before-the-cameras-nigeria-redefines-african-life.html?emc=edit_th_20160219&nl=todaysheadlines&nlid= 67135616&_r=0

Pedrosa, R. H. L. (2006, September 11–13). *Educational and socioeconomic background of undergraduates and academic performance: Consequences for affirmative action programs at a Brazilian research university.* Presentation at the IMHE/OECD general conference on values and Ethics in Higher Education, Paris. Retrieved November 2, 2006, from https://www.oecd.org/site/ 0,2865,en_21571361_37232210_1_1_1_1_1,00.html?appId=-1&token=1678498690

Pitchbook. (2014, August–September). Top universities for VC-backed entrepreneurs. *Pitchbook Venture Capital Monthly.* Retrieved from http://blog.pitchbook.com/the-top-50-universities-producing-vc-backed-entrepreneurs/

Plume, A., & van Weijen, D. (2014, September). Publish or perish? The rise of the fractional author. *Research Trends.* Retrieved from http://www.researchtrends.com/issue-38-september-2014/publish-or-perish-the-rise-of-the-fractional-author/

Porter, M. E. (1990). *The competitive advantage of nations.* New York, NY: Free Press.

Prince, M. (2004). Does active learning work? A review of the research. *Journal of Engineering Education, 93,* 223–232.

Radjou, N. (2014). Frugal innovation: A new approach pioneered in the global south. *Ideas for Development Blog.* Retrieved from http://ideas4development.org/en/frugal-innovation-new-approach-pioneered-in-the-global-south

Ramcharan, R. (2004). Higher or basic education? The composition of human capital and economic development. *IMF Staff Papers, 51*(2), 309–326.

Ramsden, P., & Callender, C. (2014). *Review of the national student survey.* London: HEFCE.

Ranis, G., Irons, M., & Huang, Y. (2011). *Technology change: Sources and impediments* (Economic Growth Center Discussion Paper No. 1002). New Haven, CT: Yale University. Retrieved from http://www.econ.yale.edu/~egcenter

Rigg, P. (2016, May 20). Where higher education is a tool for tackling poverty. *University World News, 414.*

Rodriguez, A., Dahlman, C., & Salmi, J. (2008). *Knowledge and innovation for competitiveness in Brazil.* Washington, DC: The World Bank. Retrieved from https://openknowledge.worldbank.org/bitstream/ handle/10986/6413/439780PUB0Box310only109780821374382.pdf?sequence=1

Roemer, J. (1998). *Equality of opportunity.* Cambridge, MA: Harvard University Press.

Romero, S. (2012, August 30). Brazil enacts affirmative action law for universities. *The New York Times.* Retrieved from http://www.nytimes.com/2012/08/31/world/americas/brazil-enacts-affirmative-action-law-for-universities.html

Rowan-Kenyon, H., Savitz-Romer, M., & Swan, A. K. (2010). *Persistence and retention in tertiary education.* Washington, DC: The World Bank. Retrieved from http://siteresources.worldbank.org/EDUCATION/ Resources/278200-1099079877269/547664-1099079956815/547670-1276537814548/Equity_ Tertiary_Persistence_Full_Report.pdf

Salmi, J. (2009a). *The challenge of establishing world-class universities.* Washington, WA: The World Bank. Directions in Development.

Salmi, J. (2009b). Scenarios for financial sustainability of tertiary education. Higher education in 2030. *Centre for educational research and innovation* (pp. 285–322). Paris: OECD.

Salmi, J. (2010). Ensuring the successful implementation of financing reforms. *In financing higher education in Africa* (pp. 157–170). Washington, DC: The World Bank.

Salmi, J. (2012a). *Why invest in tertiary education?* (Policy Note written for AusAID).

Salmi, J. (2012b). *Lessons from international experience: Promoting tertiary education development and reform.* Policy Note written for AusAID.

Salmi, J. (2013a, January). Welcome to the university of the future! *Handshake, 8.*

Salmi, J. (2013b). *Effective change strategies in tertiary education reforms.* Policy Note for AusAID.

Salmi, J. (2013c). *Formas Exitosas de Gobierno Universitario en el Mundo.* CYD Foundation Study # 03/2013.

Salmi, J. (2013d). *Tertiary education in Latin America and the Caribbean: Challenges and opportunities.* Washington DC, the Inter-American Development Bank. (Unpublished report)

Salmi, J. (2013e). If ranking is the disease, is benchmarking the cure? In P. T. M. Marope, P. J. Wells, & E. Hazelkorn (Eds.), *Rankings and accountability in higher education: Uses and misuses* (pp. 235–256). Paris: UNESCO.

Salmi, J. (2014). The challenge of sustaining student loans systems: Lessons from Chile and Colombia. In B. Chapman, T. Higgins, & J. Stiglitz (Eds.), *Income contingent loans: Theory, practice and prospects.* London: Palgrave MacMillan.

Salmi, J. (2015a). *Is big brother watching you? The evolving role of the state in regulating and conducting quality assurance.* Washington, DC: Council of Higher Education Accreditation.

Salmi, J. (2015b). *Study on open science: Impact, implications and policy options.* Brussels: The European Commission.

Salmi, J. (2016a). Peril and promise: A decade later. *International Journal of African Higher Education, 3*(1), 43–50.

Salmi, J. (2016b). Excellence strategies and the creation of world-class universities. In E. Hazelkorn (Ed.), *Global rankings and the geo-politics of higher education: Understanding the influence and impact of rankings on higher education, policy and society.* London: Routledge.

Salmi, J., & Saroyan, A. (2007). League tables as policy instruments: Uses and misuses. *Higher Education Management and Policy, 19*(2), 31–68.

Salmi, J., & Malee, B. R. (2014). The equity imperative in tertiary education: Promoting fairness and efficiency. *International Review of Education, 60*(3), 361–377.

Salto, D. (2014, January 17). The for-profit higher education giant. *University World News, 303.* Retrieved from http://www.universityworldnews.com/article.php?story=20140115175750863

Savitz-Romer, M., Rowan-Kenyon, H., Weilundemo, M., & Swan. K. (2009). *Educational pathways to equity: A review of global outreach and bridge practices and policies that promote successful participation in tertiary education.* Washington, DC: The World Bank. Retrieved from http://siteresources.worldbank.org/EDUCATION/Resources/278200-1099079877269/547664-1099079956815/547670-1128086743752/Jamil_OutreachandBridge2011_Nov.4.pdf

Smith, M. (2016, February 6). As Flint fought to be heard, Virginia tech team sounded alarm. *The New York Times.*

Sowell, T. (2004). *Affirmative action around the world: An empirical study.* New Haven, CT: Yale University Press.

Student International Staff (SI). (2016, December 8). Australian university becomes first education institution to issue climate bond. *SINews.* Retrieved from https://www.studyinternational.com/news/australian-university-becomes-first-education-institution-to-issue-climate-bond/

The Economist. (2013, February 2). The Nordic countries: The next supermodel. *The Economist.* Retrieved from http://www.economist.com/news/leaders/21571136-politicians-both-right-and-left-could-learn-nordic-countries-next-supermodel

The Economist. (2015, August 22). Getting to Cambridge. *The Economist,* p. 49.

The Economist. (2016, June 11). Hot to make a good teacher. *The Economist.* Retrieved from http://www.economist.com/news/leaders/21700383-what-matters-schools-teachers-fortunately-teaching-can-be-taught-how-make-good

The Economist. (2017, January 26). Grading education: A fintech startup tries to shake up American student loans. *The Economist.* Retrieved from http://www.economist.com/news/finance-and-economics/21715672-taking-risk-return-ratio-education-seriously-fintech-startup-tries?fsrc=scn/tw/te/bl/ed/

University Alliance. (2012). *The way we'll work: Labour market trends and preparing for the hourglass.* London: University Alliance.

Usher, A. (2005). *A little knowledge is a dangerous thing.* Toronto: Educational Policy Institute.

Usher, A. (2014a, November 28). Better know a higher education system: India (part 2). *HESA Blog.* Retrieved from http://higheredstrategy.com/better-know-a-higher-ed-system-india-part-2/

Usher, A. (2014b). *The Korean academic credit bank: A model for credit transfer in North America?* Toronto: Higher Education Strategy Associates.

Usher, A. (2016, February 26). A great day for student assistance. *HESA blog.* Retrieved from http://higheredstrategy.com/a-great-day-for-student-assistance/

UWN. (2016a, April 15). High MOOC completion rates in developing countries. *University World News, 409.* Retrieved from http://www.universityworldnews.com/article.php?story= 20160414211758202

UWN. (2016b, January 29). Reports count impact of advanced sciences on economy. *University World News* (Issue No. 398).

Valero, A., & Van Reenen, J. (2016, August). *The economic impact of universities: Evidence from across the globe* (NBER Working Paper Series Working Paper 22501). Cambridge, MA: National Bureau of Economic Research.. Retrieved from http://www.nber.org/papers/w22501

Vogel, I. (2012). *Review of the use of 'Theory of Change' in international development.* London: Department of International Department.

Watts, A., & Fretwell, D. (2004). *Public policies for career development: Case studies and emerging issues for designing career information and guidance systems in developing and transition economies.* Washington, DC: The World Bank.

Whitehead, J. (1998, August 27–30). *Education theories of educational change within higher education: Robustness in the Roman Ruins.* Paper Presented to the Symposium on 'Educational Change Within Higher Education' at the Annual Conference of the British Educational Research Association, Queens University, Belfast. Retrieved from http://www.actionresearch.net/writings/jack/BERA98B.htm

Wildavsky, B. (2012). *The great brain race: How global universities are reshaping the world.* Princeton, NJ: Princeton University Press.

World Bank. (1999). *World development report 1999: Knowledge for development.* New York, NY: Oxford University Press.

World Bank. (2001). *World development report 2001: Attacking poverty.* Washington, DC: The World Bank.

World Bank. (2002). *Constructing knowledge societies: New challenges for tertiary education.* Washington, DC: The World Bank.

World Bank. (2012). *Putting higher education to work: Skills and research for growth in East Asia.* Washington, DC: The World Bank.

World Bank. (2013). *ACE project: Project appraisal document* (Report No. 77422-AFR). Washington, WA: The World Bank.

World Bank & UNESCO. (2000). *Higher education in developing countries: Peril and promise.* Report of the Independent World Bank / UNESCO Task Force on Higher Education and Society, Washington, DC.

World Economic Forum (WEF). (2015). New vision for education: Unlocking the potential of technology. *World Economic Forum.*

World Economic Forum (WEF). (2016). The future of jobs: Employment, skills and workforce strategy for the fourth industrial revolution. *World Economic Forum. Retrieved from* http://www3.weforum.org/ docs/WEF_Future_of_Jobs.pdf

Yusuf, S., & Nabeshima, K. (2007). *How uuniversities ppromote eeconomic growth.* Washington, DC: The World Bank.

Zhao, C. M. (2011, January). *Updated carnegie classifications show increase in for-profits: Change in traditional landscape, carnegie foundation for the advancement of teaching.* Retrieved from www.carnegiefoundation.org/newsroom/press-releases/updated-carnegie-classifications

Zhao, X., & Yu,. R. (2016, July 30). An overseas study experience, at home. *China Daily.* Retrieved from http://www.chinadaily.com.cn/china/2016-07/25/content_26205585_2.htm

# APPENDICES

EUROPE AND CENTRAL ASIA

| Country | Survey | Year | Sample size after sample selection |
|---------|--------|------|-----------------------------------|
| Albania | Life in Transition Survey | 2006 | 8290 |
| | Albania Living Standards Measurement Surveys | 2005 | |
| | European Values Study | 2008 | |
| Armenia | Life in Transition Survey | 2006 | 1604 |
| | European Values Study | 2008 | |
| Azerbaijan | Life in Transition Survey | 2006 | 1816 |
| | European Values Study | 2008 | |
| Belarus | Life in Transition Survey | 2006 | 1599 |
| | European Values Study | 2008 | |
| Bulgaria | Life in Transition Survey | 2006 | 3946 |
| | European Values Study | 2008 | |
| | European Social Survey | 2000–2008 | |
| Bosnia | Life in Transition Survey | 2006 | 1763 |
| | European Values Study | 2008 | |
| Croatia | Life in Transition Survey | 2006 | 3493 |
| | Adult Education Survey | 2008 | |
| Czech Republic | Life in Transition Survey | 2006 | 8829 |
| | European Values Study | 2008 | |
| | European Social Survey | 2000–2008 | |
| | European Survey on Living Conditions | 2005 | |

| Country | Survey | Year | Sample size after sample selection |
|---------|--------|------|-----------------------------------|
| Estonia | European Survey on Living Conditions | 2005 | 11644 |
|  | European Social Survey | 2000–2008 |  |
|  | European Values Study | 2008 |  |
|  | Life in Transition Survey | 2006 |  |
|  | Living conditions survey of the Baltic region | 1999 |  |
| Georgia | European Values Study | 2008 | 1665 |
|  | Life in Transition Survey | 2006 |  |
| Hungary | European Survey on Living Conditions | 2005 | 13881 |
|  | European Social Survey | 2000-2008 |  |
|  | European Values Study | 2008 |  |
|  | Life in Transition Survey | 2006 |  |
| Kazakhstan | Life in Transition Survey | 2006 | 704 |
|  | Kazakhstan Living Standards Mesurement Surveys | 1996 |  |
| Kosovo | European Values Study | 2008 | 1007 |
| Kyrgyzstan | Life in Transition Survey | 2006 | 4740 |
|  | Kyrgyzstan Poverty Monitoring Surveys | 1997 |  |
| Latvia | European Survey on Living Conditions | 2005 | 6473 |
|  | Living conditions survey of the Baltic region | 1999 |  |
|  | European Values Study | 2008 |  |
|  | Life in Transition Survey | 2006 |  |
| Lithuania | European Survey on Living Conditions | 2005 | 7926 |
|  | Living conditions survey of the Baltic region | 1999 |  |
|  | European Values Study | 2008 |  |
|  | Life in Transition Survey | 2006 |  |
| Moldovia | European Values Study | 2008 | 1554 |
|  | Life in Transition Survey | 2006 |  |

| Country | Survey | Year | Sample size after sample selection |
|---------|--------|------|-----------------------------------|
| Montenegro | European Values Study | 2008 | 1812 |
| | Life in Transition Survey | 2006 | |
| Poland | European Survey on Living Conditions | 2005 | 28045 |
| | European Social Survey | 2000–2008 | |
| | European Values Study | 2008 | |
| | Life in Transition Survey | 2006 | |
| Romania | European Values Study | 2008 | 1510 |
| | Life in Transition Survey | 2006 | |
| Russia | European Values Study | 2008 | 4631 |
| | Life in Transition Survey | 2006 | |
| | European Social Survey | 2000–2008 | |
| Slovakia | European Survey on Living Conditions | 2005 | 12519 |
| | European Social Survey | 2000–2008 | |
| | European Values Study | 2008 | |
| | Life in Transition Survey | 2006 | |
| Serbia | European Values Study | 2008 | 1690 |
| | Life in Transition Survey | 2006 | |
| Slovenia | European Values Study | 2008 | 9627 |
| | Life in Transition Survey | 2006 | |
| | European Social Survey | 2000–2008 | |
| | European Survey on Living Conditions | 2005 | |
| Ukraine | European Values Study | 2008 | 4022 |
| | Life in Transition Survey | 2006 | |
| | European Social Survey | 2000–2008 | |
| Turkey | Life in Transition Survey | 2006 | 1998 |
| | European Social Survey | 2000–2008 | |
| Uzbekistan | Life in Transition Survey | 2006 | 787 |
| Tajikistan | Life in Transition Survey | 2006 | 1235 |
| | TajikistanLiving Standards Mesurement Surveys | 2007 | |

## LATIN AMERICAN COUNTRIES

| Country | Survey | Year | Sample size after sample selection |
|---------|--------|------|-----------------------------------|
| Colombia | Colombia Quality of Life Survey | 2003 | 27909 |
| Ecuador | Ecuador Living Standards Measurement Surveys | 1998, 1999, 2006 | 33043 |
| Guatemela | Guatemala Survey on Living Conditions | 2000 | 10399 |
| Mexico | Mexican Family Life Survey | 2002, 2005 | 18323 |
| Panama | Panama Standards Living Surveys | 1997, 2003, 2008 | 26123 |
| Chile | International Social Survey Programme | 1999 | 2904 |
| | International Adult Literacy Survey | 1999 | |
| Peru | Peru Living Standards Measurement Survey | 2001 | 11361 |
| Brazil | Pesquisa Nacional por Amostra de Domicilios | 1996 | 118679 |

## OECD COUNTRIES

| Country | Survey | Year | Sample size after sample selection |
|---------|--------|------|-----------------------------------|
| Austria | European Survey on Living Conditions | 2005 | 10200 |
| | European Social Survey | 2000–2008 | |
| | European Values Study | 2008 | |
| Belgium | European Survey on Living Conditions | 2005 | 11139 |
| | European Social Survey | 2000–2008 | |
| | European Values Study | 2008 | |
| Canada | Canada General Social Survey | 2006 | 12899 |
| Cyprus | European Survey on Living Conditions | 2005 | 6973 |
| | European Social Survey | 2000–2008 | |
| | European Values Study | 2008 | |

| Country | Survey | Year | Sample size after sample selection |
|---|---|---|---|
| Denmark | European Survey on Living Conditions | 2005 | 8927 |
| | European Social Survey | 2000–2008 | |
| | European Values Study | 2008 | |
| Finland | European Survey on Living Conditions | 2005 | 12 584 |
| | European Social Survey | 2000–2008 | |
| | European Values Study | 2008 | |
| France | European Survey on Living Conditions | 2005 | 15129 |
| | European Social Survey | 2000–2008 | |
| | European Values Study | 2008 | |
| Germany | European Survey on Living Conditions | 2005 | 21824 |
| | European Social Survey | 2000–2008 | |
| | European Values Study | 2008 | |
| Greece | European Survey on Living Conditions | 2005 | 11087 |
| | European Social Survey | 2000–2008 | |
| | European Values Study | 2008 | |
| Ireland | European Survey on Living Conditions | 2005 | 9467 |
| | European Social Survey | 2000–2008 | |
| | European Values Study | 2008 | |
| Italy | European Survey on Living Conditions | 2005 | 29207 |
| | European Social Survey | 2000–2008 | |
| Luxembourg | European Survey on Living Conditions | 2005 | 7601 |
| | European Social Survey | 2000–2008 | |
| | European Values Study | 2008 | |

| Country | Survey | Year | Sample size after sample selection |
|---|---|---|---|
| Netherlands | European Survey on Living Conditions | 2005 | 11569 |
| | European Social Survey | 2000-2008 | |
| | European Values Study | 2008 | |
| New Zealand | International Social Survey Programme | 1999 | 3310 |
| | International Adult Literacy Survey | 1999 | |
| Norway | European Survey on Living Conditions | 2005 | 8699 |
| | European Social Survey | 2000-2008 | |
| Portugal | European Survey on Living Conditions | 2005 | 10901 |
| | European Social Survey | 2000-2008 | |
| | European Values Study | 2008 | |
| Spain | European Survey on Living Conditions | 2005 | 23671 |
| | European Social Survey | 2000-2008 | |
| | European Values Study | 2008 | |
| Sweeden | European Survey on Living Conditions | 2005 | 8672 |
| | European Social Survey | 2000-2008 | |
| Switzerland | European Social Survey | 2000-2008 | 8935 |
| | European Values Study | 2008 | |
| | International Adult Literacy Survey | 1994, 1998 | |
| UK | European Survey on Living Conditions | 2005 | 11857 |
| | European Social Survey | 2000-2008 | |
| USA | General Social Survey | 1996-2008 | 15259 |

## EAST AND SOUTH ASIA AND PACIFIC COUNTRIES

| Country | Survey | Year | Sample size after sample selection |
|---------|--------|------|-----------------------------------|
| China | East Asia Social Survey | 2006, 2008 | 5100 |
| Philippines | International Social Survey Program | 1999 | 813 |
| Mongolia | Life in Transition Survey | 2006 | 823 |
| Timor-Leste | Timor-Leste Living Standards Measurement Survey | 2001 | 3103 |
| Nepal | Nepal Living Standards Survey | 2004 | 6850 |
| Taiwan | East Asia Social Survey | 2006, 2008 | 5573 |
| South Korea | East Asia Social Survey | 2006, 2008 | 5100 |
| Indonesia | Indonesia Family Life Survey | 2007 | 15545 |
| Japan | East Asia Social Survey | 2006, 2008 | 2879 |

## METHODOLOGY USED TO ESTIMATE LEVELS OF INEQUALITY AND INTERGENERATIONAL MOBILITY

### Empirical Specification

The following equation (1) is used to quantify the country-cohort-specific level of inequality in access to tertiary education:

$$TE_i^{jc} = \beta^{jc} TEF_i^{jc} + \delta^{jc} PRF_i^{jc} + \epsilon_i^{jc}, \qquad i = 1 \ldots N \qquad (1)$$

where $TE_i^{jc}$, the outcome variable, is a dichotomous variable taking on the value one if the individual $i$ reports having participated in tertiary education and zero otherwise. For each country the population is divided into 4 cohorts: 1969–1978, 1959–1968, 1949–1958, 1939–1948. These 4 cohorts cover individuals in age of participating in tertiary education in 4 different periods. Equation (1) is estimated separately for each country $j=1\ldots68$ and cohort $c=1\ldots4$.

The explaining variables related to the family background of the respondents, $TEF_i^{jc}$ and $PRF_i^{jc}$, refer to the educational attainment of the father. $TEF_i^{jc}$ is equal to one if the father of the respondent has attained tertiary education and zero otherwise; $PRF_i^{jc}$ is equal to one if the father has at a maximum completed primary education and zero otherwise while. The excluded category is composed of all individuals with lower or upper secondary education. $\epsilon_i^{jc}$ is the disturbance term of equation (1).

189

Equation (1) is estimated using a probit model. The analysis is restricted to adults between 25 and 65 of age at the time of the survey in the cohorts born between 1938 and 1978.

The marginal effects to be estimated, $\hat{\beta}^{jc}$ and $\hat{\delta}^{jc}$, describe the influence of the family background on the respondent's educational achievement for country $j$ and cohort $c$. $\hat{\beta}^{jc}$ is an estimate of the increased probability for individuals whose father has a tertiary education to enrol in tertiary studies compared to individuals whose father has only completed secondary education (henceforth the reference category).

Similarly, $\hat{\delta}^{jc}$ is the penalty with respect to the reference group, in terms of the likelihood of having access to tertiary studies for individuals with a low family background.

*Country and Macro Regional Estimates*

The estimated value of $\hat{\beta}^{jc}$ for a given country $j$ is given by $\hat{\beta}^{j} = (1/C)\sum_{C=1}^{C}\hat{\beta}^{jc}$, i.e., it is the average value of the estimated cohort-coefficients. The same approach is followed for $\hat{\delta}^{j} = (1/C)\sum_{C=1}^{C}\hat{\delta}^{jc}$. The same weight is given to each cohort so that $\hat{\beta}^{jc}$ and $\hat{\delta}^{jc}$ are not sensitive to the size of the cohorts. This makes country comparisons more reliable as country results will not be affected by differences in the age structure in the various surveys.

Based on these country cohort specific intergenerational education regressions, the macro regional estimate of $\hat{\beta}$ and $\hat{\delta}$ are also computed for the 4 sets of countries considered in the study – OECD Countries, Eastern Europe and Central Asia, South-East Asia, Latin America and Caribbean, measured by $(1/J_r)\sum_{j=1}^{J_r}\hat{\beta}^{j}$ and $(1/J_r)\sum_{j=1}^{J_r}\hat{\delta}^{j}$ with $J_r$ the number of countries belonging to the macro-region $r$.

A global measure of inequality of opportunity for each country $j$ is given by the sum of the absolute values of two estimated coefficients: $\widehat{INE}^{j} = |\hat{\beta}^{j}| + |\hat{\delta}^{j}|$. The macro regional measure of inequality of opportunity is equal to $\widehat{INE} = (1/J_r)\sum_{j=1}^{J_r}\widehat{INE}^{j}$.

High estimates of $\widehat{INE}^{j}$ are interpreted as significant intergenerational mobility, while low estimates of $\widehat{INE}^{j}$ suggest that educational attainment outcomes are not closely related across generations. In addition to considering the population as a whole, the study examines how the intergenerational correlations in education vary by sex. For this, equation (1) is simply estimated separately by country, cohort and sex.

*Time Comparisons*

The study computes linear time trends in intergenerational mobility by regressing for each country respectively $\hat{\beta}^{jc}$ and $\left|\hat{\delta}^{jc}\right|$ on a variable $T$ taking on the values 1 to 4, with the value 1 for the oldest cohort to attend tertiary and 4 for the youngest one. Regional linear trends are obtained by relying on similar estimates but while pooling together all countries belonging to the region $R$ and adding country fixed effects in the equations. The coefficients associated with the $T$ variable, $\hat{\theta}_{\beta}^{j}$ and $\hat{\theta}_{\delta}^{j}$, show the absolute change in $\hat{\beta}^{jc}$ and $\left|\hat{\delta}^{jc}\right|$ occurring from one cohort to the next. If $\hat{\theta}_{\beta}^{j}$ and $\hat{\theta}_{\delta}^{j}$ are positive (negative), the correlation between the probability to participate in tertiary studies and paternal education has increased (decreased) over time. The study also examines how mobility in tertiary education has evolved in relative terms by measuring the rate of change across each cohort as follows: $\dfrac{\hat{\delta}^{j}}{\hat{\delta}^{j39-48}}$ , $\dfrac{\hat{\beta}^{j}}{\hat{\beta}^{j39-48}}$ . In addition, in order to detect non-linear changes across cohorts in the estimated values of $\hat{\beta}^{jc}$ and $\left|\hat{\delta}^{jc}\right|$, the estimated coefficients $\dfrac{\hat{\delta}^{j}}{\hat{\delta}^{j39-48}}$ and $\dfrac{\hat{\beta}^{j}}{\hat{\beta}^{j39-48}}$ are plotted against $T$.

*Ranking*

Countries are ranked in three groups according to the degree of educational persistence across generations as measured by $\widehat{INE}^{j}$. The best performing countries in terms of educational mobility lie between the 100th and 75th percentiles. The worst performing countries lie in the bottom 25th percentile. The rest of the countries are assigned to the middle group.

| | |
|---|---|
| 100th percentile | Best performers in educational mobility |
| 75th percentile | Middle group |
| 25th percentile | Lowest performers in educational mobility |

APPENDIX 2 – RESOURCE DIVERSIFICATION MATRIX

| Category of income | Source of income | | | | |
|---|---|---|---|---|---|
| | Government | Students and families | Industry & services | Alumni/ philanthropists | International cooperation |
| *Budgetary contribution* | | | | | |
| General budget | X | | | | |
| Dedicated taxes (lottery, tax on liquor sales, tax on contracts, tax on export duties) | X | | | | |
| Payroll tax | | | X | | |
| *Fees for instructional activities* | | | | | |
| Tuition fees | | | | | |
| Degree/non-degree programs | | X | X | | |
| On-campus/distance education programs | | X | X | | |
| Advance payments | | X | | | |
| Chargeback | X | | | | |
| Other fees (registration, labs, remote labs) | | X | | | |
| Affiliation fees (colleges) | | | X | | |
| *Productive activities* | | | | | |
| Sale of services | | | | | |
| Consulting | X | | X | | X |
| Research | X | | X | X | X |
| Laboratory tests | X | | X | | |
| Patent royalties, share of spin-off profits, monetized patent royalties deal | | | X | X | |
| Operation of service enterprises (television, hotel, retirement homes, malls, parking, driving school, Internet provider, gym) | | | X | | |
| Financial products (endowment funds, shares) | | | X | | |

| | 1 | 2 | 3 | 4 | 5 |
|---|---|---|---|---|---|
| Production of goods (agricultural and industrial) | X | X | X | | X |
| Themed merchandises and services (smart card) | X | X | X | X | X |
| Rental of facilities (land, classrooms, dormitories, laboratories, ballrooms, drive-through, concert halls, mortuary space, movie shooting) | X | X | X | X | |
| Sale of assets (land, residential housing, art treasures) | X | X | X | | |
| *Fund raising* | | | | | |
| Direct donations | | | | | |
|   Monetary grants (immediate, deferred) | X | X | X | | |
|   Equipment | | X | X | | |
|   Land and buildings | | X | | | X |
|   Scholarships and student loans | X | X | X | | X |
|   Endowed chairs, libraries, mascot | | X | X | | |
|   Challenging / matching grants | | X | X | X | |
|   Religious donations ("Zakat") | | X | | X | |
| Indirect donations (credit card, percentage of gas sales, percentage of stock exchange trade, lectures by alumni) | | | X | X | |
| Tied donations (access to patents, share of spin-off profits) | | | X | | |
| Concessions, franchising, licensing, sponsorships, partnerships (products sold on campus, names, concerts, museum showings, athletic events) | | | X | | |
| Lotteries and auctions (scholarships) | | | X | X | |
| *Loans* | | | | | |
| Bank loans | X | X | X | X | X |
| Bond issues | | | X | X | |

# ABOUT THE AUTHOR

**Jamil Salmi** is a global tertiary education expert providing policy advice and consulting services to governments, universities, professional associations, multilateral banks and bilateral cooperation agencies. He is an Emeritus Professor of higher education policy at Diego Portales University (Chile) and Research Fellow at Boston College's Center for Higher Education (USA). Until January 2012, Dr. Salmi was the World Bank's tertiary education coordinator. He wrote the first World Bank policy paper on higher education reform in 1994 and was the principal author of the Bank's 2002 Tertiary Education Strategy entitled *Constructing Knowledge Societies: New Challenges for Tertiary Education*. Dr. Salmi's 2009 book addresses the *Challenge of Establishing World-Class Universities*. His following book, co-edited with Professor PhilIP Altbach, entitled *The Road to Academic Excellence: the Making of World-Class Research Universities*, was published in September 2011.

GLOBAL PERSPECTIVES ON HIGHER EDUCATION

Volume 1
WOMEN'S UNIVERSITIES AND COLLEGES
An International Handbook
Francesca B. Purcell, Robin Matross Helms, and Laura Rumbley (Eds.)
ISBN 978-90-77874-58-5 hardback
ISBN 978-90-77874-02-8 paperback

Volume 2
PRIVATE HIGHER EDUCATION
A Global Revolution
Philip G. Altbach and D. C. Levy (Eds.)
ISBN 978-90-77874-59-2 hardback
ISBN 978-90-77874-08-0 paperback

Volume 3
FINANCING HIGHER EDUCATION
Cost-Sharing in International perspective
D. Bruce Johnstone
ISBN 978-90-8790-016-8 hardback
ISBN 978-90-8790-015-1 paperback

Volume 4
UNIVERSITY COLLABORATION FOR INNOVATION
Lessons from the Cambridge-MIT Institute
David Good, Suzanne Greenwald, Roy Cox, and Megan Goldman (Eds.)
ISBN 978-90-8790-040-3 hardback
ISBN 978-90-8790-039-7 paperback

Volume 5
HIGHER EDUCATION
A Worldwide Inventory of Centers and Programs
Philip G. Altbach, Leslie A. Bozeman, Natia Janashia, and Laura E. Rumbley
ISBN 978-90-8790-052-6 hardback
ISBN 978-90-8790-049-6 paperback

Volume 6
FUTURE OF THE AMERICAN PUBLIC RESEARCH UNIVERSITY
R. L. Geiger, C. L. Colbeck, R. L. Williams, and C. K. Anderson (Eds.)
ISBN 978-90-8790-048-9 hardback
ISBN 978-90-8790-047-2 paperback

Volume 7
TRADITION AND TRANSITION
The International Imperative in Higher Education
Philip G. Altbach
ISBN 978-90-8790-054-4 hardback
ISBN 978-90-8790-053-3 paperback

Volume 8
THE PROFESSORIATE IN THE AGE OF GLOBALIZATION
Nelly P. Stromquist
ISBN 978-90-8790-084-7 hardback
ISBN 978-90-8790-083-0 paperback

Volume 9
HIGHER EDUCATION SYSTEMS
Conceptual Frameworks, Comparative Perspectives, Empirical Findings
Ulrich Teichler
ISBN 978-90-8790-138-7 hardback
ISBN 978-90-8790-137-0 paperback

Volume 10
HIGHER EDUCATION IN THE NEW CENTURY: GLOBAL CHALLENGES
AND INNOVATIVE IDEAS
Philip G. Altbach and Patti McGill Peterson (Eds.)
ISBN 978-90-8790-199-8 hardback
ISBN 978-90-8790-198-1 paperback

Volume 11
THE DYNAMICS OF INTERNATIONAL STUDENT CIRCULATION IN A
GLOBAL CONTEXT
Hans de Wit, Pawan Agarwal, Mohsen Elmahdy Said, Molatlhegi T. Sehoole,
and Muhammad Sirozi (Eds.)
ISBN 978-90-8790-259-9 hardback
ISBN 978-90-8790-258-2 paperback

Volume 12
UNIVERSITIES AS CENTRES OF RESEARCH AND KNOWLEDGE
CREATION: AN ENDANGERED SPECIES?
Hebe Vessuri and Ulrich Teichler (Eds.)
ISBN 978-90-8790-479-1 hardback
ISBN 978-90-8790-478-4 paperback

Volume 13
HIGHER EDUCATION IN TURMOIL: THE CHANGING WORLD OF
INTERNATIONALIZATION
Jane Knight
ISBN 978-90-8790-521-7 hardback
ISBN 978-90-8790-520-0 paperback

Volume 14
UNIVERSITY AND DEVELOPMENT IN LATIN AMERICA: SUCCESSFUL
EXPERIENCES OF RESEARCH CENTERS
Simon Schwartzman (Ed.)
ISBN 978-90-8790-524-8 hardback
ISBN 978-90-8790-523-1 paperback

Volume 15
BUYING YOUR WAY INTO HEAVEN: EDUCATION AND CORRUPTION IN
INTERNATIONAL PERSPECTIVE
Stephen P. Heyneman (Ed.)
ISBN 978-90-8790-728-0 hardback
ISBN 978-90-8790-727-3 paperback

Volume 16
HIGHER EDUCATION AND THE WORLD OF WORK
Ulrich Teichler
ISBN 978-90-8790-755-6 hardback
ISBN 978-90-8790-754-9 paperback

Volume 17
FINANCING ACCESS AND EQUITY IN HIGHER EDUCATION
Jane Knight (Ed.)
ISBN 978-90-8790-767-9 hardback
ISBN 978-90-8790-766-2 paperback

Volume 18
UNIVERSITY RANKINGS, DIVERSITY, AND THE NEW LANDSCAPE OF
HIGHER EDUCATION
Barbara M. Kehm and Bjørn Stensaker (Eds.)
ISBN 978-90-8790-815-7 hardback
ISBN 978-90-8790-814-0 paperback

Volume 19
HIGHER EDUCATION IN EAST ASIA: NEOLIBERALISM AND THE
PROFESSORIATE
Gregory S. Poole and Ya-chen Chen (Eds.)
ISBN 978-94-6091-127-9 hardback
ISBN 978-94-6091-126-2 paperback

Volume 20
ACCESS AND EQUITY: COMPARATIVE PERSPECTIVES
Heather Eggins (Ed.)
ISBN 978-94-6091-185-9 hardback
ISBN 978-94-6091-184-2 paperback

Volume 21
UNDERSTANDING INEQUALITIES IN AND BY HIGHER EDUCATION
Gaële Goastellec (Ed.)
ISBN 978-94-6091-307-5 hardback
ISBN 978-94-6091-306-8 paperback

Volume 22
TRENDS IN GLOBAL HIGHER EDUCATION: TRACKING AN ACADEMIC
REVOLUTION
Philip G. Altbach, Liz Reisberg, and Laura E. Rumbley
ISBN 978-94-6091-338-9 hardback
ISBN 978-94-6091-339-6 paperback

Volume 23
PATHS TO A WORLD-CLASS UNIVERSITY: LESSONS FROM PRACTICES
AND EXPERIENCES
Nian Cai Liu, Qi Wang and Ying Cheng
ISBN 978-94-6091-354-9 hardback
ISBN 978-94-6091-353-2 paperback

Volume 24
TERTIARY EDUCATION AT A GLANCE: CHINA
Kai Yu, Andrea Lynn Stith, Li Liu, and Huizhong Chen
ISBN 978-94-6091-744-8 hardback
ISBN 978-94-6091-745-5 paperback

Volume 25
BUILDING WORLD-CLASS UNIVERSITIES: DIFFERENT APPROACHES
TO A SHARED GOAL
Qi Wang, Ying Cheng and Nian Cai Liu
ISBN 978-94-6209-033-0  hardback
ISBN 978-94-6209-032-3  paperback

Volume 26
INTERNATIONALISATION OF AFRICAN HIGHER EDUCATION –
TOWARDS ACHIEVING THE MDGS
Chika Sehoole and Jane Knight (Eds.)
ISBN 978-94-6209-309-6  hardback
ISBN 978-94-6209-310-2  paperback

Volume 27
THE INTERNATIONAL IMPERATIVE IN HIGHER EDUCATION
Philip G. Altbach
ISBN 978-94-6209-337-9 hardback
ISBN 978-94-6209-336-2 paperback

Volume 28
GLOBALIZATION AND ITS IMPACTS ON THE QUALITY OF PHD
EDUCATION: FORCES AND FORMS IN DOCTORAL EDUCATION
WORLDWIDE
Maresi Nerad and Barbara Evans (Eds.)
ISBN 978-94-6209-568-7 hardback
ISBN 978-94-6209-567-0 paperback

Volume 29
USING DATA TO IMPROVE HIGHER EDUCATION: RESEARCH, POLICY
AND PRACTICE
Maria Eliophotou Menon, Dawn Geronimo Terkla, and Paul Gibbs (Eds.)
ISBN 978-94-6209-793-3 hardback
ISBN 978-94-6209-792-6 paperback

Volume 30
HOW WORLD-CLASS UNIVERSITIES AFFECT GLOBAL HIGHER
EDUCATION: INFLUENCES AND RESPONSES
Ying Cheng, Qi Wang and Nian Cai Liu (Eds.)
ISBN 978-94-6209-820-6 hardback
ISBN 978-94-6209-819-0 paperback

Volume 31
GLOBAL OPPORTUNITIES AND CHALLENGES FOR HIGHER EDUCATION
LEADERS: BRIEFS ON KEY THEMES
Laura E. Rumbley, Robin Matross Helms, Patti McGill Peterson, and
Philip G. Altbach (Eds.)
ISBN 978-94-6209-862-6 hardback
ISBN 978-94-6209-861-9 paperback

Volume 32
CRITICAL PERSPECTIVES ON INTERNATIONALISING THE
CURRICULUM IN DISCIPLINES: REFLECTIVE NARRATIVE ACCOUNTS
FROM BUSINESS, EDUCATION AND HEALTH
Wendy Green and Craig Whitsed (Eds.)
ISBN 978-94-6300-084-0 hardback
ISBN 978-94-6300-083-3 paperback

Volume 33
THE IMPACT OF INTERNATIONALIZATION ON JAPANESE HIGHER
EDUCATION: IS JAPANESE EDUCATION REALLY CHANGING?
John Mock, Hiroaki Kawamura, and Naeko Naganuma (Eds.)
ISBN 978-94-6300-168-7 hardback
ISBN 978-94-6300-167-0 paperback

Volume 34
GLOBAL AND LOCAL INTERNATIONALIZATION
Elspeth Jones, Robert Coelen, Jos Beelen, and Hans de Wit (Eds.)
ISBN 978-94-6300-300-1 hardback
ISBN 978-94-6300-299-8 paperback

Volume 35
MATCHING VISIBILITY AND PERFORMANCE: A STANDING CHALLENGE
FOR WORLD-CLASS UNIVERSITIES
Nian Cai Liu, Ying Chen and Qi Wang (Eds.)
ISBN 978-94-6300-772-6 hardback
ISBN 978-94-6300-771-9 paperback

Volume 36
UNDERSTANDING GLOBAL HIGHER EDUCATION: INSIGHTS FROM KEY
GLOBAL PUBLICATIONS
Georgiana Mihut, Philip G. Altbach and Hans de Wit (Eds.)
ISBN 978-94-6351-043-1 hardback
ISBN 978-94-6351-042-4 paperback

Volume 37
RESPONDING TO MASSIFICATION: DIFFERENTIATION IN
POSTSECONDARY EDUCATION WORLDWIDE
Philip G. Altbach, Liz Reisberg and Hans de Wit (Eds.)
ISBN 978-94-6351-082-0 hardback
ISBN 978-94-6351-081-3 paperback

Volume 38
THE TERTIARY EDUCATION IMPERATIVE: KNOWLEDGE, SKILLS AND
VALUES FOR DEVELOPMENT
Jamil Salmi
ISBN 978-94-6351-127-8 hardback
ISBN 978-94-6351-126-1 paperback